ZERO-BASE
BUDGETING
COMES OF AGE

ZERO-BASE BUDGETING COMES OF AGE

What It Is and
What It Takes to Make It Work

Logan M. Cheek

A Division of American Management Associations

Chapter 8, part of Appendix A, and
the Selected Readings list have been
revised for the second printing.

Library of Congress Cataloging in Publication Data

Cheek, Logan M
  Zero-base budgeting comes of age.

  Bibliography: p.
  Includes index.
  1. Zero-base budgeting. I. Title.
HF5550.C49   658.1'54   77-4362
ISBN 0-8144-5442-9

© 1977 AMACOM
A division of American Management Associations, New York. All rights reserved. Printed in
the United States of America.

Second Printing

To my many colleagues who developed and refined the zero-base approach to solving management problems at Texas Instruments, McKinsey, and other progressive organizations, as well as to those executives of vision—particularly Jimmy Carter—who saw its value and moved forcefully to implement it . . . and especially to Pam and Christen.

Preface

Budgeting rests on principles which have more in common with concepts of human relations than with rules of accounting; . . . if these principles are applied, successful practice is inevitable.
James L. Pierce, *The Budget Comes of Age*

IN his book *The Battle for Investment Survival,* Gerald Loeb states: "The difference between the investor who year in and year out procures for himself a final net profit and the one who is usually in the red is not entirely a question of superior selection of stocks or superior timing. Rather, it is also a case of knowing how to capitalize successes and curtail failures." * His dictum on successful securities investing applies equally to business planning and budgeting. For years top executives, controllers, planning managers, and budget analysts have wrestled with three similar and basic management issues:

> What new products, markets, production methods, or staff efforts offer the greatest profit potential for my company? And, in the public sector, what are the most critical needs of my constituents?

> Which approaches represent the most cost-effective and affordable way to launch that product, serve that market, manufacture those goods, or deliver that service?

> And, most important, how do I allocate resources from the marginal to the more promising efforts?

In recent years planning professionals have developed rather innovative techniques to address the first issue. From market research they

* Simon & Schuster, 1957.

can segment markets, trend income levels, and spot emerging consumer needs. Research and engineering can offer a horn of plenty of technical innovations. Economic forecasting can provide some comfort to the uncertainties of timing. The planning executive's own suspicions can be confirmed or refuted using the Delphi technique. And where doubts still remain, an army of management, marketing, economics, media, and engineering consultants stands ready and eager to bless (or damn) their proposed plans and strategies.

Yet for all the sophisticated techniques, few organizations seem satisfied with their planning efforts. In the words of one chief executive, "It's like a Chinese dinner: I feel full when I get it, but after a while I wonder whether I've eaten at all."

Responsibility for addressing the second and third issues usually rests with an entirely different individual—the controller or budget manager. His is a thankless task, and often a "no win" one. On a simplistic level, he faces the impossible responsibility of challenging numerous budget requests submitted by scores, hundreds, and sometimes thousands of professional peers, each far more expert in the various specialties of marketing, personnel, accounting, or law than he could ever hope to be. And his task is complicated in most organizations by what are admittedly horse-and-buggy budgeting approaches.

Such approaches manifest themselves in what Jimmy Carter calls the "traditional budgeting syndrome" (see his paper "Zero-Base Budgeting" in Appendix C). He describes this as follows.

- During the initial phases of the budget cycle, staff managers take the current year's spending level, increment it for inflation, and fold in a myriad of new programs.

- The results are submitted to the budgeting staff (normally well past the eleventh hour) for consolidation and presentation to the chief executive. Their analysis and presentation to him clearly show that the initial effort is totally unrealistic and usually unaffordable if not irresponsible.

- But because they're lacking a thorough understanding of which efforts are really critical, a rather distressing scenario now unfolds. Arbitrary across-the-board cuts are made, and considerable muscle and bones are sacrificed with the fat. Last-ditch Byzantine lobbying efforts occur between the CEO and his key subordinates. The controller runs out of time and patience, not to mention scarce political capital.

- Yet somehow (usually several weeks after the deadline) some sort of budget is finalized and blessed. All parties congratulate one another, and the exhausted ones slip away for a quick vacation, quietly suppressing nervous feelings of doubt. But all share a determined commitment that next year will be different—if nothing else, they will start earlier or increase the planning and budgeting staff!

The example may be overdone, but I'd argue that all major organizations have faced all these problems to one degree or another at one time or another. Let's briefly diagnose why:

1. They lack a means to translate the good intentions and objectives of their long-range plan into a practical, realistic, affordable, and achievable tactical budget.
2. They lack the means to thoroughly assess and decide on each spending request by considering small, manageable, understandable packages, each of which stands or falls on its own merits.
3. Lacking each of the above, they cannot decide how to channel their scarce resources toward the most cost-effective undertakings.

The bottom line is not surprising. Strategic planning becomes a rather academic exercise, full of unrealized dreams and short on genuine accomplishments. And budgeting becomes a hopeless last-minute political flail. Even the most experienced diplomat would find his talents sorely taxed in such an environment.

Several years ago, though, I learned of an intriguing new approach developed at Texas Instruments. Its internal logic is simple, and in concept it goes back to management basics. Of all the new ideas that have surfaced in the management literature in the last decade, I have found it to be the most practical and useful. It is called *zero-base budgeting*. It requires each manager to break up his annual budget into small understandable pieces called "decision packages." In each package he outlines what he wants to do, how he proposes to do it, other ways of doing it, how much it will cost, how it will benefit the organization, and what will happen if it's not done. The packages are tied to long-range plan objectives, then ranked and approved up to the level of affordability.

I had read of the Texas Instruments experience in an article published in the November/December 1970 issue of the *Harvard Business Review*.* Jimmy Carter, just elected governor of Georgia, also read the article and invited its author, Peter Pyhrr, to join his staff and install the system there. Although I was unaware of their efforts at that time, I began to use the concept at Xerox starting in 1971, drawing on the Texas Instruments experience, as well as several variations of it I had

---

* Peter A. Pyhrr, "Zero-Base Budgeting."

observed or used as a consultant with McKinsey and Company. My
success with the zero-base concept varied at first, but I found it useful
in several planning, budgeting, control, and operational situations as
I successively held increasing responsibilities as a planning executive,
controller, general manager of a new venture, and director of two small
companies. One of my early applications was presented in the May/
June 1973 issue of the *Harvard Business Review,* under the title "Cost
Effectiveness Comes to the Personnel Function." This opened the door
to contacts with a number of organizations and individuals, including
Peter Pyhrr.

Management Analysis Center, Inc. began its extensive role in zero-
base budgeting when Peter A. Pyhrr was hired in 1972 in MAC's
Northbrook, Ill. office. Pyhrr left in 1974, but MAC's interest in zero-
base was strongly established. Many of the approaches to zero-base
budgeting common today were MAC innovations. Clearly many organizations were becoming deeply involved, and about this time I received numerous requests for further information. With the warm
endorsement of Xerox' management, I presented the concept to some
45 organizations. By maintaining continuing contacts with most of
them, I could observe their experiences as they implemented it. And
more importantly, I began to draw some broader conclusions as to
what zero-base budgeting was really all about and what it takes to
make it work.

As I reviewed the experience of my friends in other organizations
and gained more experience in the technique, and confidence in how to
handle its subtleties, I learned that when linked to other classic management approaches, it could become a powerful weapon in my professional arsenal. For successful zero-base budgeting hinges on more
than just a disciplined, systematic set of forms and procedures. Indeed,
quite a bit more is involved. In my view, its key success factors include:

Linking to the long-range planning process. Effective zero-base
budgeting requires a closed-loop feedback system to link the organization's objectives and strategies developed during long-range planning.
Otherwise, both the plan and the budget will be out of step with each
other and probably with reality. And zero-base budgeting's key benefit
of getting better resource allocation will fall depressingly wide of the
mark. But where linked, it becomes a powerful tool in making the long-
range plan happen.

*Gaining the support, involvement, and commitment of top manage-
ment.* Without high-level support, zero-base budgeting will be viewed
as another gimmick of the budgeting staff to gore somebody's (or

everybody's) ox. But when the chief executive is involved, he will come to thoroughly understand, often for the first time, how much is being spent for exactly what and most importantly why. The quality of his decisions and their implementation will be markedly enhanced.

Generating imagination by cost center managers. An effective zero-base budgeting process hangs on the amount of innovation brought to bear by those putting together the decision packages. Without this quality, packages will more often than not merely reflect the current way of doing things. But with it, new, exciting, and imaginative approaches will surface that can lead to more productive, efficient, and profitable operations.

Selling the concept and the ideas it brings to the surface. Most importantly, an effective zero-base budgeting process requires salesmanship, both of the concept itself and to manage the inevitable changes generated by the new ideas it brings to the surface. Without salesmanship by all concerned—the chief executive, budget staff, and cost center managers—the concept and all its benefits will probably be stillborn. But with some common sense attention to the basics of human relations, the zero-base budgeting process can become a rewarding and meaningful experience rather than just another threat to entrenched baronies.

Motherhood? Yes. But translating each of these principles into practical techniques is critical to success: All are necessary, and no one of them is sufficient.

That's what this book is about. In it, I hope to share my own experiences as well as those of several progressive organizations that have enjoyed success with zero-base budgeting. In each case, I find they've all effectively met each of these challenges. They thoroughly understood the concept and carefully designed supporting forms and procedures. This area will be covered in Chapters 1 and 2. Firm understandings and agreements have been nailed down for the ranking of budget proposals. Several ideas in this area will be reviewed in Chapter 3. A clear link has been made to the long-range planning process. How this might be done is the subject of Chapter 4. Then, Chapter 5 reviews a variety of sales (or persuasion) techniques that have direct application to and are critically needed for a successful zero-base budgeting process. Chapter 6 focuses on how to foster innovation. The role of top management is discussed in Chapter 7. Chapter 8 addresses some frequently raised questions. Finally, Chapter 9 presents some concluding thoughts.

For organizations that have successfully linked the zero-base budgeting procedures with the tested management principles developed in this book, the concept has truly emerged from its infancy. For, reduced to its procedural essentials, zero-base budgeting is nothing more than the same practical, logical approach used for years by anyone who makes spending decisions, whether an astute manager or a cost-conscious homemaker. Yet by linking those procedures to preagreed realistic planning objectives, gaining the involvement and commitment of top management, and fostering an innovative staff environment, and with careful attention to basic selling skills, zero-base budgeting has truly come of age. And the new integrated process has been a lot more pleasant and enjoyable for all concerned—and profitable for their organizations.

The thinking and experience of many of my business colleagues over the past several years are heavily reflected in this book. Morris Albertson of New York Telephone, Donald Anderson of Southern California Edison, William Phelps of Combustion Engineering, and Peter Pyhrr of Alpha Wire all provided helpful guidance in several key areas of the manuscript, drawing from their direct work with zero-base budgeting. In addition, two former associates of mine at McKinsey and Company—James P. Timoney, now with International Basic Economy Corporation, and Ward L. Reed, Jr., now with Arthur D. Little—were most helpful in reviewing the manuscript. Particular thanks go to John Main of Main, Jackson & Garfield, Inc., management consultants, for permission to incorporate into Chapter 6 large parts of an excellent article, "Innovation: Circumventing the Corporate Logjam" (appearing originally in his firm's quarterly newsletter, *Management Practice,* Fall 1976). I also wish to thank the editors of the *Harvard Business Review* for their permission to include in Chapters 2 and 3 material from my article "Cost Effectiveness Comes to the Personnel Function," published in the May/June 1973 issue, and for permission to quote from James L. Pierce's article, which was published in May/June 1954 (copyright © 1954 by the President and Fellows of Harvard College; all rights reserved).

Above all, though, I am indebted to Richard A. Marlow, who is chief financial officer of Associated Products, a division of Nabisco. Dick's thoughtful criticism was prompt, tireless, and unrelenting.

I am also thankful to Cecelia Rice and Dorothy Bird of the Xerox library for their assistance in locating key reference materials, and to my secretaries over the past six years—Jean Seager, Lynne Miller, Berdena Suhr, and Bonnie Seitz—for their typing and proofing both the manuscript for this book and articles incorporated into it.

Logan M. Cheek

Contents

1

Understanding the Zero-Base Approach

The goal . . . is the discovery of elements of truth, which with the passing of the centuries and the changes in . . . custom have come down to us overgrown with falsity.
Giambattista Vico, *Scienza Nuova,* 1725

ANY management technique comes of age when, after its earlier shortcomings have been identified and broadly recognized, it is refined with a new approach that squarely addresses the basic needs of an organization and its management. Examples from the contemporary management scene abound.

◊ As organizations grow, many move to decentralize to serve their markets and customers better.
◊ The needs of managing the highly complex space programs gave rise to a number of new approaches such as program management and matrix organizations.
◊ The challenges of worker alienation have prompted a number of new exciting motivational techniques in job enrichment and team organization.

Planning and budgeting have not been immune to change. In recent years, it has become apparent that the traditional tools of the trade in this key area left much to be desired. The needs were particularly obvious to most managers and executives involved with them on a professional basis in business and government, as well as in not-for-profit organizations. Because of that need, many of them in recent years have come increasingly to employ a new technique—the zero-base approach—in their professional work. With that acceptance, planning and budgeting have now passed through a metamorphosis. Out of past problems and shortcomings has emerged a cleaner, more rational, systematic, constructive, and results-oriented approach. And where success has been achieved, the professional stature, credibility, and careers of those using it have increased immeasurably.

Understanding this new zero-base concept requires a three-pronged approach. First, we must understand the traditional planning and budgeting approaches, their underlying assumptions, and their inherent shortcomings. Second, we should trace how these shortcomings led to the zero-base approach in a number of progressive business and public organizations. Finally, we should detail what the zero-base concept offers in terms of its approach, its philosophy, and its benefits.

THE TRADITIONAL APPROACH

A broad description of traditional planning and budgeting approaches is at best a generalization. Like all generalizations, it permits exceptions. But I do believe that what follows is representative and indicative of the inherent shortcomings faced by many organizations in operational planning and budgeting.

Its Inherent Logic and Assumptions

The logic behind traditional planning and budgeting techniques is depicted in Figure 1. In simplest terms, it calls for three steps:

1. Last year's spending level (or the trend of recent years) is extrapolated into next year.
2. The trended level is incremented for wage and salary increases as well as increases in the cost of purchased materials and services.
3. That spending level is further incremented for new projects and programs. Such requests often represent 50 to 100 percent increases over the incremented trend.

Figure 1.   Traditional techniques focus on incrementing past spending levels.

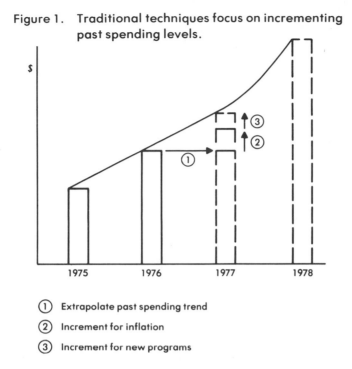

① Extrapolate past spending trend
② Increment for inflation
③ Increment for new programs

If all cost centers follow this approach (and most will) then it's clear that the initial consolidation of spending requests will raise a major issue for management decision: affordability. But let's step back for a moment and analyze the implicit assumptions made when the first step was taken. We assumed that all the activities making up last year's spending level:

◇ Were essential to achieving the ongoing objectives, strategies, and mission of organization.
◇ Must be continued during the coming year and are more urgent than newly requested programs.
◇ Are now being performed in the best, most cost-effective manner.
◇ Will continue to be cost-effective and necessary in the coming year, thus requiring budget increases only for labor and materials inflation.

Unless all these assumptions are true—and it is highly unlikely that they are—our simplistic extrapolation has generated a grossly inflated budget.

Impact on Decision Making

Let's now consider what happens when our submissions are consolidated for top management review.

The consolidated figures are normally *functionally oriented*. That means that the key decision makers know how much they're spending for marketing, finance, legal, personnel, and a host of other staff *activities*. But they don't know what they're getting in terms of *results*. And since the long-range plan objectives developed in the prior quarter normally focused on such high-minded objectives as increasing market share, penetrating new markets, or increasing productivity, linking the two is difficult, if not impossible.

As a corollary to their functional orientation, the budget is *accounting-oriented* in focusing on the issue of "how much." This kind of budget cannot answer such critical questions as "Why am I doing it?" or "Will it really make my plan's objectives happen?" We know, for example, how much we're spending for marketing staff services, but we have no means of knowing if it is the best way to launch that new product or increase market share.

And finally, at the human level, many heated arguments will now develop over the merits of those new incremental programs. Most can, in fact, withstand the test of cost-effectiveness. But the sum of all efforts, old and new, cannot withstand the test of affordability. One of my early motivations to employ zero-base budgeting in fact grew out of this problem. I was hard put to understand why managers within my organization engaged in ceaseless bickering and often childlike arguments. On the one hand, the annual budget cycle found our staff managers forcefully advocating the obvious responsiveness of their new programs to business imperatives. On the other hand, the controller and his budget staff argued the equally obvious need for an affordable, responsible budget. Yet the necessary resources were probably already there, buried in the base of last year's spending. The need, then, was for a system that rationally broke up all spending requests—both old and new—into understandable, manageable alternatives that enabled people (in the words of the scholar quoted at the beginning of this chapter) to discover the truth and falsity in each and *allowed all to compete on equal footing for scarce budget dollars.*

In sum, then, what does the traditional system provide us? In a real sense, very little. True, we do know how much is being requested, and we know that that amount is unaffordably high. But we don't know what's going to be delivered or if that's the best use of our resources. Since we don't know what's going to be delivered, we have an approach that focuses on, and indeed encourages, *activity* rather than *results,* both in putting together a budget and implementing it. Furthermore, implementing a budget with poorly allocated resources runs the serious risk of having an underemployed staff creating solutions to chase problems. And because the initial budgets are un-affordable, arbitrary tasks are now required to make the budget real-istic, often at considerable risk of missing obvious business opportun-ities.

Other Shortcomings

But even if the traditional budgeting system had merits, there are several inherent aspects of any staff organization and of its people that will subtly, but inexorably, prompt increases in overhead costs. Here are the five most frequently cited.

Staff managers are gun-shy on tough personnel decisions. When tasked with a budget reduction, the need to terminate or transfer a subordinate puts most staff managers in a painful position. It is dif-ficult to dismiss a friend, acquaintance, or professional colleague when there is little hard reason to do so. And the traditional budgeting ap-proach does little to provide the pertinent facts. (Line managers, on the other hand, are usually an entirely different matter, for their access to hard information on volume and productivity measures makes them more at ease in such situations.) Staff managers will often invent elab-orate projects to keep their people occupied.

Just as the budget is functional, so too is the organization. Being functionally oriented, most staffs focus on their service activities. Often the supplier of that service is separated from the user. A manager re-questing a data processing report rarely knows how much it costs, unless, of course, there is an internal chargeback system. Thus, he is hard put to compare its cost to the value he places on it. Moreover, the data processing manager often does not know the report's value in use, much less how the report can be improved to increase its value. Very frequently, that report continues to be provided long after its need has passed. Worse yet, it is often provided for a purpose not even justified by cost in the first place.

In one of the more amusing incidents of my consulting days, one of my colleagues was responsible for a cost reduction effort for a shipping and transportation client on the verge of bankruptcy. He noted a line item in the company's general ledger for "public ware-house rental" that the accounting staff had paid automatically for many years. The facilities manager told him that this was material stored at the request of the operations manager. But the operations manager knew nothing of it. A physical audit of the public warehouse uncovered a couple of hundred rolltop desks, several safes and rifles, and four stage coaches that had been in storage since the late nineteenth century! Shocking? Yes. But how many of us can cite less extreme incidents in our own organizations where the left hand doesn't know what the right hand is doing?

The organization staffs up with technicians and professionals. Support areas like research, engineering, data processing, and personnel are usually staffed with specialists. Such specialists are more often than not intent on advancing the state of the art in their profession. This is not all bad, but it leads to demands for and delivery of services at a quantity, quality, and level of perfection all out of proportion to the organization's real need. A new and sophisticated operations research model is of little value to the marketing managers of a product about to be written off, especially if none of them reads the reports or can make intelligent use of them.

Staff managers tend to reward responsiveness to perceived needs. Superiors often put a greater premium on quick responses than on running a tight ship. Most subordinates in fact live in fear *every day* of "looking dumb" and missing out on the next merit increase or promotion if they can't provide the boss with a quick and complete piece of thorough staff work or if they fall behind in providing their services. Only once a year, if then, during the budget cycle, might they be challenged for incurring high costs for delivering their services. So to avoid being nailed, many tend to overspend, overstaff, or at least overbudget. And if they become more proficient in their job over time and move to reduce costs, they find themselves open to the charge of having been inept managers in the past. It's not surprising, then, that few will risk taking a really critical look at their own organization.

The compensation system rewards those with large organizations. With the exception of managerial bonuses, and frequently only those at the highest level, most compensation systems are not tied to results. Rather, one's base salary is primarily a function of his expense budget or staff size. In turn, this will reinforce all the inherent organization problems outlined above.

These factors, coupled with the inherent shortcomings of the traditional budgeting system, prompt a natural tendency for staff overhead to get out of control. Thus, an effective alternative to historic budgeting practices must address shortfalls in the budgeting process *per se* as well as the dynamic peculiarities of the organization.

The Politics of Rolling Up the Final Budget

But let's now continue our discussion of the traditional budgeting approach. Once the budget has been consolidated, it is presented for

top management review. At various levels a number of events occur—
some rather ridiculous, others traumatic.

♦ At the top management level, there is quick recognition that the
budget will have to be trimmed. The system now places that responsibility on the top men. Yet because activities are buried within functions, executives lack the necessary understanding to know what to
do or how to proceed. So an arbitrary task is edicted: to cut back 20
percent or to last year's level. Whether that is the appropriate amount
is anyone's guess.

♦ The controller's staff now spend endless hours reviewing the
submissions, suggesting tasks, and coordinating the rework. Theirs is
a thankless task, for lacking intimate knowledge of what the resources
are for and why the spending is important, they must work in the dark
—and their attention to detail, nurtured through many years in accounting, makes them least likely to enjoy this. They become increasingly frustrated and irritable, which leads to high turnover and morale
problems. Extreme cases degenerate into ulcers and divorces. (I know
of one situation where the controller came to work one morning faced
with a nearly successful union organizing drive among his budget
analysts!) As a last desperate move, the order is put out to cut, shave,
chop, and trim.

♦ If the order to cut is repeated over several planning cycles, a
peculiar brand of gamesmanship develops among the cost center managers. On the one hand, an experienced cadre of clever men evolves.
Each year they substantially overinflate their budget submissions, because they know that when their proposals have been cut, they will
probably wind up with what they really needed anyway. The system
implicitly rewards their behavior. On the other hand, those who made
responsible submissions are penalized by the inevitable cuts. Few
make the same mistake twice. The unfortunate result is that dishonesty
is encouraged.

The end result of all this is that budgeting time becomes "dummy
up" time, with few straightforward answers offered to critical business
and planning issues and certainly not to the controller's staff. With
that growing polarization between cost center manager, budget staff,
and top management, there is often a total breakdown in communications.

The Traditional Approach: A Bottom Line

What is the value of the traditional approach? Beyond a set of consolidated budget submissions (minus the arbitrary cuts), most mana-

gers, controllers, and chief executives aren't really certain. To be sure, they do know how much is being spent, but they lack an appreciation of specifically what's going on, why, what better ways might be available, and which efforts are really necessary, because everything is functionally buried. And there is no understanding of how all the individual efforts relate to each other, much less a desire to talk about it openly. Nor are these efforts usually tied to broader plan objectives. In short, the system has given birth to an elephant with the muscular development of a mouse and the brain of an amoeba. Worse yet, top executives and the budget staff don't understand the creature's physiology. So they are at a loss to efficiently wield a scalpel on its fat without damaging its already overtaxed muscles. Even if he could, the chief executive is wary of stimulating the creature into charging off without purpose and in the wrong direction. And the controller fears it might viciously strike back at its tormentor as it has often been known to do.

HOW THE ZERO-BASE APPROACH EMERGED

Zero-base budgeting—to use President Jimmy Carter's words—has had a rather long gestation period and a brief infancy. Some of its principles were developed from ideas dating back decades in such areas as capital budgeting, while others are more contemporary. Figure 2 traces its recent history. Here are several budgeting techniques that either preceded zero-base budgeting or share many of its features.

Capital Budgeting. For as far back as forty or fifty years, most organizations have evaluated capital spending requests in stand-alone packages or programs. Each package describes what's being requested (say, a new lathe), what it will cost, its benefits (in increased productivity, increased volume, or decreased cost), and possibly some alternatives (for instance, a comparable lathe from other vendors). In more recent years, the financial staffs have employed increasingly sophisticated analytical techniques to evaluate the project's worth. Return on investment, opportunity costing, years to break even, cash flow impact, and net present value come to mind. If the same measure has been used across the board, all projects can be ranked quickly and objectively and the most promising ones selected. In a real sense, this is nothing more than the zero-base concept, modified to fit the needs of one particular area.

Program, Planning, and Budgeting. Many professionals have traced zero-base budgeting's origins to the Program, Planning, and Budget-

Figure 2. A brief history of zero-base budgeting.

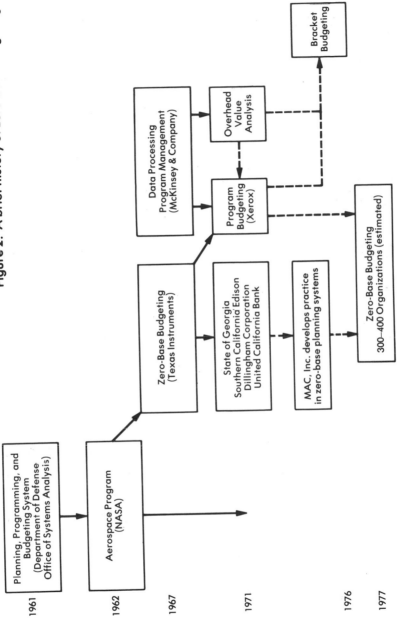

ing (PPB) system, which was developed in the early 1960s in the Department of Defense's Office of Systems Analysis and, in a refined form, broadly applied to the U.S. space program. At the risk of gross oversimplification—for there is an extensive body of professional literature * on the subject—PPB could be characterized in three ways:

1. It organized spending by *programs* rather than functional objects of expenditure as traditional budgets do. In other words, spending was classified by *outputs* tied to *objectives* rather than by *inputs* tied to *functions*.

2. These programs were extended far enough into the future to display their full resource requirements and spending implications. In other words, the cost of a new weapons system was projected over its life rather than just the next fiscal year. Using this approach would presumably avoid surprises in future budgets, as well as cost overruns.

3. All programs were subjected to a rigorous, explicit, quantitative analysis that focused on increasing the value of the program, decreasing the cost of resources required to deliver it, or both. Called *cost-effectiveness analysis*, it was (for example) used to assess several alternative weapons delivery systems (such as manned bombers, strategic nuclear submarines, or intercontinental ballistic missiles), with each compared to the required objectives of providing a strategic nuclear deterrent.†

In sum, PPB was a *program-oriented* technique with a *long-range horizon* that demanded cost justification of several alternative approaches against an established strategic need. Its primary thrust was toward *planning*, not budgeting. But where properly conducted, an operating budget was its natural fallout.

Project Management. In the late 1960s this concept came to be applied in the space program. Some of its planning techniques found use in the programming projects for the data processing departments of a number of business organizations. Again, the primary focus was on evaluating and ranking outputs (or the value of results) by program rather than summing up inputs (or costs). But the analytical techniques for ranking were further refined and expanded to include such noneconomic factors as technical feasibility (did the effort require a major state of the art effort with limited chance of success?), legal re-

---

* See, for example, Charles J. Hitch, "Program Budgeting," *Datamation,* September 1967, or Charles J. Hitch and Roland McKean, *Economics of Defense in the Nuclear Age,* New York: Atheneum, 1965.

† James G. Abert, "Structuring Cost Effectiveness Analysis," *The Logistics Review and Military Logistics Journal,* March–April 1966, pp. 19–31.

quirements (even if it's *not* cost-effective, must it be done anyhow to stay out of court?), operational feasibility (even if it *is* cost-effective, will line management eagerly accept and implement it?), as well as intangible benefits and the risks of not acting. These techniques have found direct application to ranking in zero-base budgeting and will be developed in detail in Chapter 3.

Management by Objectives. At the same time, many organizations began to instill principles of management by objectives (MBO) into their planning and performance appraisal processes. At Texas Instruments, the system was called "Objectives, Strategies and Tactics" (OST) planning system. In a nutshell, OST linked MBO and long-range planning with zero-base budgeting. In so doing, broad preagreed affordable objectives and strategies could be readily translated into a tactical operating budget.

Overhead Value Analysis. Overhead Value Analysis (OVA) emerged in its full form in the mid-1970s. It evolved from the profit improvement techniques developed by a number of consulting firms, primarily McKinsey and Company, to attack staff costs.* Its analysis focuses on programs or services and subjects each to a rigorous cost/benefit analysis. But it contains an intriguing new twist: Each manager who incurs the cost (or supplies the service) must work closely with those who benefit (the receivers or demanders) who specify exactly what's required. Although top management makes the final decision, the supplier must get the sign-off of the receiver by "selling" his service. This can have major (and positive) ramifications for the organization's human dynamics. Many organizations using zero-base budgeting have incorporated this "sign-off" technique into their procedure.

Bracket Budgeting. Bracket budgeting is a relatively recent technique † designed primarily for line (rather than staff) budgets. But it shares a similarity with one of zero-base budgeting's refinements: by using sophisticated statistical analyses, it attempts to assess the probability of a program's benefit being achieved. This is particularly critical for staff budgets, for we can be reasonably certain that while all *expenses* will happen, the *benefits* more likely will not.

And so we have set the stage for zero-base budgeting.

---

* John L. Neuman, "Time for Lasting Cuts in Overhead," *McKinsey Quarterly*, Summer 1975.

† Michael W. Curran, "How Bracket Budgeting Helps Managers Cope With Uncertainty," *Management Review*, April–May 1975.

THE ZERO-BASE APPROACH

In a nutshell, zero-base budgeting has been defined * as:

> An operating planning and budgeting process which requires each manager to justify his entire budget request in detail *from scratch* [hence zero base] and *shifts the burden of proof to each manager* to justify why he should spend any money at all. This approach requires that all activities be identified in *"decision packages"* which will be *evaluated by systematic analysis* and *ranked in order of importance.*

It's apparent from looking at some of the key phrases in this definition that zero-base budgeting has drawn heavily on some of the techniques already outlined. What's probably unique is the zero-base concept itself, although one could argue that many organizations facing a cash flow crunch have frequently reduced their capital budget to zero by deferring all such spending to another year. In many ways, it is unfortunate that the approach came to be tagged with this name "zero-base." Because of that onerous name, many budget center managers view it as another gimmick of the top brass or the controller to threaten if not eliminate their operation. One of my colleagues, incidentally, still thoughtlessly calls it "that zero-sum procedure," even after being corrected many times!

This inordinate focus on its zero-base aspect and the unwarranted perception of it as a "zero-sum" game (one in which one side must lose what the other gains) overlooks other integral parts that are critical to its success. Let's review the important ones.

Zero-base budgeting shifts the burden of proof away from top management and toward each budget center manager. But more is required than just a shift of responsibilities. If the budget center manager is going to prove his case effectively, he must become a persuasive salesman. Few, in my experience, are comfortable in this role. He must gain an appreciation of the finer points of persuasion and salesmanship before a zero-base budgeting process will be fully effective. The OVA concept of having the user and supplier of staff services jointly agree on what's required has direct application here. (Other needs are reviewed in Chapter 5.)

Activities are identified in "decision packages." For any given activity, there may be several alternative decision packages, each describing

---

* Peter A. Pyhrr, "Zero-Base Budgeting," unpublished speech delivered at the International Conference of the Planning Executives Institute, New York, May 15, 1972.

a different level of effort. Drawing on a basic feature of capital budgeting, zero-base budgeting packages are output-oriented (launching a product, improving a service, or increasing revenue, return on investment, market share, or productivity) rather than input-oriented by function. As already noted, one of the shortcomings of a functionally oriented budget is that it tends to become inflated. There is nothing to prevent zero-base budgeting decision packages from being inflated either. However, since the packages are appreciably smaller than a department's consolidated functional budget, it is much easier to understand them and so detect the "fluff" in each. And more importantly, by comparing packages, obvious redundancies can be readily identified and eliminated.

Packages are evaluated by systematic analysis. If a cost/benefit analysis can be performed on a function, it is a candidate for a zero-base budgeting package, even if the benefit is intangible. By tying costs to benefits (as did PPB), zero-base budgeting squarely addresses the key issue: "What am I getting for this expenditure?" But more than just a statement of the costs and benefits for the current mode or operation is required. Drawing on the concepts of project management, some refinements of zero-base budgeting require careful attention to legally mandated efforts, the technical "state of the art" feasibility, or such intangibles as "better human relations." These aspects of the systematic analysis become critical to the ranking process in zero-base budgeting.

Packages must be ranked in order of importance. Drawing on features of capital budgeting and project management, zero-base budgeting requires that all packages be ranked in order of importance. Sometimes that ranking is based on cost-effectiveness; other times it incorporates other criteria such as those noted above. But the ranking is critical to achieve zero-base budgeting's objective for better resource allocation. Once the ranking has been agreed to, packages can be readily approved and funded up to an acceptable level of affordability.

It's clear, then, that the process is much more than just a "zero-base" one. Because of these other aspects, it could easily have been given a number of less emotional names: Decentralized budgeting, program-based budgeting (which was my early favorite), cost-effectiveness budgeting, or budgeting to objectives, or priorities, might have been good possibilities. But with several years now of a fairly successful track record, the "zero-base" name has become indelibly fixed in the management lexicon. And those who have come to understand its full ramifications and subtleties are no longer hung up with semantic threats.

What are these subtleties? In a real sense they can be considered corollaries to each of the four characteristics discussed above. Here is what's required for successful zero-base budgeting:

A burden of mutual commitment between superior and subordinate. While the burden of proof has been shifted from top management to the staff manager, the agreement on the final ranking and resource approval represents a businesslike understanding of what results are expected. The logic is quite simple: Both jointly agree to the integrity of the packages and their ranking. Top management agrees to fund them, and the staff manager agrees to deliver the service. Now if a new task comes along, they must either (a) trade it off against (or decommit to) something else already agreed to or (b) increase the staff manager's budget. This highly positive aspect of zero-base budgeting facilitates a healthy working environment.

Innovative decision packages. Merely identifying all activities in discrete packages accomplishes little useful purpose. To be sure, more marginal activities might thus be identified for possible elimination, but truly effective zero-base budgeting should foster innovation. New and better, more cost-effective ways to perform the same function have to be conceived and captured in a decision package, and given a fair hearing. By pushing responsibility for those new ideas down to the lowest possible level, zero-base budgeting can become a broad-based suggestion plan. And with suggestions coming from those most intimately aware of improvement opportunities, zero-base budgeting affords a golden opportunity for their day in court.

Breaking up decision packages into different ways of performing the same function and different levels of effort. The concept of breaking up decision packages into different ways and levels is probably the most complex and confusing aspect of zero-base budgeting and merits extensive discussion in the next chapter. The idea is important, however, if we are to have a meaningful ranking process.

To give an example, the answer to a "make or buy" question may lead to several different *ways* of performing the same job. In security services, for example, I could (1) have a dedicated staff of my own guards; (2) hire an outside firm on a contract basis to provide guard services; (3) incorporate that job with that of the receptionists; or (4) not have a security service at all, but require everyone to have a security badge and make every employee responsible for security, with the right to throw anyone not wearing a pass out of the plant. If I decide to have a dedicated staff of my own guards, I may then build up the security budget in *levels,* starting with no security, then a skeleton force for eight hours on day shift only, then a skeleton force for the other sixteen hours, then a full increment for the day shift, then a full increment after hours, then a skeleton weekend force to be fully incremented if production goes on overtime.

Laying out all the most feasible alternative ways and levels in this fashion will facilitate quick decision making during the ranking process. But more importantly, it fosters innovation.

Tying the packages to a corporate mission or planning objectives. All packages must be ranked in order of importance. So the corollary issue is: "What's important?" This requires logical and consistent objectives, clearly transmitted to each budget center manager so that (a) he knows what the organization is trying to do and (b) he can begin to figure out some clever ways in which his budget center can contribute to meeting some of the objectives. Effective zero-base budgeting demands that those walls of Jericho between planning and budgeting must come down, that the two functions must be linked. This relationship is depicted in Figure 3 and will be expanded upon in greater detail in Chapter 4.

We've seen now that the zero-base concept is quite at odds— perhaps 180 degrees—with the traditional approach. These key differences are summarized for comparison in the following list.

Figure 3. Integration of zero-base budgeting with long-range and operating planning.

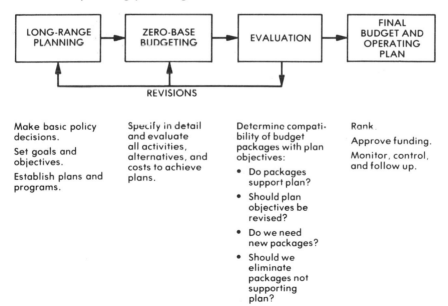

Make basic policy decisions.

Set goals and objectives.

Establish plans and programs.

Specify in detail and evaluate all activities, alternatives, and costs to achieve plans.

Determine compatibility of budget packages with plan objectives:

• Do packages support plan?

• Should plan objectives be revised?

• Do we need new packages?

• Should we eliminate packages not supporting plan?

Rank.

Approve funding.

Monitor, control, and follow up.

Source: Adapted by permission from Peter A. Pyhrr, *Zero-Base Budgeting* (New York: John Wiley, 1973), p. 3.

Aspects of the Budgeting Approach	Traditional Approach	Zero-Base Approach
Philosophy	Functionally oriented (by division and department).	Program-oriented (by production or service).
	Accounting-oriented (primary focus on "how much").	Decision-oriented (focus on "what, why, and how" issues as well as "how much").
	Focused on justifying new incremental programs.	Requires all programs, old and new, to compete for the same scarce resources.
Technique	Extrapolate past spending.	Break up budget into understandable decision packages.
	Increment for inflation and new programs.	Analyze all packages and rank them.
	Trim, usually across the board, to achieve affordable level.	Trim only discrete, marginal programs and packages, up to the level of affordability.
Linkages to Long-range Plan	Linkages to long-range plan's strategies and objectives given lip service at best. If budget indicates plan is unachievable, attempt rarely made to reconcile or rationalize the two.	Requires integrated linkages to long-range plan's strategies. By constant reiteration of the process, both plan and budget are brought into consonance.
End Product	An aggregated set of numbers, often bloated beyond affordability and understood by few, if any. Long hours often spent in bringing preliminary submissions to reasonable levels.	A clean, lean, muscular set of ranked priorities than can be rationally increased, changed, or trimmed as circumstances warrant.
Organizational Impacts	Encourages "gamesmanship":	Facilitates rational analysis and decision making:
Within staffs	–Those who substantially inflate requests, knowing they will be cut, are implicitly rewarded, for they wind up with what they probably wanted anyway.	–Those who do inflate their packages are more likely to be caught and exposed for what they are.
	–At the same time, those making responsible submissions are penalized with the inevitable cuts. Few make the same mistakes twice. Thus, dishonesty is encouraged.	–Carefully devised results-oriented packages make heroes of their sponsors.

Aspects of the Budgeting Approach	Traditional Approach	Zero-Base Approach
Organizational Impacts (cont'd.)		
Between staffs and budgeting	The situation is polarized: Budgeting time is "dummy up" time.	All options are laid out for open discussion, mutual evaluation, and agreement in businesslike atmosphere.
	Communications often break down.	Triggers need for, and use of, selling skills within and between staffs to persuade each other of merits of their proposals and to manage the changes required by the approved programs.
Between staffs and top management	The burden of proof is placed on top management to decide how much should be spent for what and why.	The burden of proof is placed on staff managers to show why they should spend anything at all—with top management making final decisions on an orderly, rational base of ranked priorities.
Personnel Impacts	Known to lead to high turnover and morale problems, not to mention divorces and ulcers.	The system is clean, responsible, and responsive. Where cuts are necessary, feedback can be more convincing and tactful because the cuts are put in the context of the organization's broader objectives, needs, and resource limitations.
Follow-up Controls	Relatively easy to translate into a follow-up control mechanism. However, the spending being controlled may not represent the best use of the organization's resources.	With appropriate procedures and forms, decision packages can be readily rolled up for a conventional follow-up control system. More importantly, specific major results-oriented programs can be monitored to make sure they achieve the crucial obtives and not just a targeted spending level.
Linkages to Other Business Systems	None known.	Allows for easy detection of duplication, thus providing a more rational basis for organization planning.
		Could logically be linked to a manpower planning and placement system that facilitates movement and develops key performers.

Using the approaches mentioned above, MAC, Inc. worked with Peter A. Pyhrr from 1972 to 1974 to refine the process. Since that time, MAC, Inc. has applied zero-base budgeting to over 100 organizations in both the private and public sectors. MAC's major role, besides providing impetus to the emerging process, was to expand the concept to emphasize organizational development and planning. At the same time, similar practices were being developed by Allen Austen of Austen and Lindberg in Salt Lake City, as well as Karl Miller of Pace Associates, in York, Pennsylvania. In more recent years, many of the major accounting firms, including Peat Marwick Mitchell & Co., Coopers & Lybrand, Ernst and Ernst, and Arthur Young, Inc., have become active, particularly in those aspects of zero-base budgeting that relate to follow-up financial controls.

CONCLUSION

What then is the zero-base approach all about? The answer is very clear. It tries to uncover what is really going on in an organization, why it's being done, what better ways might be available, and which activities are really important—as well as what they cost. If we know what these efforts are, how they relate both to each other and to broader goals of the organization, we have a powerful tool to manage and allocate our resources and, in so doing, to achieve our objectives. And this is precisely the virtue of the zero-base approach. A goal, objective, strategy, policy, decision, scheme of control—all these managerial commodities are successful only if they can be implemented. The zero-base approach provides an effective means to translate high-minded goals into reality—and with better resource allocation to boot.

2

Getting Your Zero-Base Budgeting Act Together

Do not be desirous to have things done quickly; do not look at small advantages. Desire to have things done quickly prevents their being done thoroughly. Looking at small advantages prevents great affairs from being accomplished.
Confucius, *On Government*

Confucius' ancient advice is no less true today for an effective zero-base budgeting effort. With a well-intentioned sense of urgency, many organizations attempt to adapt zero-base budgeting forms and procedures used elsewhere to their situation. The effect is a lot of unnecessary rework and redesign, for more often than not, someone else's forms and procedures were structured to meet an entirely different objective. Getting your zero-base budgeting act together, then, requires rigidly adhering to the basic steps of good systems design:

1. Define your objectives: What are you trying to do?
2. Structure your implementation strategy: How do you get there from where you're now?
3. Develop your supporting system: What's required for input?

If these three steps are followed sequentially, you'll find that zero-base budgeting can be implemented rather quickly and efficiently, with minimal risk of confusion and frustration, which often result in its being thrown out altogether. This approach and the issues to be addressed in each step are depicted in Figure 4. As can be seen from the figure, the sequence of steps in *implementing* the zero-base budgeting system is the exact reverse of the sequence followed in *designing* it. To design the system, we start with objectives and work back to our input requirements; to implement it, we start with the input—our decision

Figure 4. Sequence of steps for designing and implementing a zero-base budgeting system.

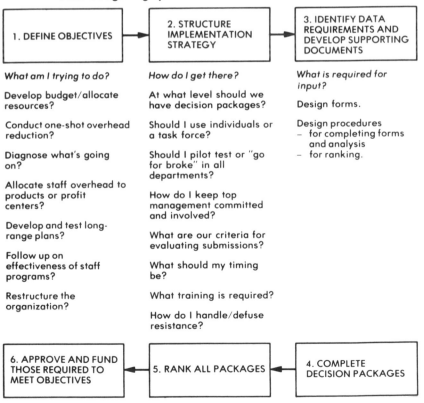

packages—and work through an evaluation and ranking to an approval of those packages that meet our basic objectives.

DEFINING THE OBJECTIVES

The first step in structuring a zero-base budgeting system is to establish objectives for the effort. This normally involves a brief informal meeting among those who will administer it as well as those who will make use of the end product. The participants generally include the controller and his budgeting staff, the planning executive and his staff, and possibly a handful of key line executives, including the chief executive. Each should come prepared with an overall appreciation of the concept and approach as outlined in Chapter 1.

The purpose of the meeting is quite simple: to gain full agreement at the outset as to what is being attempted. The zero-base approach can be applied to a variety of problems. Once agreed upon, the objectives will drive the entire implementation strategy as well as the design of its supporting forms and procedures. Here are some uses to which zero-base budgeting might be put:

1. Developing an operating plan and budget for the coming year.
2. Conducting a one-shot cost reduction effort on staff overhead.
3. Diagnosing what's really going on in the organization so as to refine policy or set long-range objectives.
4. Allocating staff overhead to product lines or profit centers on a more equitable basis.
5. Validating the feasibility of the long-range plan.
6. Auditing the effectiveness of staff programs.
7. Providing a data base to restructure the entire organization.

There are no doubt others, but these are the most common. The important point is this: Just to achieve one or two of these objectives successfully will require installing a whole new approach and developing a different mentality in the organization. Laying on additional objectives and requirements during the first year or two quite probably will prompt the system to collapse under its own weight. Restricting your efforts to one or two key objectives also facilitates a more businesslike relationship among the staff. In this regard, two of my earliest zero-base budgeting experiences come to mind.

The first case involved developing a long-range personnel department plan. Toward the end of the process, the vice president asked if all the submissions could be readily converted into next year's budget. The answer was no: Since developing a budget was not the original intent of the study, the forms did not require account-level detail. Naturally, the various personnel managers got rather annoyed when tasked for additional data, and a few probably wondered if the top man really had his head screwed on right!

The second case occurred a year later in putting together a staff budget. Right in the middle of the process, the controller came under pressure to allocate staff overhead more equitably among product lines. Naturally, I was asked whether the necessary analytical information was available in the zero-base decision packages. Again, the answer was no: The forms did not contain allocation detail. This naturally prompted concerns as each wondered whether the other knew what he was doing.

So my advice would be to start small with one or two objectives first, then expand the concept into additional areas as more proficiency and experience are gained. But be sure that all key players agree to the objectives and understand clearly that no others will be pursued.

STRUCTURING THE IMPLEMENTATION STRATEGY

Now that you know where you want to go, the next task is to determine how to get there. This requires addressing a number of subissues, including:

1. What are our decision units going to be?
2. Who should be responsible?
3. Should we pilot-test or go for broke?
4. What role will top management play?
5. What are our criteria for evaluating decision packages?
6. What's our timing?
7. What sort of training is necessary?
8. How do I handle or defuse resistance?

The answers to each of these questions will logically lead into a charter of responsibilities and an implementation schedule, as well as to basic information elements to be incorporated in the forms and procedures.

Defining the Decision Units

The simplest solution is to define decision units as the present cost centers. But this need not be the only approach, nor necessarily the best. If you remember, back in Chapter 1 we noted that the zero-base concept is *output-* or *results-oriented* rather than *input-* or *activity-oriented*. This could lead you to define decision units around products

or markets or customer groups or geographic territories or capital projects or anything else that can be logically tied to the organization's
mission or long-range objectives. While each organization must decide
for itself what is practical, my own experience leads me to suggest the
following guidelines:

Each package should stand alone. This permits you to identify
clearly all true costs of delivering a given service. From an administrative standpoint, it precludes confusion and screw-ups during ranking
if one package that supports another happens to get eliminated. For
example, let's suppose the marketing staff puts together a package to
provide market research services for "Forward Product X." The package should include marketing's effort as well as operations research
and data processing services requested from other departments, and
externally purchased consulting services. If these latter supporting
functions are developed separately but dropped during the ranking
process, marketing's package may well be an impractical headless
horseman. If the organization has no internal chargeback system, then
the decision packages should be explicitly cross-referenced to prevent
the necessary supporting packages from falling between the cracks.

*Top management should set a minimum organization level from
which decision packages are to be developed.* Normally, this would be
a section level operation of no less than five to seven people. But it
could be a substantially larger entity, such as the 100-man security
force or maintenance crew. And the decision unit could be as small as
a single staff specialist.

*Each manager should be permitted to further break down his
decision unit into appropriately smaller packages.* The minimum size
of the package would be that level of effort required to complete a job
meaningfully and provide some benefit to the organization. In my
experience, this should be *no less than a one-person package.* While
fractions of man years may be practical for analytical purposes, they
are meaningless for decision making: How can I increment or cut out
0.5 clerks? Remember, the prime objective of zero-base budgeting is
decision making. Nitty-gritty fractionalized packages defeat that purpose and create a mountain of paperwork.

Focus on staff rather than line operations. Budgeting for line operations is driven by unit volumes and standard costs and is derived by
multiplying the two. Zero-base budgeting is intended primarily for
staff functions such as the headquarters departments or the manufacturing or field sales staff. To be sure, an organization could conceivably use the zero-base technique (as no doubt many have) in
manufacturing line operations. Basically, it would mean putting to-

gether a team of smart industrial engineers to work out fundamentally different ways of manufacturing the product, seeking in all cases increases in hourly productivity or improvements to standard rates. No doubt Volvo went through a mental process similar to zero-base budgeting several years ago when it abolished assembly lines and moved to assemble cars by teams. But this use of zero-base budgeting is uncommon. Rather, it is used primarily for staff efforts, as shown in Figure 5. And here is the crux of its value: The efforts of staff manufacturing industrial engineers or personnel job enrichment specialists are highly leveraged. A one-dollar resource investment into focused efforts on their part will not unlikely yield a hundredfold return in increased line productivity. That's another good reason why the decision package must be structured to capture both costs *and* benefits of a given effort on the *entire* organization.

Stay flexible. While any procedure (including zero-base budgeting) requires a certain degree of discipline to be successful, it should not be so rigid as to stifle innovation. The zero-base forms have been designed to facilitate flexibility *within* a manager's sphere of responsibility, but suggestions for improvement opportunities that reach beyond his sphere should also be encouraged. Such ideas might include consolidating planning, data processing, or secretarial support functions within or between departments. In addition to encouraging ideas from the grass roots, many organizations charter an independent third party to identify and propose new ideas. In some cases, this role has been played by the controller's staff, in others, by a permanent profit-improvement section or an outside consultant.

One rule overriding everything, though, is not to lose sight of your preagreed objective for the zero-base effort. That objective—to put together the annual budget, achieve a one-shot cost reduction, audit the effectiveness of staff programs, or whatever—should drive your thought process as you define decision units.

Who Should Be Responsible?

A second key task in structuring an implementation strategy is to figure out who should formulate the decision packages. At first glance, you might think this should logically be the responsible manager of the decision unit (or budget center). Yet this need not necessarily be so, for you really have four alternates. You could assign the work to the individual manager, a multifunctional task force, an outside consultant, or a combination of any of the above.

The reasons for choosing one of these four vary widely between organizations but generally fit the following patterns:

Figure 5. Representative functions amenable to zero-base budgeting.

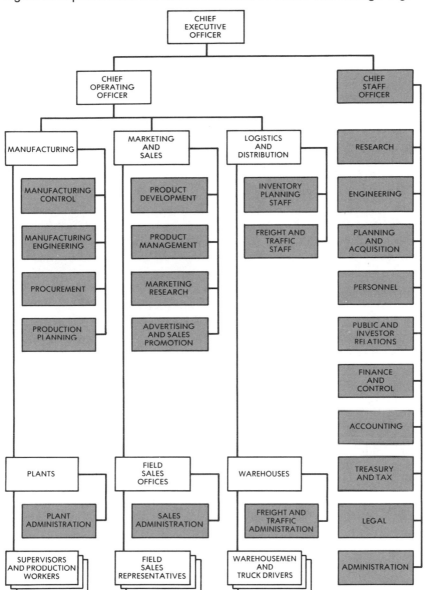

STAFF Functions appropriate for zero-base budgeting.

LINE Functions inappropriate for zero-base budgeting, but on which ZBB packages should have direct, tangible, and leveraged effects.

Using the individual managers. Those organizations which are endowed with an aggressive innovative grass-roots management team recruited and nurtured over the years; which enjoy freewheeling and open communication on tough, seemingly intractable problems; which have full and open commitment and involvement from the top to the zero-base concept; and which possess skilled administrators on the budget staff, committed to keeping the ball moving, are safe in assigning the task to their individual budget center managers. Such organizations are not infrequently the acknowledged leaders in their industry or pretty close to the top.

Using a multifunctional task force. Those organizations which have generally weak management at the grass roots (or a promising but immature one) but *do* have a number of "stars" who can innovate; which wish to give those stars a quick, challenging exposure to all facets of the organization; which need to produce their budget quickly and without extensive training; and which have a warm but not altogether total commitment from top management to test and verify the idea and debug it thoroughly before extending it to the grass roots generally opt for the task-force approach. Usually, they are average organizations—neither recognized leaders nor turnaround cases.

Using consultants. Those organizations which have a weak, complacent, lackluster, or thoroughly lackadaisical management at the grass-roots level; or which face a highly charged, polarized, political environment; or which need skilled no-nonsense expertise to produce immediate and tangible results as well as (hopefully) develop an ongoing capability and must funnel highly sensitive and confidential findings directly to the top for immediate action generally rely on a consultant. Such situations are not infrequently encountered where an immediate staff reduction is of urgent necessity or a turnaround is imperative.

Using a combination of the above. Those organizations that are very large, relatively flush in resources and time, and face highly technical or complex management problems usually opt for a combination of the above. In such cases, the key men at the top honestly admit to the human frailty of not being able to appreciate fully all the subtleties of the business, and employ a "check and balance" approach. Their hope is that in so doing, all sides of critical operational issues will be brought to the surface and will thus lead to more intelligent decisions.

For each approach, there are very real advantages and disadvantages, which are summarized in Table 1.

Table 1. Responsibility for decision packages: individuals vs. task forces vs. consultants.

Individual Effort	Task Force Effort	Consultant
	Pros	
Allows those most intimately aware of the job to suggest improvements. Clear commitment and accountability for implementation.	Minimizes training. Permits assignment of most competent people. Speeds up the process. Avoids some confusion since all members work closely under common assumptions. Increased objectivity.	No training (unless brought in to support task force). Technical proficiency. May have access to wealth of ideas for improvement from other companies. Can provide a convenient "whipping boy" for tough decisions.
	Cons	
Large-scale training and coordination efforts necessary. Individuals may hold back on best alternatives to protect their empires.	Dilutes follow-on commitment and accountability for implementation. May not be able to uncover or perceive best ideas for improvement.	End product is only as good as the man. Sometimes fails to leave ongoing capability. Often resisted as a "threatening outsider." Burden of commitment and accountability remains with organization (or CEO).

Should We Pilot-Test or Go for Broke?

The next major subissue is of less importance because more and more organizations have tried zero-base budgeting and proven its value. For those organizations where the initiative for zero-base budgeting has come directly from the chief executive, it is more often than not a nonissue. Being results-oriented, most chief executives want the system implemented yesterday!

Where the initiative, however, comes from the rank and file or from the financial staff, as it often still does, the question remains valid. And a delicate tradeoff is involved: On one hand, everybody wants quick results to look like a hero; on the other hand, no one wants zero-base budgeting to suffer infant crib death with a possible career upheaval.

Three alternatives are depicted in Figure 6. Alternative 1 represents the "go for broke" approach, where the chief executive is totally on board, management at the grass roots is strong, and the budget staff is able to keep on top of the situation. Alternative 2 represents a weak compromise, and one rarely used nowadays. But it is still appropriate where staff resources are extremely limited or where outsiders must be called in. Alternative 3 represents the "pilot test" approach. It was quite popular in zero-base budgeting's formative years but is less necessary today because more managers have become proficient in the technique.

Again, the choice of implementation alternatives must be made with careful consideration of each organization's circumstances.

What Role Will Top Management Play?

The specifics on top management's role in zero-base budgeting—particularly in ranking and deciding on packages—are the subject of Chapter 7. Top management's early commitment is critical, and it should become involved in the implementation strategy from the beginning. In my experience, three options are open, each logically following the other.

1. Where top management is the first to hear of zero-base budgeting and seize the initiative to move out on it, further efforts by others to gain top management's support are academic. Indeed, they may be counterproductive: As any salesman will tell you, once the close is made, leave. To do otherwise invites reconsideration and a reversal of the decision.

2. Where the initiative originates from a key officer or the controller, an appropriately timed copy of a brief professional article on zero-base budgeting should open the door to gaining top-level support. I say "appropriately timed" since most CEOs are very busy and possibly won't catch the full impact of what you're proposing if they're commiserating over last month's poor sales performance or preparing for a proxy fight. And I say "brief professional article" because few CEOs have the luxury of time or the interest to read a book or even entertain a full-blown proposal on the subject. The initial need is merely to spark interest, nothing more. Full technical details can come at a later and more appropriate time when the interest is real. Of course, if the CEO asks, "What can we do to improve our planning and budgeting process?" kick down the door and charge through, horse, broom, and balloons!

Figure 6. Implementation alternatives.

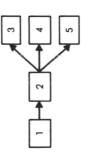

	PROS	CONS

ALTERNATIVE 1

1. Set up and train teams.

2–5. Evaluate all departments concurrently.

PROS: Rapid implementation.

CONS: High failure risk.

ALTERNATIVE 2

1. Set up and train teams.

2–5. Evaluate departments in sequence.

PROS: Low failure risk.

CONS: Slow implementation, with possible need for later reevaluation of earlier efforts.

ALTERNATIVE 3

1. Set up and train team with multifunctional membership.

2. Initial team to evaluate personnel or legal programs.*

3–5. Team members then chair and train new teams that evaluate their own departments.

PROS:
Quick feasibility test on smallest department.

Low failure risk.

Rapid resolution of "bugs"

Rapid training of departmental teams.

CONS:
Implementation shorter than in alternative 2 but longer than in alternative 1.

*These staffs selected only because of small size permitting rapid team training.

3. If there is slight interest generated but no great enthusiasm (what I'd call the "show me" attitude), then by all means, conduct a show-and-tell meeting. It should be positive and direct and include a live example of ranking decision packages from your own organization. I'd strongly urge putting the chief through a ranking exercise, using real packages. I've found that the direct, hands-on experience of working with zero-base budgeting packages and understanding what's really going on in one part of the organization inevitably leads to their enthusiastic endorsement.

And that's exactly what's needed at this stage: commitment. But it must be more than an oral commitment; it should be a memorandum, and in the obvious writing style of the CEO. It will be used to kick off the process within the organization and should be incorporated in the procedure. That it be written in his style and personally signed by him *is* important. I find that directives in the controller's style but with the chief executive's signature have a way of disappearing into numerous managers' "wait and see" files. An example of such a kick-off memo is shown in Figure 7.

Figure 7. Sample letter of transmittal from the chief executive.

MEMORANDUM

TO:	All Managers	**OFFICE:**	Chairman and CEO
FROM:	Charles E. Ott	**DATE:**	June 1, 1977
SUBJECT:	1978 Operating Plan — Zero-Base Budgeting		

Next year will be tough. As we found in the long-range plan, we've got obvious problems with competition, regulations, and spiraling costs. But we will face an even greater challenge in launching four exciting new products on which the survival of our company depends.

To ensure that our resources are being put to best use and that we can rapidly redeploy them if necessary, our 1978 Operating Plan will incorporate the concept of zero-base budgeting.

Zero-base budgeting is a challenging approach. It is one that already has clearly proved its value in many organizations. The process offers each of you a unique opportunity to make your case to me for improved, more cost-effective operations. I'm looking forward to personally reviewing your ideas for improvement and spending priorities and expect each of you to share my personal commitment.

One final thought: If the chief executive is not sold on the value of this approach and is not willing to make the effort or commitment to forcefully implement it throughout the organization, then the idea should be restricted to your own area of operations, if not dropped altogether. I personally know of no organizations that have successfully pulled off zero-base budgeting without a firm commitment from the top.

What Are Our Criteria?

Any sound planning and control system seeks both to measure costs *and* track benefits. Zero-base budgeting is no different. Identifying costs associated with a given program package is quite simply a matter of rolling up all expense accounts—labor, material, utilities, depreciation, and so on—into the appropriate decision packages. Measuring benefits, though, is an entirely different matter that merits special and early attention as we plan the forms and start setting up the procedures.

The key need is to orchestrate the effort so that all budget center managers are "singing out of the same hymnbook" if you will. If all staff managers are given free rein to come up with their own measures, you don't have to think too far into the future to imagine the confusion that will result. Suppose one manager evaluates the merits of his decision packages using ROI as he defines it while a second uses increased market share, a third, increased dollar sales, a fourth, increased unit volume, and a fifth, decreased staff costs. Even if all their assumptions and numbers are right (and they rarely are), consolidating and ranking this potpourri of apples and oranges will tax the talents of the most experienced budget managers!

What's required, then, is to reach some agreement well in advance of implementing zero-base budgeting as to just what measurements are to be used and what the value of each is. Since costs will be identified in dollars, I find it best to identify benefits in some dollar measure such as increased sales or revenue. Where the staff manager is more comfortable with other criteria (such as market share or unit volume), the budget staff should translate these into a common dollar value. This will ensure both a common framework and common values and make the job easier for all.

In measuring benefits, any one of three approaches can be pursued:

The single-criterion approach. This approach is most common where the zero-base concept is used for capital budgeting. All projects are cast in decision packages. Each is evaluated in terms of either return on investment *or* cash flow *or* years to break-even or some other quantifiable measure. Then all packages are ranked systematically from highest to lowest by that single yardstick.

The multiple-criteria approach. This approach is normally used where the zero-base concept is applied to staff budgets. Again, all projects are cast in decision packages. Each is then evaluated on any one of two or three yardsticks. Those most frequently used are increased revenue and increased productivity (or decreased costs) of line organizations. After translating these projected benefits into dollar values, costs can be subtracted and the packages ranked in descending order of net benefit.

The opportunity cost approach. This approach can be used for zero-base budgeting in both staff and capital budgeting situations. Unlike the multiple-criteria approach, it is particularly useful where you can't easily identify a benefit to the revenue line or, in some organizations, decreased costs. In simplest terms, the estimated cost of the proposed approach (say, setting up an in-house market research function) is subtracted from the actual cost of the present approach (say, a market research function that relies heavily on outside agencies and consultants) to yield a net savings.

The ideal situation is one where the organization already has a well-established long-range planning procedure. From the long-range plan, the budget staff can abstract its major objectives (which might read: "increase after-tax profits 15 percent per year by increasing unit volume 12 percent per year and productivity 4 percent per year"), translate each into dollar amounts to serve as yardsticks for the coming year, display them on a standard chart (such as Figure 14 at the end of this chapter), then incorporate them into the zero-base budgeting procedure. But even organizations with no structured long-range planning objectives can still employ zero-base budgeting effectively. In such cases, yardsticks can be identified and assigned a value based on the organization's current operating environment.

What's Our Timing?

The time required to implement zero-base budgeting during its first year will hinge in large part on the answers to the other seven issues discussed in this section. Thus, if you opt for a large number of decision units; include more budget center managers; move for a pilot test; allow top management to play a low-key role; incorporate many yardsticks to measure benefits and leave it up to the budget center managers' discretion to define them; keep procedural direction and training to a minimum; and tolerate widespread resistance to the effort, you may find the process never gets completed!

Most organizations, however, find the process takes about the same time as their old approach during the first year and somewhat less time thereafter. Table 2 outlines the time required for each of the specific planning and budgeting steps, based on the experience of a number of organizations.

Table 2. Time requirements in weeks for budgeting, traditional vs. zero-base approach.

		Zero-Base Approach	
Budgeting Step	*Traditional Approach*	*First Year*	*Other Years*
Set up procedures and forms.	2	3	2
Communicate procedure and train key people.	1	3	2
Develop "first pass" traditional budget or decision packages.	4	4	3
Consolidate submissions or rank packages.	2	2	2
Conduct top management review.	2	2	2
Develop "second pass" traditional budget or refine select packages.	4+	2	2
Consolidate submissions or rerank refined packages.	2+	1	1
	17++	17	14

These requirements represent what I feel are reasonable standards for scheduling where the effort is smoothly administered. This should not imply, however, that budget center managers will be tied up for four or more full weeks in drafting and refining their submissions; in practice, they will spend only a few days or even hours in "hands-on" efforts. The same logic applies to the rest of the steps, whether traditional or zero-base. Because of this, more time should not be allowed, for if it is, Parkinson's Law—that work expands to fill the time allotted for it—will invariably come into play.

This issue is more than just one of time: A corollary is the question of quality. Many executives, on first hearing of zero-base budgeting, somehow hope that it is a magic formula that will bring all kinds of improvements during the first year. Such is rarely the case. No doubt solid benefits will accrue in the first year, but I know of few organizations that feel they get their best mileage from the process until the third or fourth year. Those who would hope to bull their way to an outstanding first year should consider Peter Pyhrr's critique of zero-base budgeting in the State of Georgia after the first full cycle:

> Zero-base budgeting can be effective and should be continued next year. . . . The quality of the decision packages and analysis is generally poor to mediocre . . . however, these results are better than anticipated. . . . Opportunities for reducing costs and improving effectiveness were not adequately identified and evaluated. . . . Quality improvements will come naturally as agency managers continue to use this type of analysis. . . . Most of the severe problems encountered this year can be avoided next year because of this year's learning experience as well as a few minor changes in the process.*

Does this mean zero-base budgeting represents wasted efforts?

I think not. Its value will be proved in your organization to an increasing degree, but over time. Here is what I think is a fair representation of the experience of a number of organizations that have used it over several planning and budgeting cycles.

During the first year, the organization gets its feet wet in the process. The quality of the analysis is about average, and resource allocation is about the same as would have been gained with the traditional approach. But a few "star" managers are quick to seize on its value and identify key profit opportunities that can be derived from their areas. The ideas they generate probably justify the entire effort. But in some cases there may be widespread resistance to the paperwork problem.

During the second year, the organization is now riding down the learning curve. With some shakedowns of the procedures, forms, and training, more managers are attuned to the concept and its process. They begin to observe that carefully thought-out submissions get attention—and resources. Many more now seek to identify better ways of providing their services and move smartly to cultivate professional contacts outside the organization as sounding boards for new ideas. Resource allocation is better, as are the packages, but further improvements are still possible.

During the third year, the flat area of the learning curve is reached. With the exception of newly appointed managers, only refresher training is necessary. Top management can now pay more attention to follow-up controls on the best packages from prior years (to assure that the benefits identified and promised are in fact happening) and on

---

* Peter A. Pyhrr, *Zero-Base Budgeting* (New York: John Wiley, 1973), pp. 130–31.

setting up performance audits to monitor and track new programs. The accounting staff now begins to seriously entertain the idea of restructuring the chart of accounts and the financial systems to include product, program, or decision package codes as well as functional codes.*

During subsequent years, implementation is now effectively completed and maximum benefits are being achieved. Major efforts from now on are more maintenance-oriented.

As you might suspect, the most critical period is at the conclusion of the first year. It is usually at that point that most of the frustrations have occurred while the benefits have not yet been fully realized. The analogy to a capital project or the launching of a new product is apt: Most of the costs have been incurred, but the benefits have yet to be fully realized. In fact, those organizations discarding the concept have usually done so then, not realizing that the big payback is yet to come!

What Training Is Required?

Training in the concept of zero-base budgeting can encompass any of a number of alternatives such as:

◊ A well thought-out procedure with one-on-one coaching by the budget staff.

◊ A formal short classroom effort that presents the concept and its mechanics.

◊ A somewhat longer classroom effort that gets beyond the concepts and mechanics, providing an overview of the organization, its industry, economics, and plans and goals, as well as basic concepts in planning and control.

◊ An extensive formal effort incorporating all the above as well as workshop sessions in human relations, persuasion skills, and how to foster innovation.

Selecting the appropriate options depends on a careful assessment of the capability, maturity, and sophistication of the management cadre. Many of those who are well endowed have been able to implement zero-base budgeting with a good procedure and nothing more. Others have found this inadequate and have had to extend their efforts into the third and fourth level. If that is necessary, it should not be viewed

---

* A product or program code is a common identifier for all decision packages supporting a given product or staff effort. It cuts across different functional departments such as marketing, manufacturing staff, or control. Many companies doing goverment contract work already have program codes in their accounting systems to facilitate rolling up all costs for a specific effort.

as an indication of incompetence. As I noted above, many staff managers grew up in and continue to work in rather narrow technical and professional areas. They have never been challenged to look at their services from a businesslike perspective as zero-base budgeting requires. Yet this new discipline, if communicated to them in a soundly structured training program, can immeasurably increase their effectiveness and efficiency as managers.

How Do I Defuse Resistance?

Careful advance attention to all the above issues will go a long way to smoothing implementation. But no organization is perfect, and all will experience some resistance from a few key detractors. Such problem cases should not be allowed to fester; they should be identified well in advance of announcing the new approach, and a specific action plan worked out on how to handle each of them.

A plan to handle detractors can be written or simply be a set of mental notes. It should identify who they are, what their concerns will be, and how each will be addressed.

Their identity will be pretty well known from past experience. Those managers who always complain of a lack of adequate resources, who are always lobbying for more than they realistically need, who generally feel uncomfortable with business planning and budgeting, who feel they've been shortchanged in the past, or who are just plain immature, insecure, or ornery are prime candidates.

In most cases I find principal objections will center on allegations that zero-base budgeting (a) requires more time, (b) wastes a lot of time on detailed analysis of programs that probably won't be approved anyway, and (c) requires cost-effectiveness analysis where evaluation data are simply not available. How these and other concerns are handled is discussed in Chapter 8.

Even if time does not permit working up a detailed plan, responses to each of these and other anticipated concerns should be well thought out, agreed to by all managers involved in administering the zero-base budgeting process, and tactfully explained. My own experience suggests, however, that the objections most commonly raised are really covers for a more fundamental one. As J. P. Morgan once said: "A man always has two reasons for the things he does—a good one and the real one." And the real reason is often the feeling that zero-base budgeting may well wipe out their own jobs!

This concern is a valid one. Therefore, before implementing the process, many organizations have incorporated a couple of ideas to smooth the introduction. In some cases a commitment is made that no one will lose his job. If his position is radically changed or altered, one of comparable level and responsibility will be guaranteed. Manpower savings are then captured through attrition. In other cases outright bonuses are made, usually of up to 10 percent of the first year's savings.

Of overriding importance is not to play with a detractor like a cat with a chipmunk. Where that happens, the controller and his budget staff have lost sight of the concept of their duties as eliciting, rather than laying it on, and they're sure to convert the ambivalence of the organization toward zero-base budgeting and its administrators into one-dimensional hostility. Rather, what's required is to gain a quick commitment to give zero-base budgeting a fair try, then to move out smartly to develop, rank, and select the best decision packages.

The same logic applies to all other strategic issues discussed above: If a choice must be made between the fine points of how we're to get there and actually getting there, the latter is clearly preferable.

DEVELOPING THE SUPPORTING SYSTEM

If we've carefully thought out and resolved all the above issues, then developing the supporting system is merely an act of putting the meat on the bones. The supporting system for zero-base budgeting consists of two documents: a decision package form, with worksheets if desired, and a procedure manual. Let's review some basic ideas for their design and format.

The Decision Package

A decision package has been defined as a document that "identifies a discrete activity, function, or operation in a definitive manner for management evaluation and comparison with other activities." * A sample decision package is depicted in Figure 8. It is offered only as an example, for there is no such thing as a "model" decision package. Formats will vary widely among and even within organizations, depending primarily on what you're trying to accomplish.

What items should be included in a decision package? Regardless of its purpose, all decision packages will incorporate the following minimum elements:

Basic identifying data, including the program name, program number and level, a brief description of the program's goals and objectives, as well as the sponsoring organization, cost center, author, and date.

* Peter A. Pyhrr, op cit., p. 6.

Figure 8. A sample decision package.

1. Define and describe the program.	PROGRAM NAME: Service Force Job Enrichment Program Program No. 16

DESCRIPTION   (objectives, target population, implementation schedule):

To extend the job enrichment program for the service force —
as piloted in Spring Falls, Avon Hills, and Maplewood branches
— to all branches between 1972 and 1976.

2. Identify and segregate legally required efforts.

Is program legally required? ☐ Yes   ☒ No

3. Evaluate feasibility:

(a) State-of-the-art implications.

STATE OF THE ART   ☒ High   ☐ Medium   ☐ Low

(b) Ease of implementation.

EASE OF IMPLEMENTATION   ☐ High   ☐ Medium   ☒ Low

(c) Net economic benefits ...

ECONOMIC BENEFITS   ☒ High   ☐ Medium   ☐ Low

	Potential revenue impact	Probability of occurrence	Probable gross benefit (cost)
Identifiable benefits:			
Reduction in service force turnover of 1 point.	$ 450,000	.2	$ 90,000
Extension of 1.2 point reduction in absenteeism, as demonstrated in pilot project.	$ 2,132,500	.8	$ 1,706,000
Extension of 5% increase in service force productivity, as demonstrated in initial efforts.	$85,500,000	.1	$ 8,550,000
Total benefits	$88,082,500	.12	$10,346,000
Tangible costs to Xerox of acting: Group personnel staff time to develop program, and line management time to implement program in all branches.	($ 472,950)	.9	$ 425,655
Total costs	($ 472,950)	.9	$ 425,655
Probable net benefits (cost)			$ 9,920,345

... and intangibles.

Intangible benefits

Increased morale in service force, with improved customer
service and satisfaction.

"Contagious effect" of job enrichment to other groups, e.g.,
sales and clericals.

Improved service manager development with concurrent sharpening
of their motivational skills. As an extreme example, one
manager at Avon Hills increased his team's productivity 70%.

(d) Economic risks.

ECONOMIC RISKS   ☒ High   ☐ Medium   ☐ Low

Possible consequences of not acting:
Continued escalation of service costs as a percent of revenue.

ASSUMPTIONS AND OTHER CONSIDERATIONS:

Cost estimates assume 4.4 man years of group staff time, .26 man
years of branch manager time, and 15.8 man years of service manager
time to implement program in a population of 1,053 service managers.

Benefit estimates assume elimination of 3 days absenteeism per
month for each of 1,053 service teams, favorable productivity, and that
turnover experience in pilot branches can be cascaded to all branches.

Feasibility assessment, including details on the program's economic benefits and costs and the risks of not acting. In addition, many organizations require an assessment of the program's legal necessity and technical and operational feasibility.

Alternative courses of action, including a brief description of other ways considered but not recommended to accomplish the same objective.

These basic elements are incorporated in the "bare bones" decision package shown in Figure 8. Figure 9 provides a more generalized refinement.

In principle, a decision package may include any of a number of other items to facilitate administration of the system. For example, where the system is being used to develop an *operating budget,* the format of the packages might also include:

Intangibles that cannot be quantified (such as improved morale, management development, or public image). These aspects often merit heavy consideration when a hard choice has to be made between two packages of equal economic merit.

Account level detail to facilitate translating approved packages quickly into the existing accounting and control system.

Head count of exempt and nonexempt workforce associated with the program where the organization controls its operations on personnel as well as expense dollars.

Cross-references to supporting packages where the organization does not have an internal chargeback system for support services. It's preferable, though, that all packages stand alone.

Product line allocation where the organization wishes to allocate staff expenses to profit centers or product lines.

Operating ratios such as cost benefit ratios, unit volume of sales per marketing analyst, or payables processed per accounting clerk, for analytical evaluation and comparison with other packages.

Assumptions used in developing the package can be displayed and checked to ensure economic feasibility. Normally, though, I find these are better left to an attachment.

In addition, if the zero-base process is used in support or for validation of a long-range plan, some forms include a cross-reference to the organization's long-term goals. (This will be discussed in Chapter 4.)

Finally, two other elements might be considered:

Figure 9. A decision package form: "bare bones" elements.

PROGRAM NAME:		NO.			
			LEVEL_____ OF_____		
ORGANIZATION:	BUDGET CENTER	PREPARED BY:		DATE:	

DESCRIPTION OF GOALS AND OBJECTIVES:

FEASIBILITY ASSESSMENT:

   1. Is this program legally required?　　☐ YES　　☐ NO

   2. Technical feasibility　　　　　　　　☐ HIGH　　☐ MEDIUM　　☐ LOW

   3. Operational feasibility　　　　　　　☐ HIGH　　☐ MEDIUM　　☐ LOW

   4. Economic benefits (describe below)　☐ HIGH　　☐ MEDIUM　　☐ LOW

                                          Probable Gross

     Identifiable Benefits:　　　　　　　Potential　　Probability　　Benefit/(Cost)

     Total Benefits

     Tangible costs:

     Total Costs

     Probable net benefits (costs) .... _____

   5. Economic risks of not acting (describe) ☐ HIGH　☐ MEDIUM　☐ LOW

ALTERNATIVE WAYS AND LEVELS CONSIDERED		APPROVALS	
Ways	Levels		
		_____	
			Date
		_____	
			Date
		_____	
			Date
		_____	
			Date

Functional coding. Many zero-base systems—particularly in larger organizations—require that the packages be coded to indicate the service being delivered. For instance, all computer centers, employment functions, or market research functions may be assigned a unique code. When pulled together by codes and compared with each other, obvious redundancies are more readily uncovered. This is particularly appropriate in large government organizations and was first successfully tried in Georgia. Using that approach, some 43 printshops were merged into one, as were all departmental computer systems.

Follow-up control. A question frequently raised is "How do I assure achievement of benefits in the program packages when my control system is tied to functional accounts?" To those organizations doing contract work for government projects this represents no problem. But if you have only a functionally coded accounting system, a simple control block incorporated at the very end of the decision package may do the trick. One that I've frequently used looks like this:

Check one:
□ This program is ongoing
or
□ Staff work for this program will be completed
by ——————— and implemented by ———————.

Copies of all approved program packages are placed in a calendarized suspense file for follow-up when appropriate. I suggest investing in a major restructuring of the accounting system only after a couple of successful years with the process.

A supplementary decision package that incorporates all these additional elements is shown in Figure 10. Figures 11a and 11b are offered as annotated examples of how a decision package might be filled out in practice. Finally, the "model procedure" in Appendix A provides additional insights into how each section is completed.

The Worksheet

After spending a little time understanding each of the annotated exhibits and the model procedure, filling in each of the sections of a decision package should be an easy task—with one possible exception: *For every activity, zero-base budgeting requires the identification and evaluation of alternatives of accomplishing it.* The principle is simple

Figure 10. A decision package form: supplemental elements.

PROGRAM NAME:		NO.	FUNCTIONAL CODE:		LEVEL___OF___

INTANGIBLE BENEFITS:

RESOURCE DETAIL: _____ 197 _____   _____ 197 _____
                  Ja Fe Ma Ap Ma Ju Jl Au Se Oc No De   Q$_I$ Q$_{II}$ Q$_{III}$ Q$_{IV}$

Account Code

Manpower
 Exempt
 Nonexempt

CROSS REFERENCES TO OTHER PROGRAMS			DIVISION O'HEAD ALLOCATION	OPERATING RATIOS:
No.	Department	Level	☐ Prorate on Revenue OR	197____ 197____
			☐ Industrial Prod. _____ %	
			☐ Consumer Prod. _____ %	
			☐ Financial Svcs. _____ %	
			☐ New Ventures _____ %	

ASSUMPTIONS:

THIS PROGRAM SUPPORTS THESE LONG-RANGE STRATEGIES	CHECK ONE:
☐ 10% Unit Volume Increase	☐ This program is on-going
☐ 5 point Market Share Increase	OR
☐ ZEPHYR Product Launch	☐ Staff work will be completed by
☐ 5% Line Productivity Increase	_____ and implemented by
☐ 3% Staff Overhead Reduction	_____

Figure 11a. A decision package: bare-bones elements.

PROGRAM NAME: PLANT SAFETY SERVICES		NO. 38	LEVEL 1 OF 5	
ORGANIZATION: MANUFACTURING STAFF	BUDGET CENTER M-109	PREPARED BY: John Eltra		DATE: 8/15/76

DESCRIPTION OF GOALS AND OBJECTIVES:

Conduct OSHA compliance reviews -- the absolute minimum for a safety program -- under leadership of corporate medical director and corporate counsel, assisted by plant managers

FEASIBILITY ASSESSMENT:

1. Is this program legally required? [X] YES   [ ] NO
2. Technical feasibility [X] HIGH   [ ] MEDIUM   [ ] LOW
3. Operational feasibility [X] HIGH   [ ] MEDIUM   [ ] LOW
4. Economic benefits (describe below) [ ] HIGH   [ ] MEDIUM   [X] LOW

Identifiable Benefits:	Potential	Probability	Probable Gross Benefit/(Cost)
None Known	$0	–	$0

Total Benefits

Tangible costs:

Corporate medical, legal and clerical support required to conduct compliance reviews, and plant manager and staff efforts required in support	($33,000)	.9	($30,000)

Total Costs

Probable net benefits (costs) ....   ($30,000)

5. Economic risks of not acting (describe) [X] HIGH   [ ] MEDIUM   [ ] LOW

This effort is legally mandated. Failure to comply can result in protracted and costly litigation, as well as plant shutdown.

ALTERNATIVE WAYS AND LEVELS CONSIDERED

Ways	Levels
1. Assign exclusive responsibility to each plant manager.	(2 of 5): Provide safety tools, gloves and shoes to all production workers.
2. Assign work to outside counsel and consulting engineer.	(3 of 5): Add plant safety engineer to conduct safety awareness program.
Former rejected since plant's lack full-time expertise, latter is too expensive.	(4 of 5): Establish corporate safety staff
	(5 of 5): Expand plant safety staffs

APPROVALS

John Eltra   8/15/76
                  Date

P___ S____   8/20/76
                  Date

_____
                  Date

_____
                  Date

Figure 11b. A decision package: supplemental elements.

PROGRAM NAME: PLANT SAFETY SERVICES	NO. 38	FUNCTIONAL CODE: M-48	LEVEL 1 OF 5

INTANGIBLE BENEFITS:

- Maintain "good corporate citizen" image
- Positive impact on safety, employee morale and communications

RESOURCE DETAIL: _____ 197 _____   _____ 197 _____

Account Code	Ja	Fe	Ma	Ap	Ma	Ju	Jl	Au	Se	Oc	No	De		Q$_I$	Q$_{II}$	Q$_{III}$	Q$_{IV}$
3500 (Ex Lab)	0	0	0	0	0	0	0	6	3	0	0	3		0	0	9	3
3501 (NE Lab)	0	0	0	0	0	0	0	1	2	0	0	1		0	0	3	1
7000 (Supplies)	0	0	0	0	0	0	0	1	2	0	0	1		0	0	3	1
8001 (Travel)	0	0	0	0	0	0	0	3	6	0	0	1		0	0	9	1

Manpower

	Ja	Fe	Ma	Ap	Ma	Ju	Jl	Au	Se	Oc	No	De		Q$_I$	Q$_{II}$	Q$_{III}$	Q$_{IV}$
Exempt	0	0	0	0	0	0	0	2	1	0	0	1		0	0	3	1
Nonexempt	0	0	0	0	0	0	0	1	2	0	0	1		0	0	3	1

CROSS REFERENCES TO OTHER PROGRAMS			DIVISION O'HEAD ALLOCATION	OPERATING RATIOS: 197 7 197 8
No.	Department	Level	[X] Prorate on Revenue	
3	Medical	1	OR	Not applicable
15	legal	1	[ ] Industrial Prod. _____ %	
			[ ] Consumer Prod. _____ %	
			[ ] Financial Svcs. _____ %	
			[ ] New Ventures _____ %	

ASSUMPTIONS:

- We will be reviewed by OSHA (per their letter of 7/1/76) during September 1977.

THIS PROGRAM SUPPORTS THESE LONG-RANGE STRATEGIES	CHECK ONE:
[ ] 10% Unit Volume Increase	[ ] This program is on-going
[ ] 5 point Market Share Increase	OR
[ ] ZEPHYR Product Launch	[X] Staff work will be completed by
[ ] 5% Line Productivity Increase	September 1 and implemented by
[ ] 3% Staff Overhead Reduction	December 31

but prompts the most questions and attendant confusion. Yet, to a large degree it is a key building block to fostering innovation.

How do we identify and evaluate alternatives in zero-base budgeting? Alternatives to accomplish any activity are of two types. The first focuses on the *different ways of performing the same function*. In most applications of zero-base budgeting, different ways of doing the same thing are mutually exclusive. Thus, although two or three ways might be considered and evaluated, only one can be selected. If we select more than one, the obvious redundancy wastes resources. Several examples can underscore this point:

◇ If I am responsible for providing computer services, I may do it through a central facility *or* through a facilities management contract *or* through decentralized minicomputers *or* through time-sharing terminals *or* through an outside service bureau. But I will *not* normally approve and fund two or more of these alternative approaches.

◇ If market research services are required, I may use the outside services of my advertising agency *or* market research firm, *or* I may depend on an internal dedicated staff *or* the part-time support of my planning staff.

◇ If I have to hire people, I can use a skeletal internal staff supported by outside agencies and search firms, *or* I may use a larger internal staff. Alternatively, I may use something in between.

Not in all cases will the alternatives strictly exclude one another. Sometimes you may choose to have an alternative support or back up the other, but such packages should be carefully scrutinized, for the risk of redundant efforts is quite real.

The second kind of alternative focuses on the *different levels of effort* that can be used to perform one of the alternative functions. Such levels are *additive* from a minimum level that can stand alone through as many increments as are practical. Any or all of the several levels may in fact be approved. If we were to expand upon our employment example cited above and we decided to use the internal-staff alternative, the different levels might look something like this:

Level 1: Screen and refer only walk-in candidates, in sufficient numbers to meet the hiring needs (employment growth plus turnover replacement) for the budget year.

Level 2: Actively solicit the required number of candidates by targeted advertising. This would presumably enhance the quality of the personnel hired.

Level 3: Actively search out candidates with a specialized in-house staff. This would hopefully further enhance the quality.

Level 4: Provide a small budget for agency and search firm fees for candidates particularly hard to find. At the same time, offer cash bonuses to employees for referrals hired.

Level 5: Undertake an extensive personnel research effort to develop and validate tests geared to selecting those employees most likely to succeed.

As you can see, level 1 represents a "bare bones" minimum, and as we add incremental levels, we increase costs as well as benefits (through improved quality). But if really pressed for resources, we could get away with level 1 and nothing else. Figures 12a and b show how the prior example (Figures 11a and b) might be incremented to a second level.

One of the best analogies illustrating this point is the situation of the housewife who puts together her monthly grocery budget. In a broad sense, her objective is to provide her family with nutrition.

In terms of alternative *ways*, the family can eat out every day at the 21 Club *or* eat spaghetti every day *or* (most probably) do something in between. The cost can range from $6,000 down to $60 per month. Let's suppose that having spent most of her food budget last month on a new Yves St. Laurent original, she opts for spaghetti every day.

In terms of alternative *levels*, she can (1) opt in the purest sense for spaghetti with butter every day at $60, (2) add Parmesan cheese every night for an additional $2, (3) add salad every night for $15 more, (4) add meat sauce on Wednesdays for $10 more, (5) add clam sauce on Fridays for still $9 more, and (6) add meatballs on Sunday for $12 more. Each of these represents incremental levels of effort (or spending). Depending on which levels she selects, she can spend (for example) $60 (#1 only), $62 (#1 and #2), $71 (#1, #2, and #5), or she can splurge on all levels at $108!

Logic dictates that alternative *ways* be looked at first, choosing the best one of them. Then alternative *levels* are selected within the chosen way.

A question frequently raised at this point is: "Why shouldn't the manager identify the best alternative way and combination of levels and present it in one consolidated package?" Although this would appear to greatly simplify matters, it leads to two pitfalls during the review process:

1. Higher management may not like the alternative chosen but will waste a lot of time trying to come up with a better approach.

Figure 12a. A decision package: bare-bones elements, level 2.

PROGRAM NAME: *PLANT SAFETY SERVICES*		NO. *38*	LEVEL __2__	OF __5__
ORGANIZATION: *MANUFACTURING STAFF*	BUDGET CENTER *M-109*	PREPARED BY: *John Eltra*		DATE: *8/15/76*

DESCRIPTION OF GOALS AND OBJECTIVES:

Provide appropriate safety tools, gloves, shoes and goggles to all line production workers in manufacturing plants at no cost.

FEASIBILITY ASSESSMENT:

1. Is this program legally required? ☐ YES ☒ NO

2. Technical feasibility ☒ HIGH ☐ MEDIUM ☐ LOW

3. Operational feasibility ☒ HIGH ☐ MEDIUM ☐ LOW

4. Economic benefits (describe below) ☐ HIGH ☐ MEDIUM ☒ LOW

Identifiable Benefits:	Potential	Probability	Probable Gross Benefit (Cost)
• *Elimination of subsidy for safety gear formerly paid to local merchants and vendors.*	$7,350	.9	$6,615
• *Elimination of accidents and injuries identified in 1976 audit caused by not having or wearing proper safety gear.*	$78,340	.4	$31,336
Total Benefits			$37,951
Tangible costs:			
• *Tools*	$1,100	1.0	1,100
• *Gloves*	2,400	1.0	2,400
• *Shoes*	10,500	1.0	10,500
• *Goggles*	1,200	1.0	1,200
Total Costs			$15,200
Probable net benefits (costs)			$22,751

5. Economic risks of not acting (describe) ☒ HIGH ☐ MEDIUM ☐ LOW

Increased lost time accidents with lower productivity and production. Prior to 1971, we did not have safety devices. If 1970 rates were to be experienced in 1977, exposure of $850,000 ($450,000 lost production, $400,000 increased insurance and workmen's compensation claims) would result.

ALTERNATIVE WAYS AND LEVELS CONSIDERED		APPROVALS	
Ways	Levels		
1. Contract with local merchants to provide safety items at 30% discount, with subsidy. Although cheaper and free of administrative headaches, would expect fewer employees to avail themselves of opportunity.	*See level #1 package of program 38 for description of incremental levels in this area.*	*John Eltra*	*8/15/76* Date
		Th. Shandt	*8/20/76* Date
			Date
			Date

Figure 12b. A decision package: supplemental elements, level 2.

PROGRAM NAME: PLANT SAFETY SERVICES	NO. 38	FUNCTIONAL CODE: M-48	LEVEL 2 OF 5

INTANGIBLE BENEFITS:
- Positive impact on employee morale
- Maintenance of reputation as local leader in this area.

RESOURCE DETAIL: _____ 197 _____   _____ 197 _____

	Ja	Fe	Ma	Ap	Ma	Ju	Jl	Au	Se	Oc	No	De		QI	QII	QIII	QIV
Account Code 4010 (Prod.Supp.)	1.1	1.1	1.2	1.2	1.2	1.3	1.3	1.3	1.3	1.4	1.4	1.4		4.2	4.5	4.7	4.9

Manpower
Exempt   0 —————————————————————————→
Nonexempt   0 —————————————————————————→

CROSS REFERENCES TO OTHER PROGRAMS			DIVISION O'HEAD ALLOCATION	OPERATING RATIOS:

CROSS REFERENCES TO OTHER PROGRAMS

No.	Department	Level
38	Manufacturing Staff	1
24	Manufacturing Admin	3*

DIVISION O'HEAD ALLOCATION
- [X] Prorate on Revenue OR
- [ ] Industrial Prod. _____ %
- [ ] Consumer Prod. _____ %
- [ ] Financial Svcs. _____ %
- [ ] New Ventures _____ %

OPERATING RATIOS:

	197 7	197 8
Lost Time / 10^6 days	3.5	3.3
Workmens Comp claims / 10^3	0.6	0.5

ASSUMPTIONS:
* Manufacturing Admin (Program 24, Level 3) will provide support through employee store

THIS PROGRAM SUPPORTS THESE LONG-RANGE STRATEGIES	CHECK ONE:

THIS PROGRAM SUPPORTS THESE LONG-RANGE STRATEGIES
- [ ] 10% Unit Volume Increase
- [ ] 5 point Market Share Increase
- [ ] ZEPHYR Product Launch
- [X] 5% Line Productivity Increase
- [ ] 3% Staff Overhead Reduction

CHECK ONE:
- [X] This program is on-going

OR

- [ ] Staff work will be completed by

_____ and implemented by

_____

2. Higher management may not be able to afford the consolidated level of effort requested but may nevertheless be definitely agreeable to something less. Again, if only one consolidated package is presented, the burden of proof lies with the reviewer to break it up. And quite frankly, top management is *not* as qualified to do this as is the lower-level manager, who is intimately aware of the operation from daily experience.

This brings us to one final question: "Doesn't this lead us into an inordinate and wasteful number of packages to show alternative ways and levels, only one of which (if that) will be approved?"

The answer is yes, it certainly will, but only if you allow yourself to get trapped in analytical and paperwork gymnastics. A key guideline is to lay out your alternatives, then *do a thorough evaluation on only that one which in your best professional judgment represents the most feasible approach.* The worksheet shown in Figure 13 was developed to facilitate this process and might well have been used to develop the packages shown in Figures 11 and 12. It is a highly informal document intended to discipline the thought process and should not contain elaborate or definitive analysis. It is used merely to identify the best approach, which will be captured in detail in a decision package. It can also be used as a discussion backup during higher-level review to show the alternatives considered.

The Procedures

A positively written, concise, and well-documented cookbook procedure can go a long way toward ensuring success in zero-base budgeting. If carefully structured, it should (1) set the stage for a rewarding effort, (2) trigger innovative ideas to improve operations, (3) minimize the training required, (4) mimimize unnecessary questions for clarification during implementation, and (5), most importantly, guarantee a reasonably uniform quality product.

While the procedures will vary with individual circumstances, most incorporate these elements:

1. A letter of transmittal from top management.
2. A statement of the purpose and objective of zero-base budgeting.
3. An economic overview of the organization and its industry, as an introduction to planning assumptions and expense guidelines.
4. A discussion of decision packages and how they're developed.
5. A discussion of the ranking process.
6. A detailed schedule.

Figure 13. A decision package worksheet.

Objective: Provide plant safety services (Alternative #2 is recommended approach)

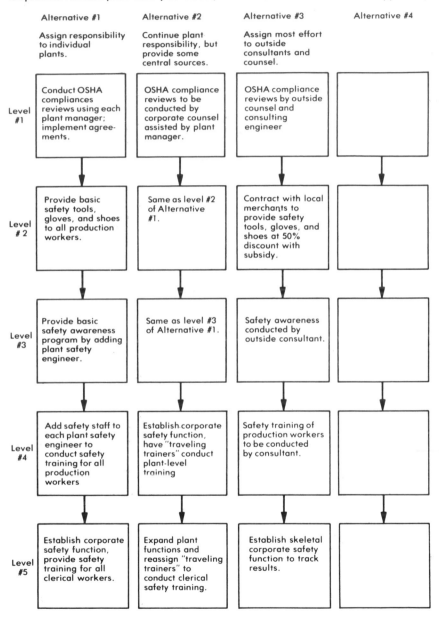

	Alternative #1	Alternative #2	Alternative #3	Alternative #4
	Assign responsibility to individual plants.	Continue plant responsibility, but provide some central sources.	Assign most effort to outside consultants and counsel.	
Level #1	Conduct OSHA compliances reviews using each plant manager; implement agreements.	OSHA compliance reviews to be conducted by corporate counsel assisted by plant manager.	OSHA compliance reviews by outside counsel and consulting engineer	
Level #2	Provide basic safety tools, gloves, and shoes to all production workers.	Same as level #2 of Alternative #1.	Contract with local merchants to provide safety tools, gloves, and shoes at 50% discount with subsidy.	
Level #3	Provide basic safety awareness program by adding plant safety engineer.	Same as level #3 of Alternative #1.	Safety awareness conducted by outside consultant.	
Level #4	Add safety staff to each plant safety engineer to conduct safety training for all production workers	Establish corporate safety function, have "traveling trainers" conduct plant-level training	Safety training of production workers to be conducted by consultant.	
Level #5	Establish corporate safety function, provide safety training for all clerical workers.	Expand plant functions and reassign "traveling trainers" to conduct clerical safety training.	Establish skeletal corporate safety function to track results.	

The procedure in Appendix A incorporates each of these elements. But here are some specific pointers on how to present each of them.

1. *The letter of transmittal* (along the lines of Figure 7) from top management should go beyond just a "call to arms" of the type "Here's what we're going to do and why we're doing it." It should explicitly signal to everyone the chief executive's full commitment to the idea and his intention to be personally involved in the review process.

2. *The statement of the purpose and objective* of zero-base budgeting should discuss in broad terms zero budgeting's philosophy, concept, and specifics, and contrast them with traditional approaches. Also, some organizations—particularly those where decentralized budgeting represents a new and unfamiliar effort—find a broader discussion of the basics of planning, decision making, and financial statements necessary to build a foundation of common understanding and expertise. Again, I cannot emphasize enough the importance of this section's message being positive in tone, focusing on what zero-base budgeting can do *for* the reader rather than what it might do *to* him. In a real sense, it will sell—or kill—the system.

3. *The economic overview* of the organization and its industry is intended to expand the basic foundation developed in the first two steps. As indicated in Chapter 1, many staff managers have spent their entire careers in specialized technical functions such as research, engineering, or data processing. While this specialization has obvious advantages, few understand and fewer have ever been told what it takes to ensure the economic success of the organization or what risks the organization faces. Even in the absence of our immediate need to put together a thoughtful, realistic budget that will improve the organization's effectiveness and efficiency, most people clearly welcome an opportunity to be treated as adults and be brought on board with an understanding of such issues as "What is our sales and expense forecast?" "What do recent trends in our market share, new-product successes, and productivity tell us?" "What major competitive threats do we face?" or, more succinctly, "What do we have to do—and do well—to succeed in this business?" Properly presented, this overview gets everyone involved and, in so doing, often sparks a myriad of new business strategies and tactics from the grass roots, aimed at the organization's most significant problems. The items shown in Figure 14 were part of a larger analysis used by a major health care company, prior to a zero-base budgeting effort, to educate its staff managers in its basic opportunities and needs, key success factors, and long-range business objectives. It can be put together rather quickly from existing information readily available to the planning or financial-analysis staff. It can also serve as a logical basis for a series of tables showing the

Figure 14. Economic overview of an organization preparing for zero-base budgeting.

1. Our environment for the last five years has faced several challenges:

   Domestic market for mainline products has matured:
   — 5 percent industry growth per year, about the same as GNP.
   — No significant change in market share for ourselves or competitors.

   Overseas markets in mainline products have exploded at 20 percent per year, but growth is moderating.

   A $50 million potential market has been identified for our new ZEPHYR product, for which we hold a 30-month technical lead and some patents.

   Unit costs have increased 4 percent per year but productivity only 2 percent. Therefore, we've had to post price increases in some areas to cover the shortfall, and accept margin deterioration in others.

2. Our recently completed long-range plan indicates that our profit sensitivities will not change fundamentally. For example, a 1 percent improvement next year in each of these areas will have widely differing bottom-line impacts:

	PROFIT IMPACT ($ MILLIONS)	EPS IMPACT
1% increase in overseas sales	10.6	19¢
1% reduction in cost of materials and services	6.4	11¢
1% reduction in selling, distribution, and administration costs	4.2	7¢
1% reduction in employment costs	4.1	7¢
1% improvement in goods-in-process inventory	2.2	4¢
1% finished-inventory reduction	2.1	4¢
1% speedup in collection of accounts receivable	1.8	3¢
1% tax reduction	1.3	2¢
1% increase in domestic sales	1.2	2¢
1% improvement in uncollected accounts receivable	0.1	0.1¢

3. In turn, this analysis suggests that the key factors to success in our business are:

   • Aggressive exploitation of overseas market potential.
   • Tight control of manufacturing labor, materials, and purchased services.
   • Increased productivity of sales force and headquarters staff.

4. Accordingly, our long-range objectives for the next five years are:
   • To increase unit volume 10 percent per year, primarily in overseas markets.
   • To increase market share in mainline products 5 points.
   • To launch ZEPHYR, achieving $25 million sales volume by 1982. At the same time, "milk" the ZEBRA product line.
   • To increase line productivity (manufacturing and sales) 5 percent per year through 1982 and cut staff by 3 percent in each of the next two years.

Strategies and tactics for next year's budget will be tied to these objectives — using zero-base decision packages.

common factors, assumptions, and guidelines for all to use in the zero-base budgeting effort.

4. *The discussion of decision packages* and how they're developed begins to bridge the gap between general concepts and specific instructions. It should include a couple of forms with specific examples showing how to present both alternative ways and levels. The examples should be easy to understand and relate to. Thus, examples of security services, maintenance services, data processing, or a new-product launch (for a major new product that has broadly involved most managers) are preferable to a highly specialized affirmative action, workmen's compensation, or patent or tax litigation example.

5. *The discussion of the ranking process* should focus on who does the ranking, the mechanism to be employed, and, most important, the common standards to be employed. Ranking will be covered extensively in the next chapter, but the procedure must lay down for all a common frame of reference to ensure the best possible allocation of resources. Some organizations will elect to have a separate stand-alone procedure to cover the details of ranking, particularly where it will be the responsibility of a special task force. Nevertheless, some minimal overview of the ranking technique can increase the "comfort factor" for those managers who formulate the decision packages.

6. *The detailed implementation schedule* is required to enforce discipline and timely completion. As discussed earlier, the overall time frame may vary somewhat between organizations and as experience is gained. Each company should tailor the schedule to meet the operating exigencies of its divisions and departments, but the schedule should be explicit and tight enough to guarantee timely completion while ensuring quality decision packages.

A common glue binding all these elements is that they be positively presented. Indeed, an unstated objective of the procedure is that it must be a persuasive document that sells everyone on the concept. Including impolitic assertions that zero-base budgeting is being installed so that we can "cut everybody's budget equitably" or "place the burden of proof for spending any money at all on all staff managers" will surely torpedo even the best-structured procedure's chances of success. It's better that such things be positively phrased: "We're seeking improved efficiency and resource allocation," or better still: "This process offers a genuine opportunity to communicate improvement opportunities to the highest level. Where clearly justified, increased resources will be approved."

And that's really the name of the game for an effective zero-base budgeting act.

3

Ranking
for Decision Making

*A wise lord cannot, nor ought he to, keep
faith . . . when the reasons that caused
him to pledge it exist no longer.*
Machiavelli, *The Art of War*

MERELY developing and compiling decision packages detailing
what the organization is up to accomplishes no useful purpose other
than providing information. What's required is to focus and direct the
organization's resources toward preagreed needs or objectives. To para-
phrase Machiavelli, "A wise executive cannot, nor ought he to, keep
the faith in efforts approved in the past when the reasons for that
approval no longer exist." That's what zero-base budgeting's ranking
process is all about. It requires that we challenge all the spending
skeletons in the organization's closet, as well as the healthy and promising requests. In so doing, we'll uncover a number of things. Some
efforts will be more relevant and necessary. Others will be more effective. Still others will be just plain misdirected or redundant. By ranking
all together, we'll be able to weed out marginal efforts and redirect
the organization's resources toward the most promising ones.

Our objectives during ranking can be best cast in Peter Drucker's famous distinction between efficiency and effectiveness. Drucker defines efficiency as "doing things right" and effectiveness as "doing the right things." This has direct bearing on our zero-base budgeting effort. Developing well-structured, innovative, practical decision packages can assure us that we're doing things right. But however *efficient* each of those individual packages is, the effort is wasted if we don't pick the most *effective* ones. Therefore, it is a well-structured, administratively simple, hard-nosed ranking process that assures us that we're doing the right things. This chapter will discuss the pivotal role ranking plays in the zero-base budgeting process, review who should do the ranking as well as some alternative ways of doing it, and conclude with some guidelines and techniques I've found helpful in facilitating the process.

RANKING'S PIVOTAL ROLE

Increasing profits and productivity is an axiomatic management responsibility. The impact of the recent economic sluggishness has intensified concerns in this area. In large part, the interest in zero-base budgeting has arisen directly out of this challenge. The reasons are quite simple: In most organizations (particularly where labor is the largest cost element), more effective and relevant staff efforts can in the *long term* significantly drive productivity and profits. In other cases, stringent controls (and in some cases reductions) on the staff are the most practical *short-term* option open to keep the bottom line black.

Yet all those concerned with managing staff organizations— department heads, controllers, or top executives—find their efforts too often stymied either because of inadequate resources, inability to understand what's really going on, or, most importantly, inability to channel what resources are available to the most necessary undertakings. If this happens, crucial profit opportunities are lost. Capitalizing on such opportunities requires that key decision makers continually address the central issue of zero-base budgeting's ranking process: "How may we best allocate our scarce resources toward the most cost-effective and productive undertakings?"

Productivity (or lack of it)—whether in staff or line organizations— continues to be a fashionable topic in business circles. It is management's whipping boy to which a host of economic ills of this decade have been ascribed, including squeezed profit margins, slackening revenues, mushrooming public service bureaucracies, inflation, and (earlier in the decade) the evaporation of our balance of trade surplus. Some disturbing figures lend weight to management's concern:

♦ After averaging gains of 3 percent a year between 1950 and 1965, the productivity growth rate dropped to 2.1 percent between 1965 and 1970. Had we experienced this latter rate during the entire postwar period, the improvement in American standards of living would have been 30 percent less. Even our 3.1-percent rate of the 1960s was outstripped by Britain, Canada, Switzerland, Germany, Belgium, Italy, the Netherlands, Sweden, and Japan.

♦ While the 1971 and 1976 rates jumped sharply to about 4.0 percent, this improvement was expected for recovery years. Unfortunately, they compare unfavorably to 1955's 4.5 percent and 1962's 4.7 percent increase.

♦ For the longer term, the outlook is not favorable. A well-publicized Bureau of Labor Statistics estimate forecasts a net potential decline of 0.2 percent in the rate. Translated into dollars, this could lower the economic output by $120 billion in the 1970s.

Clearly, the primary responsibility for driving the productivity of the entire organization falls within the charter of its staff management. Yet while techniques abound and many are being tried, the overall effort in most organizations is piecemeal at best. The result is unfortunate. In rushing headlong into implementing what is the latest fad—be it job enrichment, a new packaging approach, sales force reorganization, or product repositioning—staff resources often become stretched beyond their capability or capacity. Quality suffers, and management's patience is tested as deadlines are missed. And if the effort (or program or decision package) is one that has a marginal impact on the company's profit performance, the long-term result is often an underemployed staff focused on activity rather than results. In short, by failing to employ staff resources effectively, both staff and line productivity suffer.

In addition to the productivity problem, a structural shift in the character of the labor force has kindled management's interest in zero-base budgeting. The majority of workers in the United States and most other Western economies now earn their living by their brains in white-collar, staff, knowledge-intensive office positions rather than by their brawn in blue-collar, line, labor-intensive factory positions. Budgeting techniques developed in the past to plan and control resources for the latter group are inappropriate, if not totally irrelevant, to the former. And it is zero-base budgeting—particularly its ranking process—that specifically focuses on this problem and permits management to get on top of it.

However, ranking is no easy task for a number of reasons. In the first place, both during the budgeting process and over the course of a year, a number of bright new ideas will surface from the various staff functions of marketing, finance, personnel, logistics, or legal or manufacturing services. At the same time, any of a number of outside consultants' recommendations may have to be evaluated. Each will no doubt have intrinsic merits, but the sum of all will probably be unaffordable.

Furthermore, in a qualitative sense, the problem of managing staff functions has been compounded in recent years as each has moved more and more away from traditional housekeeping and administrative chores and into increasingly sophisticated areas. An example might be made of the personnel function: Due in large part to the impact of the behavioral sciences, personnel has moved increasingly into such complex and sophisticated efforts as job enrichment, selection research, assessment centers, and executive career planning and development. Other functions have not been immune from this thrust. Whereas the manufacturing staff may once have been little more than a safety and security staff, it now may well encompass such areas as operations research, production planning and control, inventory control, and advanced manufacturing engineering. Similarly, whereas accounting formerly kept the books and little more, its function has been broadly expanded to incorporate such sophisticated disciplines as financial planning, budgets and forecasting, profit planning, tax, and data processing. The conclusion is simply this: *As the sophistication of the various staffs and their efforts has increased arithmetically, the complexity of choosing the best programs and managing their implementation has increased geometrically.*

Finally, the intrinsic nature of many staff efforts is such that while all their costs are direct and visible, many of their benefits are indirect or intangible. Delving further into the personnel department as an example, the linkage between the costs of undertaking a comprehensive clerical or factory job-enrichment effort and improved profits is elusive at best. And because of past difficulties in establishing a clear linkage, staff organizations are usually the last areas to be augmented in an upswing and the first to be trimmed in hard times. This, I feel, is shortsighted. Leverage suggests the reason, for costs of line operations constitute between 40 percent and 70 percent of total costs in most business enterprises. On the other hand, staff costs of any *one* function usually range between 1 percent and 5 percent of the total. Such a relationship suggests that productivity and profit improvements resulting from more effective and relevant staff efforts can significantly affect revenue and profits. *Zero-base budgeting's decision packages, if well thought-out, structured, and ranked, establish that link.*

It is in this context that the key decision maker must compile a cogent, manageable action program from what is often a bewildering array of constantly changing alternative packages. The purpose of ranking is quite simple: to allocate and channel staff resources into the most worthwhile undertakings. To carry our analogy further, if the decision packages are the links between staff costs and profitable results, the ranking process forges those tactical links into a chain of the most feasible, practical, productive, and worthwhile strategies.

WHO SHOULD RANK . . .

Responsibility for ranking can be assigned to an individual budget center or decision unit managers, to small two-man teams, to a special intradepartmental or interdepartmental committee or task force, or to the organization's budget staff. Here are some observations on when and where each alternative is appropriate.

Individual budget center manager. The initial ranking should be the responsibility of the manager developing the packages. This allows him to crystallize and communicate his own views on the relative importance of each of his efforts. Of course, his ranking is subject to reordering during the review process at higher levels.

Small two-man teams. The strengths of using individual budget center managers can be reinforced by including a second manager. In larger organizations, this is usually the full-time departmental planning and budgeting manager, while in smaller ones it is a financially knowledgeable individual detailed for this special assignment during the budgeting cycle. What's important about this approach is that the two work as a team, with each man's capabilities complementing the other's.

On the one hand, the budget center manager remains the most knowledgeable of his decision packages' objectives, their technical aspects, the behavioral subtleties of the target population, and the timing and scheduling problems that might inhibit implementation.

On the other hand, the planning and budgeting manager's credentials dovetail his colleague's. Through his expertise, he should command a wealth of detailed information on the organization's objectives and strategies; on product, profit, market, pricing, expense, and work-force projections; and on more mundane items such as salaries, productivity, absenteeism, and turnover rates. All these will be critical ingredients to an intelligent review and ranking of each decision package.

This approach may seem a trivial variation of the first, but my experience suggests that two heads are better than one. Both together often wind up identifying better solutions and creating wholly new alternative decision packages. And the planning and budgeting manager can inject a higher degree of consistency and discipline into both the packages and their ranking throughout the department.

Special committee. As the ranking process moves upward through larger organizations, the needed expertise may require a larger committee. Obviously, as the number of packages increases, no single manager can be intimately familiar with all of them. The committee can be staffed at the discretion of the department's top man but normally includes the key managers in each subunit as the process moves from the bottom to the top of the organization. How this might work is depicted in Figure 15. Alternatively, the flow might well be structured around logical cross-functional groupings of similar activities (such as computer services), business areas, markets, or products.

Budget staff. A fourth alternative is to assign responsibility to the budget staff or a select committee within the controller's organization. This is the least desirable solution for two reasons. First, although one logical end product of a zero-base exercise is usually a budget, the approach is primarily intended to be an *operational planning and*

Figure 15. Ranking by special committee.

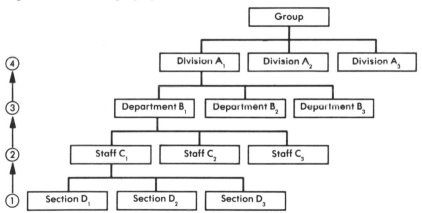

① Initial ranking is conducted by individual section managers.

② Initial consolidation is made by committee of section managers chaired by manager of staff C_1.

③. In turn, staff manager C_1 joins his peers to further consolidate in committee chaired by head of Department B_1.

④ This same process continues up to division, group, or even corporate level.

decision-making technique. Since it is the operating staff managers who will have to live with the approved ranking and implement the decision packages, assigning responsibility to the budget staff diffuses accountability for the entire effort. Those organizations choosing this option run the risk of accusations by their staff managers that the final product is not their own but "another unrealistic control budget." Equally important, few controllers or their staffs are equipped with the necessary breadth or depth of expertise to fully appreciate the subtleties of every package. Nevertheless, if the organization must execute a critical turnaround or already faces a highly charged political environment, this approach may be imperative. A better method would be for the controller to set up an independent review committee to play the role of the "organization conscience" in scrutinizing the packages and their ranking. Final approval, though, must remain with the key staff managers and the top man.

Regardless of which approach is taken, your focus should remain set on one key objective: Ranking must produce an end product that permits a quick, intelligent, rational, and definitive decision and approval by the chief executive.

. . . AND HOW IT'S DONE

Program ranking can be accomplished through any of a number of techniques. The seven sample programs depicted in Table 3 were selected to illustrate each of four alternative ranking systems. As each technique is based on different assumptions as to how organizations really work and what they need, the end product of each approach varies, in some cases widely. Under a theoretically "ideal" technique, only those programs of the most significant economic promise are ranked high, with more marginal ones accorded lower priority. Obviously, if our sole objective is to maximize profits or increase short-term cost-effectiveness, this approach has its merits.

The practical aspects of running an organization usually require an entirely different tack. Some efforts, while less worthwhile in the long term, offer more immediate and tangible results. Others will require special treatment as they may be mandated by law or policy. Still other highly leveraged and worthwhile efforts, when reviewed closely, may well be impractical to implement, due to the inability of certain key managers to accept major changes and implement the effort.

Does this mean there is no such thing as an ideal ranking system? Absolutely. Does that in turn mean that zero-base budgeting is im-

Table 3. Example of seven programs for ranking.

Program Number	Description	Estimated Accrued Net Benefit (Cost) *		
		1 Year	5 Years	Average
1	A new occupational health and safety program.	$(0.6)	$(1.4)	$(0.3)
2	Salary, benefits, secretarial and office-support costs for key departmental executives and their direct subordinates.	(2.8)	(14.0)	(2.8)
3	A new executive retreat at Disney World (or Vail, if you wish!).	(0.3)	(1.0)	(0.2)
4	A new product for which you have 30 months technical lead and some key patents.	(1.5)	25.0	5.0
5	A new approach to physical distribution that pays for itself in the first year.	0.9	2.8	0.6
6	A major blue-collar job enrichment program.	(0.5)	5.5	1.1
7	Repositioning an old reliable breadwinning product with flat sales.	3.8	17.0	3.4
	Total	$(1.0)	$33.9	$6.8

* In millions of dollars.

practical? On the contrary: Zero-base budgeting is highly practical *if* you adopt the appropriate ranking approach and tailor it to your specific needs.

What are the most common ranking approaches? Basically, four enjoy the most widespread use: the single-standard approach, the voting system, the major-category system, and the multiple-standard approach. Let's now review each of them.

Single Standard

The single-standard approach is the simplest and most appropriate to families of similar programs (like capital budget requests). All programs are evaluated by one (*but only one*) criterion. This may be return on investment, absolute dollar savings, net present value, discounted cash flow, or cost benefit ratios. Thus, if we're served up a dish of two dozen capital investment programs and we're in agreement that each package is internally sound and consistent, ranking is a simple five-step process:

1. Gain agreement on the standard to be used (ROI, DCF, etc.).
2. Rank all programs from top to bottom based on that standard.
3. Determine the cutoff point, considering available resources or affordability.
4. Approve and fund all programs above the cutoff level and defer or eliminate all others.
5. Communicate the decision to the proper managers.

Where might this be used? Aside from the classic capital budgeting example, several areas come to mind. In corporate development, strategic planners have used this concept to lay out and select from several alternative forward products. Among staffs more attuned to near-term operations, the approach is usually appropriate for sorting out a series of sales-motivational programs, advertising strategies, or compensation and benefits packages for an operating plan.

For all these cases, comparing similar types of programs under the same criteria is practical. But if we try to compare and rank *different* types of programs, the concept doesn't hold water. To illustrate this, Table 4 ranks our seven sample programs on the basis of their five-year estimated net benefit.

Table 4. Ranking of seven sample programs under single criterion.

			Estimated Average Net Benefit (Cost) *	
Program Ranking	Program Number	Program Name	1 Year	5 Year Average
1	4	New-Product Launch	$(1.5)	$5.0
2	7	Old-Product Repositioning	3.8	3.4
3	6	Job Enrichment Program	(0.5)	1.1
4	5	Physical Distrib. System	0.9	0.6
			(CUTOFF) †	
5	3	Executive Retreat	(0.3)	(0.2)
6	1	Health and Safety	(0.6)	(0.3)
7	2	Executive Core Staff	(2.8)	(2.8)
		Total	$(1.0)	$6.8

* In millions of dollars.
† Subtotals to $2.7 million in budget year and $10.1 million per year over the next five years.

By approving the four highest-ranked programs, it looks as if we'll improve operations $2.7 million next year. So on first pass, we pat each other on the back in mutual congratulation for being so clever. But let's see what's been chopped. Starting from the bottom, we've eliminated all key managers and their direct reports. Depending on whom you talk to, this may (but probably won't) increase the organization's effectiveness! And while leaderless, we've also provoked the ire of the federal regulators in OSHA, who may opt to close the company down altogether as a safety hazard. And after being closed, we can't even commiserate over our problems or prepare our resumés at the Disney World executive retreat!

This example was purposely overdrawn to illustrate the real-world practicalities of budgeting. Being penny-wise, we've also proven ourselves pound-foolish in eliminating our executive cadre and inviting a government shutdown. Carried to an extreme, had we ranked strictly on first-year returns, our new product would have been eliminated, probably prompting a slow and painful death by profit emphysema for the organization. For some executives who overcontrol their organizations, this too often happens. That's why the single-standard approach can be labeled the SINGE system, with the acronym standing for Simple and Involving No Great Effort. Unfortunately, those organizations electing to use it in complicated budgeting situations—for which it isn't intended—usually find themselves treating severe cases of burns.

Voting

Such difficulties have led to developing more sophisticated ranking procedures. Probably the earliest and still most widely used is the voting or pointscore system developed by Peter Pyhrr and used by him in zero-base budgeting's formative years at Texas Instruments and in some agencies of the State of Georgia. In honor of its originator, let's call it the P 5 system—or Pete Pyhrr's Pragmatic Pointscore Procedure, if you will. P 5 is particularly appropriate for organizations that are ranking by committee and have to quickly array a large number of packages, usually over 50. But it is also useful for an individual manager or two-man team having to cope with large volumes of packages. Basically, it works like this at the first review level:

1. Each member is provided with a complete set of decision packages and ranking sheets.
2. For large volumes of packages, each is copied on acetate slides for overhead projection.
3. The committee meets, discusses each package to gain a thorough

understanding of it, then votes on a fixed scale with either the average or the total points determining the ranking. An example of the scale is shown in Figure 16.

4. The preliminary consensus on ranking is copied on a ranking sheet and projected on the overhead.
5. The discussion then hinges on resolving principal differences to make sure that there were no major misunderstandings. Some packages may be reordered at this point.
6. On resolving those differences, a final ranking is reached, cast in hard copy, and passed up to the next higher level for consideration and final decision.

How our seven sample programs might be ranked under voting is depicted in Table 5. This ranking might be viewed as more realistic in a legal sense, as well as from the standpoint of practical budgeting politics. But insofar as it drops two programs (the launching of the new product and the job enrichment effort), its economics might be challenged during higher-level review. The point is this: Ranking by voting is admittedly not an objective procedure, being subject to the inherent biases of the committee members. If it is to be of any use, it must be reviewed carefully at higher levels to correct those biases. Alternatively, the standards for voting—say one or three or six points—

Figure 16. The P⁵ voting scale.

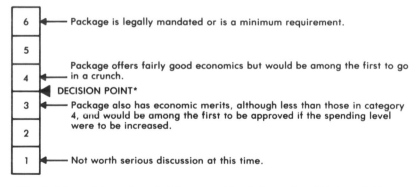

*The decision point may be set at the current level of spending. This is useful in that it forces each committee member to evaluate whether a new or expanded effort is important enough to be voted a rank of 4 or higher, with the implication that the additional resources are obtained by reducing or eliminating current efforts. Naturally, the final decision will be determined by *affordability*, which may be greater than, equal to, or less than the current spending level.

must be explicitly spelled out, tightly administered, and understood by everybody if the end product is to be of any value.

Table 5. Ranking of seven sample programs under voting mechanism.

Program Ranking	Program Number	Program Name	1 Year	5 Yr Aver.	Average Vote
				Estimated Average Net Benefit (Cost) *	
1	1	Health and Safety	$(0.6)	$(0.3)	6.0
2	2	Executive Core Staff	(2.8)	(2.8)	5.6
3	7	Old-Product Repositioning	3.8	3.4	5.0
4	5	Physical Distrib. System	0.9	0.6	4.5
			(CUTOFF @ 4.0) †		
5	4	New-Product Launch	(1.5)	5.0	3.6
6	6	Job Enrichment Program	(0.5)	1.1	2.1
7	3	Executive Retreat	(0.3)	(0.2)	0.6
		Total	$(1.0)	$6.8	4.0

* In millions of dollars.
† Subtotals to $1.3 million in budget year and $0.9 million per year over next five years. This is a substantial deterioration from our earlier example (Table 4), but we have met legal as well as minimum "requirements." On the other hand, we've deferred launching our new product.

Major Categories

Explicitly predefining major categories into which decision packages will be slotted and ranked is a variation of the voting approach. It can in part overcome some of the games managers are known to play during voting sessions. One of the most common of such games is rather clever: Most (or all) managers involved in ranking tacitly (or sometimes explicitly) agree to give high ratings to marginal efforts and low ones to those of obvious worth. Unless this nonsense is smoked out during higher review, the budget will grow out of hand. It's better to prevent the nonsense in the first place by forcing those responsible for ranking to dump each of their decision packages into major "buckets" or categories. In so doing, we're quite logically assuming that some packages, in Orwell's words, are more equal than others.

Some major categories that might be predefined could include (in order of importance):

All efforts explicitly required by law.

All efforts, however small, that pay for themselves in the first year.

All "requirements" for a core management cadre.

All efforts of substantial long-term economic merit.

All efforts of average, but positive, long-term economic merit.

All other efforts.

To continue our mathematical acronyms, let's call it MC ^{2}—or the "Major Categories" approach.

The analogy to relativity theory is not unintentional. Considering the highly charged political environment of putting together a budget, it is often better to control the reaction with a couple of well-placed control rods rather than let the reactor core explode in an uncontrolled chain reaction of emotions. To be sure, some energy (or resources) will be channeled off and lost forever, but we can afford to lose a skirmish or even a battle if it helps us win the war. The third of the major categories performs a role analogous to our control rods. It permits the organization's atomic pile to sustain an energetic level of output without tearing itself apart at the seams.

In this connection I'm reminded of Antony Jay's comparison of organization politics (or budgeting politics if you will) and the defecatory habits of the hippopotamus:

> The male indicates to other hippopotami the extent of his own territory by defecating all around its perimeter. Outside that ring they can go where they please, but if they come inside it, he will fight them to the death. So, too, nations make a ring around their territory: To Elizabeth I, the wars in Holland were beyond the ring, but the Armada came inside it. No doubt the United States government wishes it had left Viet Nam outside its defecatory ring. And so, too, industrial corporations, consciously or unwittingly, make some sort of ring around products and sales territories and sections of the market.*

To which I can only add that many department and section heads will often brook no discussion, compromise, or budgetary scrutiny of certain sacred cows within their territory.

The third category—"all 'requirements' for a core management cadre"—is designed for just such situations. It outranks efforts of substantial economic merit but is limited to a small amount of dollar resources so that its impact will be insignificant. Even though decision packages in this category may well be of lesser economic merit, by

---

* From *Management and Machiavelli* by Antony Jay, p. 32. Copyright © 1967 by Antony Jay. Reprinted by permission of Holt, Rinehart and Winston, Publishers.

assuring the core cadre that a limited number of decision packages are secure and within its protected ring, we may gain agreement to far more drastic and needed changes in other areas. That may be a small price to pay for substantial savings or if our political capital is in short supply.

This third category might be limited to the core cadre or incorporate any relatively inexpensive requests that might generate a significant level of emotion, controversy, and wheel spinning if proposed for elimination. It might well include our Disney World retreat, the corporate aviation program, or a recently approved management training program that is the chief executive's current "hot button."

What's critical about this category is that it must be judiciously employed: The detractor should be given only enough to distract him while we go on to more substantial matters.

Our seven sample programs have been slotted and ranked into major categories in Table 6. All decision packages remain unchanged from previous examples with one exception. We have split the core staff into two packages, with 2a including key men, secretaries, and support costs, while 2b incorporates all people reporting directly to them, and their support costs. The former has been slotted in category C, the latter much lower in E. Within categories D and E, the packages have been ranked in order of long-term economic merit, using the approaches discussed earlier.

Strategically, however, we've accomplished quite a bit more. By splitting the requests for the core staff and reranking them, we managed to free resources to fund both our new-product launch and our job enrichment program. More importantly, our profit improvement for the next year is up $300,000 to $1.6 million while the average for *each* of the next five years is up *$8.4 million* to $9.3 million. As Hannibal once said: "I will find a way or make one." Having meandered along the mountain trails with our first two ranking techniques, we have perhaps found a pass with our third!

Multiple Standards

As we've progressed through each of the first three ranking techniques, we've developed a capability to evaluate programs intelligently on more than just their economic merits. But while we've begun to consider other factors (such as legal necessity), we've not yet rigorously incorporated them into our evaluation process. Several years ago, Harvey Golub, then a partner at McKinsey, developed such an approach for data processing program management. I subsequently applied Harvey's concept to some specific budgeting problems at

Table 6. Ranking of seven sample programs into major categories.

Program Category	Program Ranking	Program Number	Program Name	Estimated Net Benefit (Cost) *	
				1 Year	5 Yr Aver.
A	1	1	Health and Safety	$(0.6)	$(0.3)
B	2	5	Physical Distribution System	0.9	0.6
C	3	2a	Executive Core Staff (Level 1 of 2)	(0.5)	(0.5)
D	4	4	New-Product Launch	(1.5)	5.0
D	5	7	Old-Product Repositioning	3.8	3.4
E	6	6	Job Enrichment	(0.5)	1.1
				(CUTOFF) †	
E	7	2b	Executive Core Staff (Level 2 of 2)	(2.3)	(2.3)
F	8	3	Executive Retreat	(0.3)	(0.2)
			Total	$(1.0)	$6.8

* In millions of dollars.
† Subtotals to $1.6 million in budget year and $9.3 million per year for the next five years. We've not only improved our profit outlook substantially over Table 5 but managed to fund two additional profitable opportunities. This underscores the importance of zero-base budgeting's requirement to break programs into discrete incremental levels of effort.

Xerox in the personnel and planning areas. Within the data processing profession, some have dubbed it the G [3] approach (for Golub's Guiseful Game), although one of my budgeting colleagues prefers C [2] (for Cut the Clamjamfry *).

The idea is basically this: Success in implementing any decision package will depend on five issues, not all of which are economic. These are:

Is the program legally required?

Do we have the necessary technical skills?

Will line management accept and execute the program?

* Clamjamfry is from the Scottish dialect. The nearest American equivalent is rubbish.

Will the program be cost-effective?

Can we afford not to act?

Although it appears quite complex, the underlying idea is simple. Even the most cost-effective program is useless if it will not be implemented by line management or bought by the consumer. The Edsel is an obvious example. In the same vein, a program's value is doubtful if it involves major state-of-the-art risks in untried areas. In this regard, the recent financial woes of several leading nuclear power plant contractors come to mind. On the other hand, a program of negative economic value may nevertheless be necessary if mandated by law. Examples in this category are plentiful—and growing.

To explain how this approach works, let's use the decision package shown in Figure 8 and observe how it was evaluated and ranked in a zero-base planning exercise undertaken several years ago in Xerox' personnel department. Note that the decision package includes assessment sections for each of the five issues discussed above. Here's how each was handled.

1. *Is the program legally required?* More than at any other time in history, many of the organization's staff resources must be allocated to decision packages required by public law. The bulk of such legislation and regulation has been enacted in the past decade in such areas as affirmative action, labor relations, pension vesting and portability, and SEC reporting. Requirements in this area will probably increase in future years, particularly among larger enterprises as their traditional economic role is enlarged to include a social one, as has occurred in Western Europe and Japan. Legislated requirements may reasonably be expected in such areas as broadening of workforce training and development programs, new regulations for health care insurance, and safety and environmental standards. The job enrichment program detailed in Figure 8 clearly was not a statutory necessity. But for other efforts—labor relations, affirmative action, workforce and SEC reporting, and payroll administration—legal requirements obviously have to be met. Such programs often have no net economic benefit to the business. Indeed, what benefits they do have are usually intangible in nature. Under these circumstances, evaluating them with conventional economic yardsticks would result in their being assigned a low priority. The potential legal exposure, coupled with its impact on the company image, dictates the need for special treatment. Accordingly they are segregated from all other proposals and assigned the highest priority.

While a full discussion of the spectrum of public regulation of business is beyond the scope of this book, a few illustrative examples of legally required decision packages are:

◇ Programs for maintaining records of hours, earning, overtime, union dues collected, and the financial health of existing or proposed pension plans.
◇ Financial reports to securities regulatory agencies.
◇ The company's affirmative action plans to hire and upgrade minorities and females.
◇ Validation efforts to make sure that pre-employment selection tests or standards comply with federal guidelines.
◇ Programs to eliminate recognized hazards likely to cause death or injury and efforts to ensure a safe workplace and environment.

At this point, one small word of caution is in order. Packages that are legally required should be just that and no more. One game frequently played by some staff managers is to piggyback nonstatutory efforts onto these decision packages. For instance, part of the regular employment budget may get buried in the affirmative action hiring plan, or part of the financial analysis function may be hidden in the SEC reporting package. And so the bloated budget and burgeoning empire syndrome begins to creep back into the picture. Careful scrutiny of each legally required decision package during the review process can prevent this. Having identified and segregated efforts clearly required by law, we are ready to focus on the heart of the process and its most challenging aspect: the feasibility evaluation.

2. *Do we have the necessary technical skills?* Resolving this issue requires considering the decision package's "state-of-the-art" implications. What are the technical problems involved? Do we have access to the skills within the organization or outside (for instance, consultants) to overcome these problems? If data processing support is required, is the appropriate equipment available, and how complex is the programming? By way of an example, developing or maintaining the company's compensation administration system normally involves no dramatic state-of-the-art effort. Must companies can handle it with their existing resources. In contrast, when the Tax Reform Act of 1969 (or the more recent Employee Retirement and Income Security Act) was enacted, many companies found that the timely modification of their compensation and benefits systems required bold, imaginative, conceptual thinking beyond the capability of their own staffs. To restructure their systems promptly, many relied on outside experts—attorneys, tax accountants, or consultants—who were fully knowledgeable in the subject.

In the case of the job enrichment program shown in Figure 8, qualified technical talent was already available on the personnel staff; hence the state-of-the-art factor was evaluated as "high." Had such an undertaking been attempted eight or ten years ago, its evaluation probably would have been "medium," for we would have had to either hire a qualified individual or retain an expert consultant. And had job enrichment been attempted fifteen or twenty years ago, the evaluation clearly would have been "low" since at that point in time it would have been a major state-of-the-art undertaking.

These differences in the availability of qualified technical talent are reflected in the evaluation of the program's state-of-the-art implications. The technical feasibility for all programs must be consistently evaluated against the same yardsticks. These standards, which should be applicable to most organizations, are as follows:

◊ Evaluate technical feasibility as *high* if the program appears simple, skilled personnel is currently available within the company, and EDP programming, if required, is simple and hardware available within the company.

◊ Evaluate technical feasibility as *medium* if the program appears complex, skilled personnel is not available in the company but available outside, or EDP programming, if required, is difficult or hardware is not available within the company but is on the market.

◊ Evaluate technical feasibility as *low* if the program involves a major state-of-the-art effort, personnel is not available on staff or outside, or EDP programming, if required, is very complex or hardware is not available.

3. *Will line management accept and execute the program (or will the customer buy the product)?* Resolving this issue requires a frank assessment of potential behavioral problems. What are the attitudes, policies, and management styles characterizing the line organization? What is its structure, and how does it operate? And for product marketing programs, the customers' purchasing habits must be considered. Since these elements are the most difficult to change, this issue is probably the most critical of the five. This is particularly true for programs in such new areas as job enrichment, organization development, assessment centers, selection research, but also for new production methods or dramatically different forward products. Clearly, successful implementation of such advanced concepts hinges on line management's acceptance or willingness to change its attitudes, or on customer acceptance of the new product. Unfortunately, reorienting

personality traits, management styles, or purchasing habits that have been ingrained over the years is entirely different from gaining acceptance of a slightly changed production process, a repositioned product, or a modified billing system. Most of the latter can be sold exclusively on their economic merits; changing behavior is a far greater, often impossible, challenge. Given an unwillingness to change (or, conversely, a need for aggressive promotional efforts on the part of the staff to effect the necessary changes), the sponsoring budget center therefore should waste little time musing about the value of such efforts, regardless of the imaginativeness of the decision package or its economic worth.

Again, let's look at how this factor was handled in our job enrichment program. The proposed program had been pilot-tested, and we had learned that selling the concept to management was sometimes an uphill fight. (This was less a problem of staff to line relationships than it was a behavioral one; some supervisors and key line managers will inevitably balk at the idea of assigning greater responsibilities to their subordinates.) But we knew that our successes had won converts and thus increased the program's credibility throughout the organization. On that basis, our evaluation of this factor was a qualified "low"—one that injected a sobering element (for instance, the critical need for missionary work) should the program pass its other tests and be given the green light. In other words, the high risks identified in this factor appeared warranted if and only if the anticipated rewards could be demonstrated to be exceptionally high.

As with the state-of-the-art evaluation, the standards for evaluating the operational feasibility are generally applicable to most organizations. They are as follows:

◊ Evaluate operational feasibility as *high* if implementing the program requires *little or no effort* to effect a change in line organization attitudes, policies, structure, operating environment, or management styles, or in customer purchasing habits, and *does not imply a radical departure* from historic company or market practices.

◊ Evaluate operational feasibility as *medium* if implementing the program appears to require *moderate efforts* to effect a change in line organization attitudes, policies, structure, operating environment, or management styles, or in customer purchasing habits, and *implies some departure* from historic company or market practices.

◊ Evaluate operational feasibility as *low* if implementing the program appears to require *substantial efforts* to effect a change in line organization attitudes, policies, structure, operating environment, or management styles, or in customer purchasing habits, and implies a *radical departure* from historic company or market practices.

4. *Will the program be cost-effective?* Here, we consider the proposal's net economic benefits, using cost/benefit analysis with appropriate modifications. For all our programs, including the service force job enrichment proposal, the specific issue to be resolved is: What probable dollar impact can reasonably be expected from implementing the program? To answer this question, the sponsoring budget center, assisted by planning and financial personnel, identifies potential benefits and costs, estimates the probability of each benefit and cost, and calculates the probable dollar impact. In our job enrichment example, hard quantitative data were readily available, documenting the effect such a program had had on turnover, absenteeism, and productivity in three pilot-project branch offices. For other programs, estimating potential benefits is often difficult. Overcoming this problem requires that benefits be estimated by either of two approaches: *identifiable* benefits or *target* benefits.

Identifiable benefits are used whenever possible. They must be tangible and clearly attributable to implementing the proposal. An example of an identifiable benefit would be the direct savings achieved by eliminating redundant functions in a proposed reorganization. For other proposals, it may be possible to take the *cost* (that is, value) of the present approach and subtract from it the estimated cost of the proposed approach. For example, suppose an employment manager feels he can achieve significant savings by relying less on outside agencies. In this case, an identifiable benefit can be developed using the fees paid to outside employment agencies as well as other expenses associated with the present approach. The estimated costs of additional internal staff and support costs to implement the proposed approach are then subtracted from this to develop a net economic benefit for the proposal. Finally, if a pilot test has been conducted on a small group of employees with favorable results, a plausible benefits estimate can be developed by cascading the savings identified in the pilot test over the entire organization. (This last approach was used for the job enrichment proposal.)

Target benefits are used in the absence of hard experience. In essence, these are preliminary estimates of results that the responsible staff manager promises to deliver if given the resources to pilot-test his proposal. (As soon as the pilot test has been completed, benefits can easily be reevaluated and the target estimate replaced by those benefits that have been firmly identified.) An example of a target benefit would be a 1 percent increase in revenue or a one-point decline in turnover resulting from a motivational or training program for the company's sales force. In some cases, the responsible manager can develop such estimates for each of his programs with assistance from the controller's staff or the long-range planning staff. In other cases, some staff managers will be able to support their claims for target benefits by drawing on the experience of their colleagues in other companies or by reviewing the professional literature. Here, the controller or the planning staff must make sure that the sponsoring manager's target estimate is reasonable, attainable, and if anything conservative. If that isn't done, the credibility of the entire effort will suffer. If, however, management does challenge the estimated target benefit as being overly ambitious, it is critical not to become lost in a banyan grove of quibbling over its decimal accuracy. We must remember that the goal of the procedure is to allocate resources toward those projects most likely to yield the greatest *relative* benefits and commit our managers to results.

A given company might set the following standards for categorizing net economic benefits:

◇ Evaluate a proposal's net benefits as *high* if they exceed $600,000.
◇ Evaluate a proposal's net benefits as *medium* if they exceed $100,000 but are less than $600,000.
◇ Evaluate a proposal's net benefits as *low* if they are less than $100,000.

Unlike the standards for evaluating state-of-the-art implications or ease of implementation, these yardsticks will be unique for each organization. Very large organizations will have higher levels than small companies. The appropriate standards can be very easily developed as follows: When all packages have been developed and scrutinized, rank them from top to bottom on net economic benefits. The first cutoff point will be the average between the last program in the top third and the first program in the second third. The same logic holds for the second cutoff level.

Lastly, intangible benefits and risks are described. While some of these items may appear to be platitudes, specifying them is nevertheless useful. Often, when a choice must be made between two programs of almost equal merit, the intangibles—if properly framed—

become a key factor in swinging the decision to one decision package over the other.

5. *Can we afford not to act?* Finally, we consider the *economic risks* we incur by not implementing a given package. For example, a failure to continually reevaluate the company's pre-employment selection standards may result in the hiring of less qualified employees with subsequent declines in productivity, for which costs could be estimated. Similarly, a failure to implement a manufacturing capital improvement program could result in unacceptable cost exposures. (This approach was used for the job enrichment proposal.)

As with net economic benefits, the standards for classifying economic risks are unique to any one organization. Banks and insurance companies, for example, would probably have relatively high risk standards in the personnel area, since their operations are highly sensitive to payroll costs, which distinguishes them from oil refineries. Similarly, a service organization such as an airline is more vulnerable to strike losses than a tangible-goods enterprise, which can meet such risks with inventory. For a given organization, the standards might be as follows:

◇ Evaluate risks of not acting on the proposal as *high* if they exceed $1,000,000.
◇ Evaluate risks as *medium* if they exceed $100,000 but are less than $1,000,000.
◇ Evaluate risks as *low* if they are less than $100,000.

The cutoff points are developed as described for net economic benefits.

Having evaluated every program on its own merits, the overall feasibility of each must now be determined. The decision table shown in Figure 17 (highlighted to depict the job enrichment proposal) was developed as a convenient tool to accomplish this. The table is structured so that a high rating in any one factor would not conclusively decide in favor of the program, but a low rating in any one of them would very possibly eliminate the program from consideration. The end result is that each program can be categorized into one of five categories: legally required, very desirable, moderately desirable, marginally desirable, or not worthwhile.

In turn, these categories are used as major classifications into which each program will be pigeonholed in the program ranking schedule shown in Figure 18. The legally required programs appear at the top of the schedule, and all other programs are ranked within the appropriate overall feasibility category by their economic benefits. As

Figure 17. Decision table for determining program feasibility.

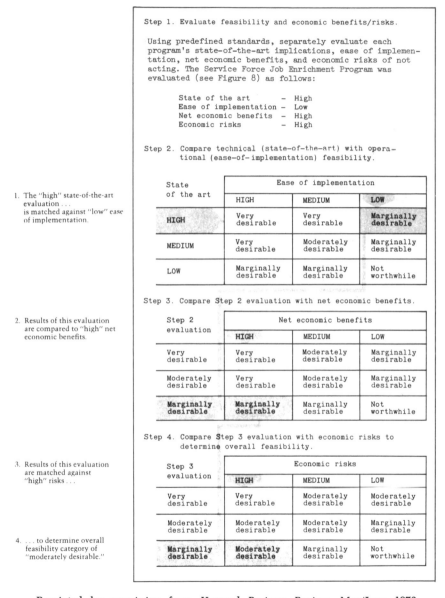

Figure 18. Program ranking schedule.

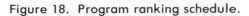

ACTION PROGRAM	Priority	Timing 1972	1973	1974	1975	1976	1977	Net annual dollar benefit	Cost/ benefit ratio (1:n)
LEGALLY REQUIRED PROGRAMS									
Labor Relations Strategy	x							($ 619)	n/a
Protect Right to Select Employees	x							($ 86)	n/a
Continue Validation of Selection Tests	x							$35,000	78.17
Redesign Personnel Data System	x							$ 273	1.78
Develop Part-Time Female Employment Approaches	x							$ 227	4.16
VERY DESIRABLE PROGRAMS									
Restructuring Service Force	1							$14,608	9.6
Service College Coop Program	2							$ 4,490	2.74
MODERATELY DESIRABLE PROGRAMS									
Service Job Enrichment	3							$ 9,920	24.3
Assessment Center	4							$ 4,946	15.40
Education & Training Center	5							$ 4,780	3.57
Clerical Selection Program	6							$ 1,799	19.94
Develop College Campus as Primary Employment Source	7							$ 834	2.06
Interfunctional Moves & Fast Track Program	8							$ 679	7.54
Selection Standards for New Sales/Tech. Rep. Types	9							$ 520	11.6
Improve Economics of Field Employment Operations	10							$ 472	1.42
Build Better Technical Recruiting/Selection Capability	11							$ 222	2.48
Monitor Sales & Tech. Rep. Selection Tests	12							$ 211	0.06
MARGINAL BUT DESIRABLE PROGRAMS									
Implement Executive Search Function	13							$ 177	1.67
Refine Career Path Guides	14							$ 110	1.75
Continue National Trend Attitude Surveys	15							$ 107	1.33
Reevaluate Overall Organization Approach	16							$ 93	2.37
NOT WORTHWHILE									
Executive Retreat	x							($ 450)	n/a
Corporate Jet	x							($ 769)	n/a
Savings Plan	x							($ 75)	n/a

Left margin annotations:

1. Legally required efforts come first . . .

2. . . . then, other programs are ranked by overall feasibility category . . .

3. . . . and within feasibility category by net benefits.

4. Priorities are indicated here.

5. Starting from the lowest priority program, marginal efforts may be trimmed as required by the budget.

6. In any case, these programs are eliminated.

||||||| Program and design development
▬▬ Program Implementation

a result, we are able to order our efforts by priority against our five criteria. Those programs evaluated as "not worthwhile" appear at the bottom of the schedule—for elimination. And if affordability dictates belt tightening when the budget is put together or an austerity program is mandated during the year, the marginal programs can be readily trimmed, starting from the bottom.

This program ranking schedule is the basic tool for allocating and deploying resources. Using it effectively implies that management must undertake some tough-minded actions, specifically:

Trimming marginal programs. This is often difficult because it may involve some sacred cows, for example, the executive jet or weekend retreat. But we must remember that increasing productivity is one important way of achieving the organization's primary objective of profitable or effective operations.

Allocating and deploying staff resources toward the most worthwhile projects. While some programs will have been trimmed, others will warrant implementation. Accomplishing this on a timely basis requires that staff resources be deployed only for the higher-ranked undertakings. Some staff might be pulled from programs that have been trimmed; other personnel—particularly in highly technical areas —might have to be hired from outside. Furthermore, additional resources might be allocated to worthwhile projects in order to speed up their implementation. For instance, in our job enrichment example, some highly favorable benefits have been identified. But because only one man is assigned to the effort, achieving these benefits will require four years. Thus, additional resources may appear justified to assure an earlier payback. This can be handled through an incremental-level decision package.

Evaluating all new program proposals and reordering priorities as necessary. To be successful, this procedure must be viewed as a dynamic one. As new proposals are developed during the budget year, they must be scrutinized, using the same standards, and they must be ranked and accepted or rejected, based on their value relative to all other efforts. As a consequence, priorities may in fact be frequently changed and staff resources be redeployed during the budget year.

Reevaluating the entire effort as appropriate. Just as the program priorities must be flexed to handle new programs, the evaluation of existing programs will change over time. For example, the appointment of a new key executive in an operating department may alter the operational feasibility of a particular program. Similarly, the personnel staff may hit on a crucial breakthrough that raises the technical feasibility, or public regulation may mean establishing a new legally required program. Any of these events could trigger a chain reaction of reordered priorities by altering the feasibility evaluation of one aspect of a particular program. Normally, these adjustments will be handled during the next budget cycle, but they may well be revised during the year if warranted.

Finally, and most important, the acid test of an approved decision package's value is its execution. Progress in executing each package must be carefully monitored to identify bottlenecks as they develop, to chart alternatives where necessary, and to ensure timely implementation and the achievement of planned benefits, particularly among high-payback packages. It is in this area (and not in developing and ranking packages) that the budget staff or controller will be the prime mover.

The ranking process described here may not on first pass appear to be an improvement over the other approaches discussed earlier, but in practice, its advantages will become quite obvious. By enforcing proper consideration of technical feasibility as well as of the behavioral subtleties of the organization and its markets, a wholly different ranking might be developed. Using our seven sample programs, Table 7 depicts how such a ranking might look. In it, we have:

◊ Segregated all legally required efforts and put them at the top of the list in category A. Unless we plan on going out of business, these packages will be approved and funded without further discussion.

◊ Identified all efforts that pay for themselves during the budget year and placed them in category B. No matter how small their impact, their benefits are obvious and can be captured.

◊ Approved core requirements for a management cadre—but only at a minimum—and placed them in Category C.

◊ Ranked everything else in the remaining four categories D through G (from "highly desirable" to "not worthwhile"), using the evaluation approach and decision tables discussed.

Having gained agreement on the ranking, we can approve all programs up to the affordable level of spending.

One final thought on ranking: Several years ago, before I had come to fully appreciate the benefits of zero-base budgeting, I worked with an organization whose top executive went through endless grief every year when reviewing budget submissions. With the burden of proof on his shoulders to control spending, a frequent comment to his key lieutenants making incremental resource requests was: "Any-

Table 7. Decision package ranking.

Category and Rank	Package Number and Name	Estimated Net Benefit *		Budget Year		Cumulative Budget Year Expense
		Budget Year	5 Yr Average	Expense	People	
A 1	Legally Required Programs #1 Health and Safety	$(0.6)	$(0.3)	$(0.6)	4	$(0.6)
B 1	Immediate Payback Programs #5 Physical Distribution System	0.9	0.6	(0.1)	3	(0.7)
C 1	Core Requirements #2a Executive Core Staff	(0.5)	(0.5)	(0.5)	13	(1.2)
D 1	Highly Desirable #7 Old-Product Repositioning	3.8	3.4	(1.2)	22	(2.4)
E 1	Moderately Desirable #6 Job Enrichment	(0.5)	1.1	(0.6)	8	(3.0)
E 2	#4 New-Product Launch	(1.5)	5.0	(1.8)	32	(4.8)
F 1	Marginally Desirable #2b Executive Core Staff	(2.3)	(2.3)	(2.3)	50	(7.1)
G 1	Not Worthwhile #3 Executive Retreat	(0.3)	(0.2)	(0.3)	2	(7.4)
	Total	$(1.0)	$6.8	$(7.4)	134	(7.4)

* In millions of dollars.

body can manage a business with a bag of gold; your job is to achieve the same results with less than a full bag!" That directive is the object of zero-base ranking. To be sure, our priorities must be tempered by judgment and common sense. But if the process is well structured and administratively simple and the packages are given hard-nosed scrutiny, ranking will indeed facilitate managing for improved results with something quite less than the full bag of gold few organizations enjoy—and none can afford.

SOME GUIDELINES . . . AND A TECHNIQUE

Having gained an understanding of who should rank and how it's done, some final observations are in order that may help facilitate ranking:

Don't waste time arguing over priorities. Programs ranked high, whether for legal, economic, or other merits, are going to be approved and funded. The same principle applies, in reverse, to low-priority programs. Zero-base budgeting is, above all, a *decision-making tool.* Thus, the review process should focus on those dozen or so programs above or below the decision point or affordability level.

Don't quibble over the decimal accuracy of benefits. To be sure, accurately specifying the *costs* of each decision package is important to the mechanics of rolling up a final expense budget. But a quick review of the program ranking schedule in Figure 18 shows that even a major shift in net benefits—sometimes of 100 percent or more—will *not* change the rankings. In other words, comparability rather than accuracy is the main consideration in package analysis and ranking. While accurately estimating expenses will be important in consolidating the final budget, only a reasonable judgment of each program's cost/benefit or net benefit is necessary for sound ranking and resource allocation. To spend an inordinate amount of time on the latter is to lose sight of the forest for the trees.

Keep your strategic objectives in mind. This is a corollary to the last observation. Many organizations spend an inordinate amount of time during ranking arguing over the merits of a proposed decision package. Yet a quick appraisal of many such programs would quickly indicate that they are peripheral or absolutely irrelevant to the organization's long-range needs and objectives. For example, a sophisticated operations research marketing model intended to support a dying product line is best ignored altogether.

Stay flexible. It is a bad plan that admits no modification. Similarly, it is a bad system that allows no user interdiction. Well-designed zero-base budgeting forms and procedures will indeed facilitate administering the process, but they must not become an end in them-selves. Those responsible for ranking should challenge the packages and demand changes where warranted. The final ranking should not be considered sacred. If the situation dictates belt tightening when the budget is put together, if an austerity program is mandated during the year, or if new improvement opportunities are identified, the dynamics of zero-base budgeting permit a change. New packages can be structured and reranked against older ones. Old packages can be trimmed to more affordable levels. Indeed, many organizations with extensive experience in zero-base budgeting find their annual budget cycle drastically altered. Rather than reworking all packages every year, they adopt an annual cycle that consists very simply of (a) verifying the costs and feasibility of all old programs and (b) reranking them against new proposals.

Above all, follow the KISS principle. Like any planning and budgeting technique, your zero-base budgeting system can easily become entangled in analytical gymnastics—both in formulating decision packages and in ranking them. This will defeat zero-base budgeting's prime objective of more rational resource allocation and quick decision making. To prevent this, both forms and ranking procedures should be kept as simple as possible.

I encountered one such situation in one of my earliest attempts at zero-base budgeting. Although all the mechanics of forms and procedures were well documented and key managers thoroughly briefed and trained, I found that ranking, reranking, and consolidation created a heavy burden on my secretarial staff. After each meeting of the various ranking committees, secretaries found themselves spending many overtime hours retyping the newly agreed-to program ranking schedules.

The decision card system depicted in Figures 19, 20, and 21 was created to solve this problem. The system basically works as follows:

1. After all decision packages are clearly defined and formalized, the key data contained in them are abstracted and captured in decision cards such as that shown in Figure 19.

2. Each decision card summarized the proposed program, its goals, and the recommended approach for *one level of effort.* For example, let's suppose your proposed approach to marketing research is to conduct it in-house (rather than through outside consultants and your advertising agency). Let's further suppose that you define five alternative levels of effort for this solution. There would then be five cards (1 of 5 through 5 of 5), each summarizing one level.

Figure 19. A decision card.

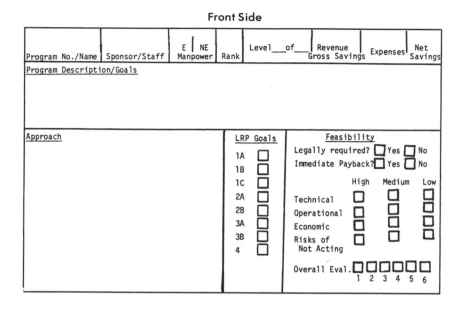

Front Side

Program No./Name	Sponsor/Staff	E | NE Manpower	Rank	Level __ of __ Revenue Gross Savings	Expenses	Net Savings

Program Description/Goals

Approach

LRP Goals

1A ☐
1B ☐
1C ☐
2A ☐
2B ☐
3A ☐
3B ☐
4 ☐

Feasibility

Legally required? ☐ Yes ☐ No
Immediate Payback? ☐ Yes ☐ No

	High	Medium	Low
Technical	☐	☐	☐
Operational	☐	☐	☐
Economic	☐	☐	☐
Risks of Not Acting	☐	☐	☐

Overall Eval. ☐ ☐ ☐ ☐ ☐ ☐
                1 2 3 4 5 6

Back Side

ACCOUNTING DETAIL

General Ledger Number	Description	Dollars 197__	197__

Figure 20. Using the decision card system.

Step 1. Abstract key information from the master decision packages on the decision card.

Step 2. Rank (or rerank) the cards, using data contained in the top margin.

Figure 20. Using the decision card system (continued).

Step 3. Where questions arise, refer to the "description" section of the decision card.

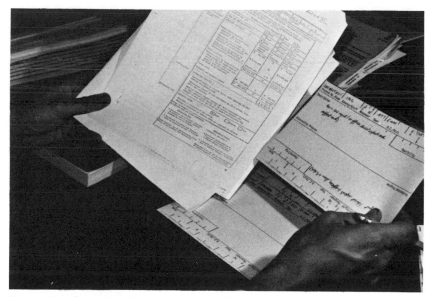

Step 4. Details can be obtained from the decision package.

Figure 20. Using the decision card system (continued).

Step 5. Expense detail is summarized on the back of each decision card.

Step 6. If the total budget is unaffordable, lowest-ranked cards can be set aside...

Figure 20. Using the decision card system (continued).

Step 7. ...or wholly new decision packages and cards can be created (either during the budget cycle or during the year).

Step 8. Once finalized, the ranked cards can be taped together and copied to create a program ranking schedule, shown in Figure 21.

3. The cards are *not* intended to give definitive or exhaustive information (for instance, on consequences of disapproval, alternatives considered, or intangible benefits). To get this information, you should refer back to the detailed decision package.

With these caveats in mind, decision cards can be ranked as shown in Figure 20, and a "program ranking schedule," shown in Figure 21, can be created by copying the ranked cards in their final order. Aside from savings in secretarial overtime, the true value of this approach has been proven to me over the years for several other reasons.

First, in small organizations where all key managers are fully intimate with each other's operations, the decision card format (used with the decision matrix to discipline the thought process) can totally replace the formal detailed decision packages with all the attendant paperwork.

Second, during the ranking sessions in larger organizations, it is

Figure 21. Program ranking schedule created from decision cards.

Program No./Name	Sponsor/Staff	Manpower E	Manpower NE	Rank	Level	Gross Savings Revenue	Gross Savings Expenses	Net Savings
#1 Health and Safety	Mfg. Staff	2	2	A-1	Level 1 of 1	0	0.6	(0.6)
#5 Phys Dist System	Inventory Pln	2	1	B-1	Level 1 of 1	1.0	0.1	0.9
#2a Exec Core Staff	CEO	6	7	C-1	Level 1 of 2	0	0.5	(0.5)
#7 Product Reposition	Prod. Mgmt.	14	8	D-1	Level 1 of 1	5.0	1.2	3.8
#6 Job Enrichment	Personnel	5	3	E-1	Level 1 of 1	0.1	0.6	0.5
#4 New Prod. Launch	Prod. Mgmt.	22	10	E-2	Level 1 of 1	0.3	1.8	(1.5)
#2b Exec Core Staff	CEO	25	25	F-1	Level 2 of 2	0	2.3	2.3)
#3 Executive Retrt	Staff Svcs	1	1	G-1	Level 1 of 1	0	0.3	(0.3)

Program Description/Goals

To purchase Rolling Hills Country Club and convert it to an Executive Retreat and Employee Recreation Center in 1978. Recreation Center concept will be implemented in 1979; Executive Retreat will be immediate.

Approach

- *Close purchase 10/15/77*
- *Solicit and select remodeling bids 12/1/77*
- *Retain golf architect 12/1/77*
- *Complete remodeling and tennis courts 4/1/78*
- *Complete refurbishing of swimming pool 5/1/77*
- *Complete golf course layout 5/1/77*
- *Opening party for key executives 5/3/77*

Feasibility

Legally required? ☐ Yes ☒ No

Immediate Payback? ☐ Yes ☒ No

	High	Medium	Low
Technical	☒	☐	☐
Operational	☒	☐	☒
Economic	☐	☐	☒
Risks of Not Acting	☐	☐	☒

Overall Eval. ☐ 1 ☐ 2 ☐ 3 ☐ 4 ☐ 5 ☒ 6

far easier to use decision cards as a *working tool* for finalizing your priorities than it is to work with overhead projectors, blackboards, or paper easels. Managers can then quickly get into a discussion of the gut issues and priorities instead of having to attend inordinately to administrative mechanics.

Finally, after the budget has been nailed down and agreed to, the cards can be used during the budget year to identify potential trade-offs, or they can be reranked quickly as priorities and objectives change.

But more important than these advantages is the impact I've found this approach has on the top-level decision maker. I suspect that for years many have wished to have a simple system that would allow them to dig deeply into the details of staff expenses, understand what's really going on, and make some basic resource allocation decisions on their own. More than anything else, this system does just that. The first time I tried it was at a final budget meeting with my group's top executive. I was allowed two hours of his time. Fortunately, the meeting was scheduled late in the day. After I briefly explained the mechanics of how to handle the decision cards as well as the preliminary ranking arrived at by his key lieutenants, he began to make his usual probing questions. The questions led to juggling a few cards. Then more questions. It was apparent after two hours that the process was only beginning. We broke for dinner. Six hours later, after reordering practically every card, sometimes digging back into the master decision packages for further details and often discussing how a particular effort supported our organization's long-range profit and marketing goals, we finally wrapped up the effort.

I will never forget his final comment as we rode down the elevator at midnight. "Suddenly, everything I've been trying to get my hands around in thirty-five years of management and ten years of running this smoke factory crystallized and came alive tonight."

Machiavelli would have been proud.

4

Applying Zero-Base Budgeting to Planning Problems

I don't know as I want a lawyer to tell me
what I cannot do. I hire him to tell me how
to do what I want to do.
J. P. Morgan *to his attorney*

MORGAN'S quandary in putting together a financial deal was shared by many of his management contemporaries in putting together their strategic plans. To be sure, the art of long-range planning has come a long way since the late 1960s when it swept through business and government organizations and was hailed as the wellhead, if not touchstone, required for future operational success. Being management's newest fad, it was quickly embraced as the means to overcome a broad range of problems. With it, the organization could "be the master of its own fate . . . to penetrate the darkness of uncertainty and provide the illumination of probability." * Yet, in my view, fond expectations for it are still too often a distant hope and lack of tangible results an oppressive reality. Aside from increasing top management's comfort factor in the short term, the most frequent practical use of the long-range plan is as a document to brief the newly hired college graduate when he walks in the door one week earlier than expected.

To be sure, these assertions may be overdrawn. Some chief executives and most planning executives would disagree with these comments privately, and probably all would loudly disagree in public. But with all due respect to the ghosts of J. P. Morgan's lawyers, long-range planning still inordinately focuses on what the organization can or cannot do with its markets, products, and technologies to boost profitability. Two key issues are often shortchanged, if not missed completely: (1) Are the plan's assumptions realistic, and (2) more important, through what tactical programs are the plan's high-minded objectives and strategies to be implemented?

Zero-base concepts can go a long way toward overcoming these problems, and this is the main thrust of the present chapter. But before we discuss how to apply these concepts, let's review some shortfalls of long-range planning as practiced in many organizations.

A RETROSPECT ON PLANNING

That many strategic planning efforts are of limited practical use stems from one pitfall: Most merely extend the current annual operating plan into a five- or ten-year horizon. To be sure, if we have nothing better, this can be a valuable exercise, for it can identify tomorrow's expense and revenue problems that might result from today's spending and marketing decisions. Obviously, if revenue is growing at 10 percent while expenses are climbing at 15 percent, it is only a matter of time before the bottom line turns red. More commonly, though, these relationships are reversed to indicate an unbelievably robust bottom-line growth!

Many organizations, however, quickly recognize these extrapolations for what they are: nothing more than five- or ten-year financial forecasts. As planning tools they are ineffective (indeed irrelevant) for one fundamental reason: They assume no significant changes in labor standards, inflation rates, competition, or the regulatory environment. To be sure, each component of the plan may indeed make

* S. R. Goodman, quoted in Louis Gerstner, "Can Strategic Planning Pay Off?" *Business Horizons*, December 1972.

eminent sense, but the sum of them makes no sense at all in the real world. Figure 22 provides some food for thought on this problem.

In a very real sense, such approaches to long-range planning are nothing more than the first cousin of the traditional budget approach described at the beginning of Chapter 1. As they offer no overview of the company, its industry and economic climate, no insights into external trends, no hard-nosed assessment of the organization's strengths and weaknesses and, most importantly, no suggestions on how to make the plan happen, they fall far short of practical strategic planning.

A quick review of most organizations' final plans can readily surface many symptoms of this approach. Page after page of five-year financial forecasts is carried to account-level detail with little or no explanatory information. Graphs of future sales and profits show either of two trends. If recent performance has been good, the trend is continued, sometimes at geometric rates beyond the second or third year. If recent performance has been so-so, a couple of years is allowed for a turnaround and usually followed by similarly sharp growth rates to make up for past shortfalls.

In seeing the future through rose-colored glasses, formulation of tactical action programs to capitalize on opportunities or minimize risks is of course unnecessary. The result is not surprising: With the credibility of the plan's outer years seriously questionable, top executives ignore the outer years as an academic pipe dream and concentrate solely on the current budget year. Where that happens, a logical question is then, "Why do we need to duplicate staffs (in planning *and* budgeting) to produce what are essentially two operating plans?"

Faced with these problems, many organizations have moved to implement more pragmatic planning efforts aimed at constantly reassessing their environment, reestablishing their basic objectives, and using them as a springboard to assemble targeted action programs. But how does all this relate to zero-base budgeting? The answer becomes quite apparent when we review several key features of zero-base budgeting. As we discussed in Chapter 1, zero-base budgeting involves more than just building a budget from scratch. It also incorporates a systematic analysis of both costs and benefits of a given effort for the *entire* organization. Rigorous problem-solving techniques are required to state the need or objective for each proposal, identify several alternative solutions, and choose the most cost-effective one. In the ideal circumstances, zero-base budgeting requires that decision packages be linked to the organization's long-range goals and objectives. In fact, approved decision packages represent a compilation of all the tactical actions required to make the long-range objectives

Figure 22. Maurits C. Escher's "Ascending and Descending Waterfall" provides an example from contemporary lithographic art suggesting that while individual pieces of a budget may be sound and logical, the "big picture" makes no sense at all. Linking the zero-base decision packages to the organizaion's overall strategic planning objectives helps resolve this anomaly. Reproduced with the permission of the Escher Foundation, Haags Gemeentemuseum, The Hague.

happen. Reduced to its essentials, the business planning approach of the more progressive organizations therefore is really zero-base budgeting, simplified as to the level of detail but stretched to encompass their long-range planning horizon!

How can zero-base principles be incorporated into the long-range planning process? Two approaches can be isolated, each representing the experience of a number of organizations. The first, clearly more of an ideal approach, represents a very fundamental grass-roots restructuring of the entire planning and budgeting systems from *scratch*. The second allows the old planning process to remain in place but sharply challenges its findings, using a *programmatic* approach and incorporating zero-base concepts. Let's now review how each works.

SCRATCH APPROACH

While the zero-base concept, as developed at Texas Instruments, is often viewed as a budgeting technique, it was in fact integrated into the company's broader system called OST. OST (or Objectives, Strategies, and Tactics) may well sound a lot like management by objectives, or Program, Planning, and Budgeting: it basically involves three steps:

1. *Develop and define your organization's major objectives, or its mission.* During this phase of the planning process, hard-nosed assessments are made of key environmental issues. Several come to mind: What is the economic outlook? What key threats do we face from government, labor, or competitors? What major technological forces are at work? What significant marketing opportunities or threats seem to be emerging? What do we expect our customers to demand? What are our own emerging strengths and weaknesses in personnel, technology, and finances? From this analysis emerges a crisp statement of three or four major goals to be pursued during the planning horizon. They may be financial or nonfinancial in nature. Here are some possibilities:

◇ Increase earnings-per-share growth at an average of 15 percent per year during the next decade (a publicly held company).
◇ Increase book value $100,000 per year and raise the return on shareholders' equity one point per year for five years (a family-owned company).
◇ Increase cash flow from present levels by 20 percent per year (a government enterprise).
◇ Increase sales 15 percent per year for five years, then net income 20 percent per year thereafter (a mutual company).

◇ Develop and maintain a working environment that will attract and retain high-talent employees at all levels (an oil company).
◇ Upgrade recognition of our profit performance by the investing public (a utility).
◇ Sharply increase the perceived level of customer service to exceed that of our major competitor (an insurance company).
◇ Achieve full affirmative-action compliance in all organizations and levels within three years (a medical supply company).

These goals basically reflect *what* we want to do. So far, Morgan's ghost remains unsatisfied. But while stating them explicitly may sound as platitudinous as praising the virtues of motherhood, it is nevertheless valuable in that it (1) defines the organization's character, (2) serves as the basis of targets for high-level executives, (3) provides planning benchmarks to screen product development and acquisition opportunities, (4) establishes standards for measuring overall performance, and (5) serves as a means of communicating to all managers what the company is trying to achieve. But more important than any of these aspects, *without objectives it is hard to formulate a strategy.* And that's what the second step of OST is all about.

2. *Establish complementary supporting strategies.* For each of the three or four major objectives we select, we can now consider up to a half-dozen strategies to accomplish each. A growth strategy should specify in broad terms how the organization plans to achieve its goals over the planning period and should (1) identify which businesses, products, market segments, and geographic areas are to receive attention, (2) indicate relative priorities for investment in alternative sources of earnings growth, and (3) specify activities that will *not* be pursued. This last requirement is important, for it will eliminate much wasted effort when the time comes to develop decision packages. Here are some alternative strategies that might be pursued to achieve the most common business and financial objectives:

Expand unit volume while maintaining the market share.
Increase market share.
Increase prices.
Reduce costs or increase productivity.
Integrate forward.
Integrate backward.
Expand geographically.
Reposition product to increase the market share in a different sector.

Introduce new products.
Enter into joint ventures.
Acquire or merge with other companies.
"Milk" or divest an existing product line.

Strategies for nonfinancial objectives (increase customer service, upgrade recognition in the investing community, achieve full affirmative action) must also be developed and quantified where possible.

Selecting appropriate supporting strategies to meet each objective established in step one is required to (1) provide middle managers with guidelines for developing their own plans, (2) permit optimal allocation of capital and personnel resources, and (3) harness the organization's talents and energies effectively.

However, the words *appropriate* and *complementary* are used advisedly. For before proceeding to the final step, a rather intensive check must be made focusing on one key issue: *Are the objectives and strategies mutually supportive and consistent, or do they in any way work at cross purposes?* Conflict among objectives and strategies (where they are pursued) often leads to unexpectedly poor if not disastrous results. For example, a shift in product emphasis to a line requiring higher than historic rates of capital spending may jeopardize earnings-per-share objectives; a high dividend payout rate may conflict with conservative debt policy and high earnings-per-share growth objectives; sales growth *per se* will not necessarily increase earnings or net worth.

Figure 23 depicts a live example of this problem, drawn form the long-range plan of a European high-technology conglomerate. There are serious questions about the internal consistency of objective 1 and strategies a, b, and c. Even if such inconsistent strategies are not pursued, just one thoughtful question from an astute cadre of operating managers will make the planning staff look silly and destroy the credibility of the entire effort.

With the consistency issue satisfactorily resolved, we have constructed the top of our planning pyramid, the objectives at the apex being supported by complementary strategies in the middle. We can now proceed to build our base of tactical supporting programs, or decision packages.

3. *Develop appropriate and realistic tactical programs to support each strategy.* It is in this step that zero-base budgeting as described in the first three chapters comes into play. Unless all the objectives and strategies are translated into meaningful action programs *by the manager responsible for implementation,* they will neither be acted

upon nor influence the organization. Equally important, unless they realistically reflect the true capabilities of the operating departments and staffs, the long-range plan represents only hope rather than honest goals. It is in this step that the elusive "how" demanded by Morgan of his lawyers is achieved. The process should be viewed as a two-way street, for decision packages may well have to be added (or cut) to facilitate achieving the goals. Not infrequently, the objectives and strategies themselves may in fact have to be modified, based on the detailed analysis of the decision packages, but this option should only be taken as a last resort.

When undertaken as a stand-alone exercise independent of a long-range planning process as described earlier in this chapter, one of zero-base budgeting's many strengths is its capability to identify

Figure 23. Corporate business objectives and strategies (extract from a long-range plan).

Objectives

1. To increase earnings per share at an average compound growth rate of 9 percent to 10 percent a year.

2. To improve earnings stability and avoid past cyclical swings in profits (this year's profits must never be less than last year's).

Strategies

1a. Increase return on stockholders' equity from 13 percent in 1966, to 16 percent in 1972, and 19 percent by 1977.

1b. Expect a minimum of 9 percent return on investment (at book value) from further capital expenditures.

1c. Maintain a ratio of debt to total capital (equity plus debt) no greater than 33 percent.

1d. Build a minimum 10 percent share in any primary market served.

1e. Increase the proportion of our business in upgraded products from 40 percent to 60 percent, and in specialty and proprietary products from 15 percent to 30 percent.

1f. Move into three new business areas — (1) animal medicine, (2) industrial gases, and (3) water management — by acquiring companies with minimum sales volumes of $10 million.

duplication of similar efforts. As decision packages are developed, ranked, and consolidated, we may logically challenge the need for (or affordability of) private secretaries (when word processing pools may be better), centralized computers (when decentralized mini-computers may be more responsive), or market research decentralized among product managers (when a central function may yield the critical mass). On the other hand, when the zero-base budgeting process is linked to the long-range planning framework, we gain an added capability to identify *duplication of different efforts.* This curious but potentially more costly redundancy is depicted in Figure 24. A short word of explanation is in order.

Let's suppose we've agreed that one of our major objectives is to increase earnings 20 percent in the coming year. During our planning process, we also agree to five strategies to support that objective, one of which is to "increase unit volume 8 percent and sales productivity 5 percent." To achieve this strategy, the staffs then develop any of a number of very worthwhile and exciting tactics, or decision packages, some of which are noted in the figure. (In actual practice, the number of supporting packages is usually substantially higher than in our example.) Now it's clear that if just three or four of these packages could in and of themselves achieve the unit volume and sales productivity objectives, then all others would be redundant. Paying for the others would be paying for overkill. *Yet the redundancy is not apparent,* even to the most seasoned observer, who sees one product planning function, one product manager and staff, one advertising function, one selection research function, or one field operations manager, each busy in his own unique way. Linking the plans and budgets in this framework of objectives, strategies, and tactics is the only practical way I know to bring to the surface such redundancies; it is certainly not possible under traditional approaches.

Implementing this approach overnight would, however, represent a substantial if not 180-degree turnabout for most organizations. Burning the bridges of return to past approaches may well be an undertaking few organizations care to risk. For this reason, some might consider what I call a "programmatic approach" on a transitional basis. This allows you to keep the old planning system in place while blending into it some of the principal strengths of the zero-base concept.

THE PROGRAMMATIC APPROACH

Let's suppose that all key players on the staff responsible for planning have put together a strategic plan. By making some key

Figure 24. "Scratch approach" to planning, using OST framework.

Objective

Increase earnings per share 20 percent per year from 1978 through 1983.

Strategies to Achieve the Objective

1. Increase unit volume 8 percent and sales productivity 5 percent per year.

2. Decrease direct labor costs 3 percent.

3. Increase market share 4 points.

4. Decrease prices 1 percent.

5. Decrease shares outstanding by 300,000.

Tactics for Strategy 1

1a. Redirect sales compensation.

1b. Launch new product ZEBRA.

1c. Reformulate/reposition old product LEOPARD.

1d. Implement customer feedback program.

1e. Implement pre-employment selection testing.

1f. Redirect sales training.

1g. Increase advertising.

1h. Implement direct mail program.

1i. Implement sales force job enrichment.

1j. Reorganize sales force.

1k. Implement quarterly sales promotions.

1l. Increase level of customer service.

1m. Weed out marginal sales performers.

1n. Provide 8-hour van delivery to major dealers.

assumptions on market growth, market share, and prices and developing expenses based on unit volume and standard cost trends, they can display the consolidated long-range profit outlook as in Figure 25. Careful scrutiny at the top level, however, raises a number of questions. Of particular interest are the following issues:

◇ Why does the profit plan show a significantly favorable variance to the profit trend?
◇ How will our sharp profit growth of 1976 be sustained?
◇ Is the continuing deterioration of margins through 1979 good from the point of view of investor relations? Why will it continue to deteriorate, and why does it rise after 1980? What are the forces at work after 1980, and how can we bring them to bear today?

Figure 25. Summary profit plan showing substantial growth.

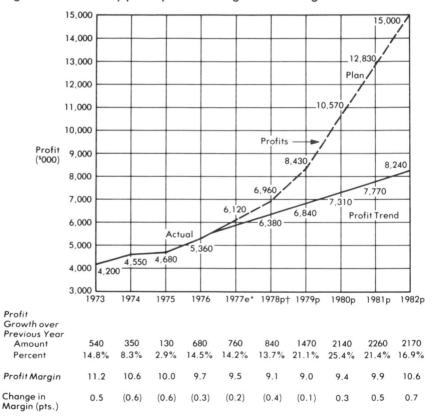

	1973	1974	1975	1976	1977e*	1978p†	1979p	1980p	1981p	1982p
Profit Growth over Previous Year Amount	540	350	130	680	760	840	1470	2140	2260	2170
Percent	14.8%	8.3%	2.9%	14.5%	14.2%	13.7%	21.1%	25.4%	21.4%	16.9%
Profit Margin	11.2	10.6	10.0	9.7	9.5	9.1	9.0	9.4	9.9	10.6
Change in Margin (pts.)	0.5	(0.6)	(0.6)	(0.3)	(0.2)	(0.4)	(0.1)	0.3	0.5	0.7

*e = expected
†p = planned

But all these issues can be distilled down to one of far more fundamental and strategic importance: *Is this plan realistic?* An assessment
of our strategic plan requires answering five questions:

1. What are the plan's central assumptions?
2. What other key risks does the organization face?
3. What is the probability of occurrence for each risk?
4. What would be the net economic impact of each?
5. What do we have to do today to capitalize on opportunities or
   minimize risks?

Let's review now how to deal with each of these questions.

What are the plan's key assumptions? Assessing what the future
holds in store need not be an entirely free-form creative process reserved for blue-sky conceptual types. Indeed, quite to the contrary,
it can be accomplished with a disciplined analytical framework.
Table 8 is intended to give an overview of what I mean, although it
has been simplified to omit a lot of detail. This hard-nosed assessment
of each of the plan's underlying assumptions may well indicate that
with overly ambitious assumptions, revenue has been overstated and
expenses have been understated. In a more positive vein, this exercise
may also uncover untapped opportunities. The gross economic impact
of each of these "what if" questions should be quantified. That is, for
each assumption that might go awry, what would happen to the appropriate revenue and expense and profit accounts?

What other key risks does the organization face? While an assessment of the plan's financial assumptions will probably bring to light
several major risks, a review of outside factors not obvious from the
profit-and-loss or balance sheet projections will no doubt indicate additional significant risks. Several come to mind. What if a recession
cuts into unit volume two years hence? What if a key competitor makes
a breakthrough on a technology rumored to be in development for the
last five years? (Remember Xerox' impact on Kodak's Verifax copier?)
What might be the impact of increased regulation, and in what areas
can they be expected? How will the consumer movement affect us, or
employee demands focusing less on bread-and-butter and more on
"quality of life" issues? (Here the 1976 automobile industry negotiations come to mind.) What if higher tax rates accelerate a continuing
flight of industry from the community, thus leaving those remaining
with substantially higher property tax assessments? (This is a very
real problem faced by many New York based organizations, private
as well as public.) What if international currency exchange rates

Table 8. Evaluation of the plan's underlying assumptions.

Major Plan Assumptions	Assessment	Impact on Proposed Plan	Net Assessment of the Plan
1. Market size to grow 6.5% per year.	Consistent with last five years.	None.	*Substantial risks to profit plan: revenue overestimated, expenses underestimated.*
2. Market share up to 15% by 1982.	Not likely: down from 10% to 6% in the last five years.	Unit volume, and hence revenue, overstated.	*Unlikely that market share can be increased without price cut.*
3. Prices can be increased 2½% per year.	Very unlikely: no price increases in the last five years.	Prices, and hence revenue, overstated.	*Competitive threats inadequately addressed—if significant, price war may be imminent.*
4. New product will capture 28% of potential market.	Unlikely: new-product penetration has been no greater than 15%.	Revenue overstated; manufacturing and sales expenses also overstated if 28% not achieved.	*Productivity action programs must be developed.*
5. Europeans will not enter our Asian markets.	No confirmation.	Unknown.	
6. Manufacturing and sales productivity will rise 4.5% per year.	Internal rates flat for the last five years; plan rate is well above industry averages.	Expenses possibly understated.	
7. Materials costs will rise at 3.5% per year.	In line with 5-year trend, but below last two years' experience.	Expenses substantially understated.	

continue to fluctuate widely? Questions such as these are obviously more of a blue-sky nature than those raised earlier, but their impact is no less real and often more expensive. Again, a hard-nosed quantification of their potential impact must be made in each case. Many will no doubt have minor economic impact, but the major ones should now be subjected to further analysis.

What is the probability of occurrence for each risk? Assessing probability is best approached using the so-called "Delphi technique." * Although I do not generally feel committees or task forces to be the best means to reach quick decisions or ensure accountability for results, they offer strong advantages as a forum for exchanging and refining ideas. The Delphi approach basically calls for assembling a panel of all the resident staff experts. The individual members review each risk and come to a full understanding of its nature. Some will no doubt have slightly differing ideas. These should be encouraged. After gaining agreement on a crisp description of each risk, an initial vote is taken by secret ballot of each man's probability estimate (on a scale from 0 to 1.0) of each event's actually occurring—*in the absence of any positive management action.* (Management actions will be the subject of decision packages to be developed later in the process.) The range of votes is then displayed for all to see, and each panel member is asked to offer his explanations of why he voted the way he did. In this regard, one caution is in order. For every issue discussed, one or two members of the Delphi panel will be acknowledged by their peers as greater among equals. For a pricing issue, it may be the revenue or marketing manager, while the plant manager will pull a lot of weight on factory productivity. Because their opinions may well sway others, they should not contribute to the initial discussions. After those discussions, a second vote is taken and displayed. Usually, the results show a narrowing of the range of probabilities. It is at this point that the expert is invited to reveal his vote and the logic behind it. Then (and only then) a final vote is taken, and the results are displayed and averaged to reflect the panel's consensus on the probability of that particular event's occurring. Figure 26 depicts how this process works for one example.

What would be the net economic impact of each risk? Estimating the probable profit impact is a simple arithmetical exercise. Each risk's gross profit impact is multiplied by its preagreed probablity. The product (or net profit impact) is ranked and displayed for higher

* For a more comprehensive discussion of this approach, see Alan R. Fusfeld and Richard N. Foster, "The Delphi Technique: Survey and Comment," *Business Horizons,* Vol. XIV, No. 3 (June 1971), pp. 63–74.

Figure 26. Using the Delphi techniques to assess risks.

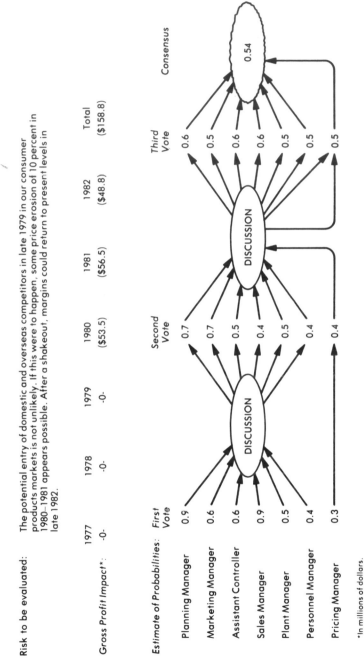

Risk to be evaluated: The potential entry of domestic and overseas competitors in late 1979 in our consumer products markets is not unlikely. If this were to happen, some price erosion of 10 percent in 1980–1981 appears possible. After a shakeout, margins could return to present levels in late 1982.

	1977	1978	1979	1980	1981	1982	Total
Gross Profit Impact*:	-0-	-0-	-0-	($53.5)	($56.5)	($48.8)	($158.8)

Estimate of Probabilities:	First Vote	Second Vote	Third Vote
Planning Manager	0.9	0.7	0.6
Marketing Manager	0.6	0.7	0.5
Assistant Controller	0.6	0.5	0.6
Sales Manager	0.9	0.4	0.6
Plant Manager	0.5	0.5	0.5
Personnel Manager	0.4	0.4	0.5
Pricing Manager	0.3	0.4	0.5

Consensus 0.54

*In millions of dollars.

review and discussion, as shown in Table 9. But the panel's work is not yet complete.

Table 9. Summary of key risks, 1977–1982 plan.

Event	Gross Profit Impact [*]	Probability	Net Profit Impact [*]
1. Market share reaches only 10% by 1982.	$2,438.0	0.90	$2,194.2
2. 18% market share on new product.	1,546.0	0.74	1,144.0
3. Sales and plant productivity flat.	896.1	0.81	725.8
4. 1980–1982 price cuts.	158.8	0.54	85.8
5. Raw materials costs up to 7% in 1977–1979, 3.5% thereafter.	118.4	0.68	80.5
6.	. . . .	. . .	. . . .
7.	. . . .	. . .	. . . .
8.	. . . .	. . .	. . . .
Total	$5,560.0		$3,336.0

[*] In thousands of dollars.

What do we have to do today to capitalize on opportunities and minimize risks? In the OST example described earlier (see Figure 24), each objective and strategy led naturally to a series of supporting tactical action programs, as well as to decisions on each. Likewise, in this approach, each recognized risk or problem must lead to identifying and approving a series of corrective action programs required *today.* For our pricing example, several possibilities are arrayed by functional department in Figure 27. A review of those programs suggests the degree of depth in this organization's strategic thinking and problem solving. Clearly, management has not forfeited its responsibilities by lying back and matching the competition's price cuts. Rather, the company has decided to embark on a strategy of enhancing its product, level of service, and internal cost structure so that it will be able to maintain premium pricing if and when the price war comes.

Each of these action programs is the subject of any of a number of decision packages which are developed along the lines described in the first three chapters. Once they're developed and costed out, three decision options are available: (1) the costs of the proposed programs can be traded off against the "business as usual" spending base, (2) costs can be added to the existing base as an investment in the future, or (3) the underlying strategy of enhancing the product and level of service can be discarded altogether, along with the required incremental spending, and a wholly new alternative strategy substituted. Such alternatives might involve:

Lowering prices now to build market share and preempt new entrants.

Raising prices now and milking the product.

Taking the ostrich approach and hoping the problem never materializes.

One would hope, though, that the depth of discussion during the Delphi panel's work would have led the committee to arrive at the most practical strategy in the first place, thus avoiding the need for unnecessary rework.

At the beginning of this chapter, I noted that the basic weakness of most organizations' strategic plans is that they do not foster decisions required today to assure future results. More often than not, planning

Figure 27. Proposed action programs by functional department.

Event: Price cuts result in 10 percent revenue reduction in 1980–1981, 2 percent in 1982. Shakeout and aggressive business actions thereafter eliminate short-falls.

Marketing/ Operations	Dealer Service	Manufacturing and Distribution	Finance	Personnel and Public Relations
Institute strategic pricing options.	Increase level of service to dealers.	8-hour van delivery to major dealers.	Develop zero-base contingency plan for expense reductions in all other areas.	Institute selection research program for sales and service force, focusing on skills required to successfully handle premium-priced product.
Focus sales training on product value.	Provide free after-hours service.	Increase productivity and quality levels in all plants.		
Increase applications selling.	Initiate targeted customer education program.			
Institute product repositioning; increase features options and upgrade product.				Institute job enrichment program for sales and service force.
Sales reorganization: – Eliminate sales representatives' responsibility for administrative and billing problems.				

results in an elaborate documentation of revenue, expense and profit projections, graphs of strategic shortfalls, and flowery statements of objectives—period. Nothing much else usually happens, except for a lot of mutual congratulation and some short-lived feelings of security that usually evaporate with next month's sales report. Unfortunately, warm felicitations and feelings of security do not make earnings or results happen.

What will make things happen are decisions. And decisions are the end product of a practical long-range planning effort. To accomplish this, the plan should clearly identify critical alternative courses of current action, establish the best ones as major objectives and goals, and lead to approval of a series of tactical programs necessary to achieve each one of them. This innovative (and reiterative) linkage between planning and budgeting is the one that too many organizations fail to forge. The key issue they omit to ask is, "What do I have to do on Monday morning to pull off all these good things?" They fail to recognize that the end product of all the long-range graphs, charts, analyses, and scenarios should not be a planning document but current decisions. It is through applying the zero-base concepts outlined in this chapter that our planning and budgeting waterfall can be made into a cascade of results rather than remain a gristmill of problems.

5

Selling the Concept— and the Ideas It Generates

It is not from the benevolence of the butcher, the brewer, or the baker that we expect our dinner, but from their regard to their own interest. We address ourselves not to their humanity but to their self-love, and never talk to them of our own necessities but of their advantages.
Adam Smith, *The Wealth of Nations*

YOU know what makes leadership?" Harry Truman once asked. "It is the ability to get men to do what they don't want to do and like it." The need for this quality is never more critical than in a highly charged budgeting environment, particularly when it comes to introducing zero-base budgeting. Everyone will eagerly concur on ambitious spending programs, but few will readily accept the fact that the resources to do everything are usually not available. Hence the con-

108

troller's repeated assertions of poverty are met with skepticism and claims that "we can't afford not to do it" or quotes from Vince Lombardi that "if you want to be number one, you've got to pay the price." As one program manager in my organization remarked during a budget review, "Everybody wants to get to heaven, but no one wants to make the sacrifice."

Successfully executing the delicate balance-beam maneuver between the costs of all the decision packages and their affordability requires a maximum of human-relations skills. Some would call these skills leadership, others tact and diplomacy, still others the art of persuasion. My personal preference is to call them what they are: salesmanship. Why? Because the techniques used by any successful salesman in closing an order can be directly applied to zero-base budgeting. But there's also a more practical reason. While a few business organizations' training programs may include some courses in "leadership," "management," "human relations," "persuasion skills," or "discussion skills," virtually all have some sort of sales training program. And rather than taking the time and expense to design a special training program for the staff managers involved in zero-base budgeting, most can simply draw on the resources of their sales training staff. My own experience suggests that the basics of staff salesmanship can indeed be taught in such a course—although learned only through hands-on experience.

Why is salesmanship important? Two reasons come to mind. First, zero-base budgeting—both as a concept and as a working management tool—must be *sold* to the budget managers who will be the prime movers in making it succeed. Of course, any new approach can be mandated by edict, but you do not convert a man by silencing him. And although you may in fact create the trappings of a zero-base budgeting system, the quality, thoughtfulness, thoroughness, and creativity of the decision packages will invariably suffer.

In this regard, the experiences at Texas Instruments and the state of Georgia are to the point. At the former, many disgruntled department heads voiced several concerns to top executives when the new zero-base budgeting system was first installed. In turn, they were informed that if they felt they were not up to the task, a replacement could be found. Initial resistance was similar in Georgia. But the political framework of the executive branch—with some department heads appointed by the governor, others elected directly, and still others with close ties to key committee chairmen in the legislature—created an almost unmanageable challenge. Both cases could have best been handled through artfully employed persuasion skills.

Secondly, when those reluctant brides among the department heads and budget center managers have been won over, a curious phenomenon occurs. Once they begin to employ zero-base budgeting techniques successfully, they too must put those persuasion skills to use in selling and managing the implementation of new ideas that the process will inevitably generate.

In both situations, gaining *commitment* rather than generating *conflict* is critical to success. Faced with a choice between the two options, each of us would surely pick the former. Yet for most organizations—particularly during the budget cycle—the latter too often prevails. Whether on the line or in the staff, failing to nail down a colleague's commitment invariably results in shortfalls to the sales plan, budget overruns, labor disruptions, turnover, and, most important, a failure to deliver on profits or services. In many cases, failure to get a colleague's commitment may be caused by faulty perceptions rather than by facts. However, in the world of human relations and organization dynamics, perceptions are far more important than facts.

The approach described in this chapter evolved out of several years as a management consultant and as an executive responsible for various staff and line organizations in a large industrial corporation. It specifically began to firm up several years ago when I assumed responsibility for the budgeting function. I was impressed by the technical sophistication of our company's planning and control systems and the quality and creativeness of its staff, but I was quite perplexed about the lack of line management's commitment to achieving the plans we worked so hard to develop. The annual budget cycle invariably seemed to deteriorate into polarized camps of "we-they" advocates, marked by games of "dummy up" or "cover up." The situation cartooned by Mort Walker is not unlike those faced by my own as well as many other organizations during the budget cycle. Even when the ice was broken and agreements were reached, commitment to making the final plan happen was a rare and cherished state.

My solution? I turned to our sales training people. Over the years they had developed and refined a rather powerful technique and packaged it into a course called Professional Selling Skills. I wondered whether their technique could be adapted more broadly to gaining commitment and motivating people in other day-to-day operations outside the selling environment. Over a period of weeks, I worked with them to tailor the technique to the needs of my own staff, and indeed, I found that the same selling principles apply elsewhere, particularly to making a success of zero-base budgeting!

How is this to be done? At the risk of oversimplifying, it is through

following that cardinal principle of human motivation espoused by Adam Smith in 1776. Translating it into the contemporary environment of zero budgeting, it means that you address yourself to your colleagues' needs rather than your own. In other words, you talk about what zero-base budgeting (or any other new approach) can do *for* him rather than *to* him. In a similar vein, applying the salesman's jargon to the staff environment suggests differences only in semantics, not substance:

◊ What a salesman calls a close is nothing more than gaining commitment. And his closing techniques apply equally well to a staff environment.

◊ A successful sale starts with probing and listening rather than fast talk. So does gaining a fellow manager's commitment.

◊ Where disagreements arise, they are refuted with facts—quickly and tactfully—so as to prevent later smoke screens.

◊ And, most importantly, commitment and motivation result from identifying, underscoring, and reinforcing benefits of interest to your colleague rather than to yourself.

Successfully employing these principles—and particularly during a zero-base budgeting process—is the key ingredient in generating the motivation and commitment critical to achieving the organization's goals, both strategic and tactical. But let's get down to specifics.

Salesmanship involves a three-step process: fashioning the discussion to your colleague's style; persuading him by carefully listening, drawing out all pertinent information, and speaking to his needs; and asking for his commitment. Let's elaborate on each of these steps.

FASHIONING THE DISCUSSION

If we want to gain the agreement of others, we must first assess and speak in their style. Our need here is to *communicate* in a manner with which our colleague is comfortable. That style may or may not be our own.

To illustrate this, let's look at the framework depicted in Figure 28. What we've structured here are four "ideal personality" types based on (1) an action versus idea orientation (the vertical axis) and (2) a short- versus long-range horizon (the horizontal axis). These four personality types (or leadership styles, if you will) are:

The "implementer" (short-range horizon, action orientation)
The "overseer" (short-range horizon, but idea orientation)

Figure 28. Four ideal personality types.

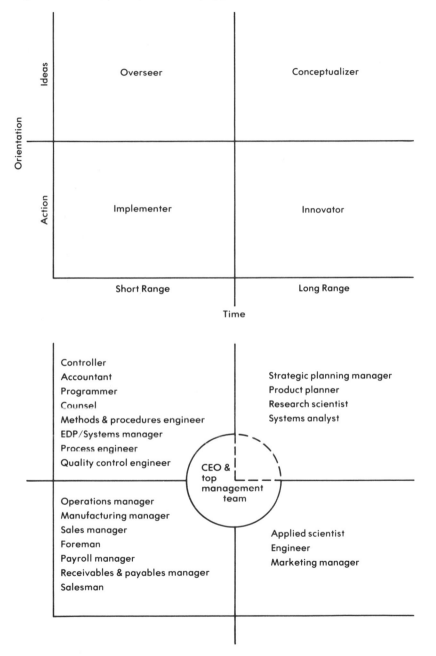

The "innovator" (long-range horizon, action orientation)
The "conceptualizer" (long-range horizon, idea orientation)

Going up the right side, we might see an Edison, then Newton and Einstein; from lower left to upper right we might first see Andrew Jackson, then Woodrow Wilson; going up the left side we might first see Theodore Roosevelt, then Franklin Roosevelt; while across the bottom Andrew Carnegie, then Henry Ford, then Alfred P. Sloan might successively appear.

But let's not fool ourselves by oversimplifying and trying to fit any one individual inexorably into only one block. While almost all of us probably *can* be slotted into one of these primary management styles, each of us will from time to time fall back into one or two others. Several examples come to mind.

Having drawn on his wisdom as a great conceptualizer to structure a constitution along federal lines, and abhorring a strong role for the national government, particularly its executive branch, Thomas Jefferson in fact executed a very pragmatic flip-flop into the "implementer" role when Napoleon offered him Louisiana—and he did this without consulting Congress!

In the contemporary business world, Edwin Land could override the objections of his overseers within Polaroid to conceptualize, innovate, and in many cases actually work directly on implementing the technologies necessary to create the SX-70 camera and bring it to market. Similarly, Harold Geneen could first draw on his overseer strengths in finance and control to pull together ITT, then move swiftly into the action orientation of an implementer to translate them into hard results.

But the framework is more than just a plaything for idle academic amusement. Let's discuss four fictional characters (one for each quadrant) who are frequently encountered in zero-base budgeting environment.

Sheldon Cowboy. Sheldon is the action-oriented implementer—a latter-day gunslinger if you will. Often he is the plant manager, general manager, or sales manager. His competence as a line executive is often outstripped only by his ego. Sometimes he even lets that ego get the better of him by overcommitment to his plan or fantasizing on past accomplishments as a manager, football hero, or war ace. But when it comes to zero-base budgeting, he will be intrigued by the idea of its capability to allow him to quickly reallocate resources, make fast decisions, and achieve better profitability. On the other hand, he will not particularly care to hear of the thought processes behind it, of its requirement for rigorous cost/benefit analysis, how to fill out a decision package to account-level detail, or the possibility that it may reduce his resources.

Sherlock Greenshade. Sherlock is usually found on the operations staff, perhaps as the accountant, controller, manufacturing engineer, or quality control manager. He's the hardheaded pragmatist, sharing a "today" orientation with Sheldon Cowboy. Often, though, he'll drive Sheldon up the wall with his attention to detail and thoroughness, which Sheldon sometimes perceives as nit-picking, often to the point of calling Sherlock a Shylock. When exposed to the concepts of zero-base budgeting, he will warm to its capability to increase his base of analytical information, to be able to track costs by function as well as program, and to be able to cut costs to the bare bone. Sherlock may even get excited about managing the paperwork, which others may see as an attempt to build his empire. Without question, the challenge of a new administrative system puts Sherlock in pig's heaven. But zero-base budgeting's strengths as a planning tool for building closed-loop hierarchies of objectives, strategies, and supporting tactics and for surfacing innovative new concepts to improve the business will probably not excite him any more than it does Sheldon.

Sherman Newthought. Sherman is the organization's down-to-earth innovator. His intellect allows him to take two seemingly unrelated concepts which nobody can ever seem to get off first base, tie them together, and come up with a wholly new approach—perhaps a new marketing strategy or a new product or design. He may be the applied scientist, engineer, or marketing manager. As the action-oriented idea man, he will perceive zero-base budgeting as a means to sell any of his many bold approaches that have been shelved in the past, or to institute dramatic new programs to resolve the long-term risks faced by the business, or to effect fundamental shake-ups in the organization's basic strategy. In short, Sherman will be thoroughly turned on to zero-base budgeting as a vehicle allowing him to communicate his ideas upward to the key decision maker and to compete equally for scarce resources. He will usually not, however, warm up to filling out the paperwork. Nor will he listen at length to any discussions of zero-base budgeting's capability to track programs across functions or cut costs. In this regard, a reminder to him is in order that zero-base budgeting may well result in his getting *increased* resources for clearly justified efforts. And he'll gladly assert that his efforts are indeed just that, as he's been doing for several years now, often unsuccessfully.

Sterling Brightman. Sterling is the organization's grand conceptualizer, often found in its research labs, planning staff, or advanced-products area. Being something of a futurist, he will warm to the idea of zero-base budgeting's capability to tie his plans and concepts to concrete action programs, to conduct a thorough closed-loop systems analysis of costs and benefits across all of the organization's functional entities, and above all to bring out bold innovative ideas. But he will be indifferent to the administrative chores of zero-base budgeting and may well be a problem when it comes to actually sitting down and translating his concepts into hard-copy decision packages. This is not because he fears the system; men of his intellect rarely feel threatened by zero-base budgeting. Rather, details (whether they be forms or the need to specify costs to the account level) simply bore him.

With four individuals so very different as these, one might ask, "How can we possibly pull off zero-base budgeting?" Yet, the task is not quite as complicated as it would first appear. Once you've assessed each of your colleagues' style (as well as your own) and tailored your approach to each of them by speaking in their style and not yours, the foundations for success have been laid. Some call this tailoring process "chemistry," others would call it "getting on the same wavelength," but the result is the same. In each case, your colleague will feel more comfortable (or certainly less ill at ease) when faced with this new and uncertain thing called zero-base budgeting—or for that matter any proposal for a new way to run the business. And once that chemistry is established, the approach taken for the balance of the discussions will be the same, whether you're dealing with a Sheldon, a Sherlock, a Sterling, or a Sherman.

PERSUADING FOR COMMITMENT

Any successful management discussion will incorporate five elements:

Stating benefits, both at the start of and during the discussion.
Probing or questioning to determine your colleague's needs.
Supporting his statements of need—where your proposal can meet that need.
Encouraging objections as a means to defuse them by taking up the benefits of your proposal.
Proofing your claims by citing facts that your colleague believes, so as to refute his objections tactfully.

Figure 29 provides a graphic summary of how the discussion is structured around all these elements. Let's now review each of them in detail.

Stating Benefits

A benefits statement is a remark which gains your colleague's attention, arouses his interest, and creates a favorable atmosphere in which you can present your proposal. Benefits statements can be made either at the outset of the discussion or during it. Depending on the timing, benefits statements will differ in emphasis, although not in substance.

An *initial benefits statement* will kick off the discussion. It begins with a general statement related to your colleague's needs, then leads into a specific reference to your proposal, be it zero-base budgeting or whatever. The general statement might be a broad remark on the need to increase profits, meet interest requirements, reallocate resources, cut costs, launch a new product successfully, manage the business more effectively, or increase productivity. The statement then (and only then) leads into the specifics of how zero-base budgeting and many of the ideas it will generate can help accomplish those needs.

When you refer specifically to your proposed approach, do not refer to its detailed features such as decision packages or ranking techniques. That would be premature at this point. Rather, focus on the

Figure 29. A persuasion model.

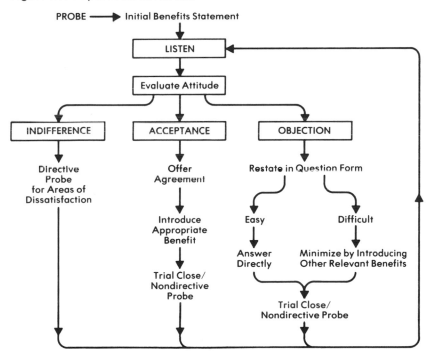

value of hard-nosed planning and creative resource allocation. By referring to some nitty-gritty aspect, you may get sidetracked and allow an untimely objection to be raised. You do not want the initial momentum of the discussion to bring to the surface possible problems; rather, you want to talk in generalities about what the process of zero-base budgeting is and what benefits the approach can offer that will be relevant and meaningful to him.

Starting strong is important for pulling off a good initial benefits statement. Did you ever begin a conversation with a friend or your wife or girlfriend and end up not covering what you started out to say? The same happens all the time in management meetings. Here are the advantages you create for yourself by starting with a strong benefits statement:

◇ You can control the discussion by first talking about what you feel is important to your colleague.
◇ You don't get sidetracked into discussing things that are unimportant, irrelevant, or detrimental to your goal.
◇ You impress your colleague with your results-oriented professionalism; consequently he'll be more likely to consider your proposal seriously.
◇ You create a positive, receptive environment for the balance of the discussion.

Alternatively, what happens if you start off weak? In addition to losing all the advantages discussed above, it will be very difficult to recover from a bad start and easy to get sidetracked further or to lose control by talking of negative features instead of benefits. The impact of all these negatives will make getting his commitment difficult if not impossible.

A *specific benefits statement* can be woven into the discussion at any appropriate moment. Because the ice has already been broken, broad general remarks about the need for better profits or productivity are no longer necessary: Their value has been agreed to. Rather, we can now get very precise on benefits.

For example, if your colleague raises an objection by asserting that this looks like another gimmick to cut budgets, you may agree but then state that in many cases increases to budgets are certainly going to be approved where the spending will clearly be cost-effective. You might also note that the primary responsibility for zero-base budgeting is shouldered by line managers and not the budget staff. Hence it is an operating tool rather than a control gimmick.

If he agrees (or states) that bright ideas for improving operations seem to have dropped off in recent years, an appropriate benefit to be introduced would be zero-base budgeting's usefulness as a vehicle to communicate new ideas to the top.

If he notes that the planning process seems to be an academic activity that generates mostly paperwork, a remark on zero-base budgeting's decision-making orientation is appropriate.

If he notes that he has never understood what results are being delivered by each department (or can't understand how zero-base budgeting will identify what's really going on), an appropriate benefits statement would be that the process breaks up the operation into small understandable elements, called decision packages, that tie together costs and benefits.

These are only four of a number of possible benefits statements. You may wish to stop briefly at this point and construct several others, based on your knowledge of your own organization and perhaps also on your recent experience in trying to "sell" some new approach to managing the business.

Probing

Probing is nothing more than a questioning technique to help you control and direct the discussion. All good salesmen use it, whether they call it probing or not. Just as in a successful sale, probing techniques in a management discussion are executed in a planned and systematic manner. This will make the difference between idle chitchat and an effective, persuasive meeting.

Why do we need to probe? Probes are employed for three purposes:

To direct the conversation. If you learn to probe effectively, you'll be able to control the conversation without making your colleague consciously aware that this is happening. It will enable you to focus the discussion as tightly or keep it as loose as you desire and channel it toward your goal of getting commitment.

To uncover relevant information. Whether or not you gain commitment will depend on your ability to demonstrate the benefits of your approach—based on your colleague's needs. Probing identifies those needs by getting him to open up and identify and discuss them.

To understand reservations and objections. An intelligent, meaningful probe woven into the conversation can help clarify your colleague's concerns. It can help you understand exactly what may be bothering him and exactly what information he's seeking. Once you understand his specific concerns, you're on the way to addressing his reservations squarely.

These are the key benefits of probing. But when is it in order? A probe is appropriate in several circumstances. You probe:

To evaluate your colleague's style or attitude. Earlier in this chapter we discussed four different personality types. If you don't know the style of your colleague, probing can help identify it. But even after you have identified his *general* style, you will still need to understand from time to time his specific thoughts on your proposal so that you can either support him in areas where you agree or allay his concerns. Probing draws out those thoughts.

To set up supporting statements. You can probe to gain a response that you can support affirmatively. Supporting will be discussed in more detail later in this chapter. At this point, it's sufficient to note that a benefit will seem more important to your colleague if he brings it up first and then you support it rather then if you introduce it and seek his agreement.

When proof statements are not accepted. Proof statements will also be discussed later in this chapter. Let's suppose, though, that you have made one and your colleague disagrees with it. You must fully appreciate why he did so before you attempt to refute him or offer a second line of reasoning focused on a benefit. The simplest way to find out is to ask. In other words, you must probe.

After failing to gain his commitment. Again, in order to continue the discussion and hopefully gain your colleague's agreement, you must know why he refuses to commit himself. The knowledge necessary to keep the discussion rolling is gained by probing.

Now that we understand why probing is important and when it's appropriate, the next question is, how do we do it? There are two types of probes: *nondirective* and *directive*. Nondirective probes are open-ended questions: They cannot be answered by yes or no. But they do enable your colleague to elaborate on his concerns, and particularly to raise issues *he* feels are important. Directive probes, on the other hand, can generally be answered by a straight yes or no. You use them to direct the discussion into an area of your choice. It also forces your colleague to discuss things *you* feel are important.

It is best to begin with nondirective probes and then become more directive. In this way, your colleague develops a sense of importance. He is able to discuss things he feels are important, and he will be more than willing to let you zero in on his specific needs. This, of course, is the ideal situation. However, if your colleague is reluctant to open up and offer his thoughts, you should probe more directly in order to elicit statements you can support. In the following, I list fourteen probes that might be commonly encountered in a planning and budgeting discussion. Decide for yourself which are directive and which are nondirective.

Why do you say that?

Wouldn't it be useful to have some sort of contingency plan on the back burner if next year's profits aren't that good?

How does that sound to you?

What else are you concerned about?

Did you ever wonder why we never seem to achieve the goals of our long-range plan?

Getting that cost estimate shouldn't be a problem, should it?

How do you like the concept?

Have you ever noticed how initial budget requests always seem at least 50 percent higher than last year's spending?

Oh?

Do you like the idea of being able to flex the budget during the year as the sales volume rises or falls?

But I don't understand!

Do you remember how we didn't finalize last year's budget until April?

Did you ever wonder why our overtime expenses shoot up during the budget cycle?

Is there anything we haven't covered?

Supporting

Using supporting statements skillfully gives your colleague a feeling that he is "buying" and not "being sold." Your role suddenly becomes that of an informed problem-solving consultant helping him reach an important decision rather than an eager huckster pushing for a sale. If you have ever made a major purchase yourself, you can appreciate the difference.

In addition, supporting statements are useful in developing and cultivating your colleague's thoughts. When you can agree with one of his remarks, you build it up in importance in *his* mind. Then, when you introduce an appropriate benefit of your proposal (zero-base budgeting or whatever) that is keyed to his thinking, you've got him agreeing about how *your* approach can solve *his* problems.

The timing of a support statement is easy, for your colleague will always provide the cue. Whenever he makes a favorable remark about either your proposal or your kind of approach, the door has been opened for you to introduce a supporting statement. There are times, however, when offering a supporting statement is not in order: if your colleague makes a remark that is irrelevant and therefore pointless to support; if his comment is unimportant and would only detract from the point you're trying to make; and if his comment is an unfavorable one, indicating that he likes the present way of doing things or sees a weakness in your approach. Handling objections such as these is discussed in the next section.

In general, then, you should not support any comment that will not directly aid you in getting your colleague's commitment. There are two steps in offering support: (1) indicate agreement, (2) introduce an appropriate benefit. Offering agreement can be accomplished easily with expressions such as "I couldn't agree more," or "Exactly," or "You're right," or any other such comment. This part of supporting merely sets the stage for you to introduce an appropriate benefit that reinforces his thought process. What's required is a statement that makes it clear how zero-base budgeting can provide that benefit. In other words, you'll want to introduce a benefit appropriate to his earlier remark. This helps build it up in importance and is far better than asserting a benefit and seeking his agreement. If you succeed, he will be left with a feeling of having bought rather than having been sold. Some examples of supporting statements in a zero-base budgeting environment follow.

Statement: "I'm quite particular about putting together a responsible budget to present to the president."

Offer agreement: "I couldn't agree more!"

Introduce benefit: "This is one of zero-base budgeting's greatest strengths. All spending requests are explicitly arrayed, with each tied to benefits as well as consequences if not approved. In that way, the wheat can be readily separated from the chaff, if you will."

Statement: "I need a budgeting system that is flexible, one that I can change quickly and easily as circumstances warrant during the year."

Offer agreement: "Exactly!"

Introduce benefit: "Unlike our present approach, zero-base budgeting will allow us to increase or cut spending during the year, starting with the most marginal efforts. Thus, arbitrary cuts that might well eliminate muscle and bones with the fat are avoided."

Statement: "Our problem is that we never seem to get our investments to hatch. And when they do, they often turn out to be snakes and lizards rather than fat hens!"

Offer agreement: "You're right!"

Introduce benefit: "No system will absolutely guarantee success. But zero-base budgeting requires explicit statements as to what's going to be done, as well as how and when. These statements, contained in our decision packages, provide a convenient tool for follow-up on cost and performance."

Statement: "I'm interested in controlling my costs."

Offer agreement: "Of course you are! What businessman wouldn't be?"

Introduce benefit: "By providing you with a ranked set of spending priorities, zero-base budgeting helps you approve and fund only those efforts that you feel can be afforded."

Handling Objections

As you talk with your colleague and discuss the benefits of your proposal, he will react in one of three ways: acceptance, indifference, or objection. (These three different possibilities are shown in Figure 29).

As we have seen, *acceptance* is handled by making a supporting statement, then either by probing nondirectively to open up other areas for discussion or, if all areas have been covered, by asking for commitment. *Indifference,* we said, is handled by a series of directive probes to uncover areas of satisfaction or dissatisfaction. Once uncovered, appropriate proof statements, benefits statements, or support statements can be introduced. Handling an *objection* successfully will require all the skills we've discussed.

You can observe whether your colleague is inclined to accept, be indifferent, or object by watching his facial expressions, observing his overt actions, evaluating his "body language" (if you believe in that concept), and alerting yourself to what he does *not* say. But more than by any of these methods, his attitudes can be assessed simply by *listening to what he has to say.*

Evaluating your colleague's attitude is important because it tells you how to respond effectively. You would not consciously want to support a hidden objection or fail to ask for his commitment to your proposal when it's obvious that he likes it. Therefore, by evaluating your colleague's attitude—particularly when he's raising an objection —you can best determine what approach to use to gain his agreement.

But how do we handle objections? Depending on the kind of objection, in two ways. There are two kinds of objections: easy and difficult. In either case, the first thing you want to do is restate the objection in question form, and for two reasons: It clarifies for you what your colleague is concerned about, and it reassures your colleague that you are concerned about and listening to his needs.

The second step after restating the objection is to answer it. If it is an easy objection, you should answer it directly, offering proof if necessary. (Proof statements are discussed in the next section.) A difficult objection should be minimized by stressing any number of other relevant benefits.

Finally, in both cases, you either probe nondirectively to open up other areas for discussion or, if all areas have been satisfactorily covered, ask for his commitment.

The following dialogue illustrates how to deal with an objection. In fact, it turns out to be two objections: an easy one and a difficult one, both of which are handled using our approach.

Your colleague: "Your new budgeting system is too complicated." (Objection)

Response: "Oh? In what ways?" (Nondirective probe)

Your colleague: "I don't see how it's any different from our old approach. If the staff could inflate their old budget forms, what's to stop them from inflating their decision packages?" (Objection)

Response: "Let me see if I understand you correctly. You feel that it will be just as easy to inflate decision packages? (Restate objection in question form)

Your colleague: "Yes."

Response: "Of course, that may well happen, but unlike in the old budgeting system, when it happens it will be obvious and easily detected during the review process. And nobody wants to look stupid." (Easy objection)

Your colleague: "But doesn't zero-base budgeting require a lot of paperwork?" (Difficult objection)

Response: "Your concern is well advised. You mean the time and effort required to fill out the decision packages?" (Restatement)

Your colleague: "Yes."

Response: "Well, my professional colleagues in other companies that have already used zero-base budgeting did have a paperwork problem. We hope to learn from their experience by simplifying the forms, providing explicit procedures and one-on-one coaching. More importantly, though, they found that describing the spending requests in detail disciplines the thought process and often generates new and better ideas. And only by specifying all our spending requests in detail can we fully understand what's being spent, why it's important, and how the benefits of the spending are to be achieved. With the information that the decision packages will provide, we can make smarter business decisions and create a more responsible and responsive budget. So there is a tradeoff—but one that I think is certainly worthwhile! Wouldn't you agree?" (Minimize by introducing other relevant benefits, closing with a directive probe)

One final thought on handling objections. Smart salesmen *encourage* objections. They know that an easy objection can be readily turned around into a strong selling point. A difficult objection is an indication that your colleague is interested enough to ask a question about a possible problem area. His concern can then be minimized by introducing still other benefits. In either case, objections allow you to talk about benefits. And with enough benefits, getting commitment is easy!

Proofing

A proof statement is merely what the name suggests. It is a factual offering of proof by you to your colleague. An important criterion for a good proof is that the source be acceptable and credible to the listener. Thus your vice president of research will probably believe a proof citation from *Scientific American* but not one from *Better Homes and Gardens*. Only when a proof source is credible does it have any meaning and fulfill its basic objective.

Why are proof statements made? Basically, for four reasons:

◇ To convince your colleague that your approach can deliver the benefits which you talk about and which are important to him.
◇ To add credibility to your statements and your whole persuasive presentation.
◇ To gain the respect of your listener as a "pro" fully knowledgeable of your subject and able to prove what you say.
◇ To add importance to suggested benefits by expanding on them.

Proofs must be offered in a sincere and meaningful tone, for they have no value when given haphazardly and carelessly. They should build a bridge that translates perceived benefits into real benefits. By proving what you say, they will help cement a rapport between the two of you. And just as this is important to a salesman, so it is to you.

When do you offer proof? Two conditions will be necessary for a well-timed proof. First, your listener must consider the benefit under discussion important. (Obviously, it is silly to offer proof of a benefit when your colleague doesn't consider it relevant or important. That's why recognizing the differences in styles and needs of a Sheldon Cowboy versus a Sterling Brightman is important.) Secondly, he must be skeptical that your proposal can provide that benefit. He may well come right out and tell you this (particularly if he's a Sheldon Cowboy), but more likely he will inadvertently convey this impression through his facial expressions or overt actions. In either case, it's important to offer proof only if he reveals skepticism. It would be meaningless to prove something he has already agreed to. In short, then, a proof is appropriate when your listener agrees that a benefit is important to him but is skeptical that your approach will provide it.

Proofing requires (1) restating the benefit, (2) proving it, and (3) expanding (not expounding) on it. Let's look at each step separately.

Restating the benefit. Restating is a reference of any kind to the benefit under discussion. It acts as a bridge between what your listener said his need was and what you're about to say.

Proving it. This is probably the easiest step. It can be a graph, a testimonial, a case history, a pilot test, a demonstration, statistics, a professional article, or merely further elaboration. You may draw from printed material or merely talk about past experience (preferably his own) to support your point. If your colleague does not accept your proof statement, probe to determine why. But if he agrees, expand on the benefit.

Expanding on it. This is without doubt the most important step in a successful proof, and unfortunately the one which is most often forgotten. By expanding on a benefit that your listener has already agreed is important to him, you (a) make the benefit seem even more relevant and important to him and (b) allow yourself to introduce additional reasons that possibly had not previously been brought out as to why he should agree to your proposal. Actually, the last response (to the difficult objection) in our sample dialogue is an example of a proof statement. Table 10 details several features of zero-base budgeting, ties each to related benefits, then offers some expansions on each of these benefits. To help develop important skills for this, you might try compiling several features of any recent staff proposal you were involved in, detailing the related benefits of each feature, then listing several possible expansions that might have been appropriate.

ASKING FOR COMMITMENT

If you've done everything right so far with good timing, your persuasion job is completed. But you have not gained commitment (or closed, as the salesman would call it). In simplest terms, getting final agreement means *simply asking for your colleague's commitment to your proposal.*

Table 10. Summary of features and related benefits of zero-base budgeting.

Zero-Base Budgeting Features	Related Benefits	Possible Expansions
Budget developed from scratch.	All proposals compete equally for scarce resources.	Detects obsolete efforts. Detects duplicate efforts.
Burden of proof shifted to decision unit manager.	Forces development of more cost-effective ways to improve operations.	Minimizes reworking of budgets at eleventh hour. Relieves top management from "working in the dark." Leads to open two-way communication and better cooperation.
"Requires paperwork."	Probably requires less paperwork than traditional systems, considering time spent during the year, under such approaches, for incremental requests, analyses, and other planning efforts. Allows tight control of specific program efforts.	Easy detection of inflated budget requests. Decision packages can be tied to organizational goals and help make them happen. Provides a basis for ongoing analysis during the year aimed at improving operations. Focuses on "what, why, and how" as well as "how much" issues.
Requires systematic analysis of impact of effort on entire operation.	Identifies all impacts of a spending decision, leading to better decisions.	Uncovers major hidden opportunities that may merit additional resources. Plan is more responsive to market needs and more sensitive to profit needs.
Decision packages are ranked in order of importance.	Improves resource allocation and profitability: marginal efforts are cut.	Ranked packages are a contingency plan for use during the year if resources go down—or up.

Unfortunately, it doesn't always work out so easily. Where you fail to gain commitment, it is usually because of three common mistakes: You have failed to (1) display a positive attitude, (2) summarize all the benefits that your colleague has accepted as important to him, or (3) ask for his agreement.

With this in mind, a good closing statement incorporates three parts. They are:

Assume that your listener will agree to your proposal and commit himself to it. Some call this "positive mental attitude." It is not a specific step. Rather, it is the attitude you project when you ask for his support. It will be indicated by the words you use. Therefore, in asking for commitment, nothing you say or do should reflect hesitation or uncertainty.

Summarize the benefits your colleague thought were important. Remember Adam Smith? Speak only of benefits that are important to your listener, not of those you think are important. Why should they be summarized at this point? Simply because summarizing them reinforces your colleague's inclination to agree—at the psychologically crucial moment.

Request his agreement. Since getting his agreement to your proposal has been the purpose of this whole exercise, it is indeed strange that this step is omitted as often as it is. Yet it is the most important step of the whole persuasion process. No matter who your listener is or what his responsibilities are, you can *always* ask for some sort of commitment. Perhaps it is his initials on your proposal or permission to do a pilot run in his department; it may be his acceptance of your decision packages or hopefully his agreement to implement the concept fully throughout the organization. *Whatever you want, ask for it.*

One final thought. The persuasion model outlined here can be a powerful tool in selling zero-base budgeting, the ideas it will inevitably generate, or any other new approach to running the organization. Reduced to its essentials, its power is derived from the fact that you use your colleague's *own logic* to gain his agreement on doing something that he may well have been reluctant to do—and like it. If he recognizes this, it may well be psychologically devastating to him and even result in an emotional outburst.

So proceed forcefully and with determination—but stay alert and sensitive.

6

Fostering Innovation

*What is unique about a company is not
products or patents. . . . What is unique is
always the same thing: it is people, the
brains and talents of people. . . . Good
ideas come from smart people. Sometimes
these people produce patents, sometimes
they produce a reputation for service, but
they always produce something that cannot
be easily duplicated by anyone else. In
other words [you must] find yourself some
smart people. This is one of the most important of the irregular rules of business,
because if you can do that, you can forget
a lot of the other rules.*
Adam Smith [pseud.], *The Money Game*

ZERO-BASE budgeting lays down a gauntlet to the organization
to innovate. The challenge is posed through the four sobering questions contained in any decision package form:

◊ What is your objective for this effort?
◊ What are the alternative ways of accomplishing this objective?
◊ How cost-effective and feasible is your chosen alternative?
◊ What will happen if your request is disapproved?

To be sure, zero-base budgeting—even without innovation—can indeed be an effective means for improving operations through short-run cost cuts. By capturing all activities in decision packages and ranking them, it doesn't take a terribly astute manager to spot and cut obvious areas of redundancy and fat. But after a year or so of wielding the hatchet, the issue then becomes, "What do we do for an encore?"

That's why innovation is important. Cutting costs is simple; improving profits is quite another matter, for it will usually require increasing costs in the short term to increase long-term revenues by a greater amount. This essential difference is captured in Shaw's words, "Some look at things that are and ask, 'Why?' I dream of things that never were and ask, 'Why not?' " The former is the task of accountants and staff analysts, whereas the latter is in the realm of visionary planners. For zero-base budgeting, this innovative process is the responsibility of the organization's rank-and-file managers as they put together their decision packages.

If, then, we are to have a successful zero-base budgeting effort that remains in place over the years, we must understand how to nurture innovation throughout the organization. This, in turn, requires an understanding of (1) what innovation is and what it is not, (2) why it's a particular problem for most organizations (particularly larger ones) that use zero-base budgeting, and (3) some guidelines on how to foster it.

WHAT INNOVATION IS—AND WHAT IT ISN'T

For the vast majority of organizations—public or private, profit-making or otherwise—the word "creative" or "innovative" generally provokes all kinds of nasty connotations. Employees with this trait are often viewed as irresponsible, unmanageable, mercurial, clever, or even weird, yet somehow indispensable. Some key managers find it quite discomforting that the organization's destiny will depend on such incorrigibles.

And yet leadership at all levels is becoming more and more attuned to the necessity of coping with and managing change, particularly when faced with the prospect of implementing a zero-base budgeting system. Change means innovation, whether it be a new way to cast engine blocks, a wholly new means of automotive power based on something other than internal combustion of gasoline vapor, a new system for distributing welfare checks, or asking if a negative income tax (or employment tax credit) would be more cost-effective than the overhead associated with the welfare solution.

Innovation can be viewed as either substantive or procedural; but we can also view it as either creative or imitative. You can copy your competitor's new product or you can come up with one of your own. Either way, you are being creative in the fullest sense. And successful organizations have found that innovative, creative change and change management are not something to be relegated to an annual off-line skull session conducted as part of the long-range planning process. Rather, creating new ideas and managing their implementation is part and parcel of the idea of leadership. In Antony Jay's words:

> To describe a man who left things exactly as he found them as a "great leader" would be a contradiction in terms. A leader may change the map of Europe, or the breakfast habits of the nation, or the capital structure of an engineering corporation; but changing things is central to leadership, and changing them before anyone else (or at least before the rest of the pack) is creativeness.*

Nor need the change necessarily be drastic; it can be as mundane as reorganizing the typing pools into word processing stations (to save money), converting the surface of the school's football field to Astro-turf (to save maintenance and prevent injuries), or consolidating redundant computer reports.

Understanding how to foster innovation can best be developed by appreciating what innovation is. Perhaps the seminal work on this subject in recent years was Arthur Koestler's *The Act of Creation.*† In it, Koestler develops the thesis that innovation is *not* the exclusive property of the creative artist, musician, scholar, or research scientist. All these professionals, as well as successful business executives, managers, and rank-and-file employees arrive at creative solutions to problems through a common, logical approach. Koestler calls this the "Eureka Process." In grossly oversimplified terms, the act of discovery or innovation can be classified into two types.

First, and most uncommon, are fundamental discoveries of basic principles. In this category we can place Einstein's development of relativity theory as well as the mathematical discoveries of Galois (in higher algebra), Poincaré (in Fuchsian functions), and Ampere (in

---

* Antony Jay, *Management and Machiavelli*, p. 83. Copyright © 1967 by Antony Jay. Reprinted by permission of Holt, Rinehart and Winston, Publishers.
† New York: The Macmillan Company, 1965.

game theory). They spring, perhaps once in a century, from the deep inner thoughts of a genius. Often they have little practical application, at least not until the rest of the world can understand them and begin to employ them profitably. In this category I would place much of the early work done by Bell Laboratories on network theory. This seemingly abstract concept is the basis for almost all modern telephone communication switching systems, but it applies equally well to any situation where I have to get something—be it a message, binary blip, or freight car—from here to there. Fortunately for our communciations system, AT&T was quick to grasp the implications of the concept and incorporate its principles into its forward systems-design effort. (But when they exposed the concept to a select group of railroad executives, not the slightest interest was evident. The Rock Island Line was indeed a mighty fine line, *wasn't* it?) That innovations of this type are normally in the purview of the longhairs, the unmanageables, the incorrigibles, and the mercurials is probably why creative types are looked upon with disdain by most managers.

It is the second category of innovation, however, from which over 99 percent of all new ideas come. And it is this type that all of us can use every day, with or without zero-base budgeting. To Koestler, it incorporates the principle of *bisociation,* or putting together two seemingly unconnected ideas or facts to form a single new idea. It can best be explained through some examples, a review of which will suggest that innovation is not as earthshaking as you might think.

1. Koestler cites the case of Gutenburg puzzling over how to reproduce the written word while watching grapes being pressed; suddenly, by bisociating grape juice with ink and the Rhine maidens' feet with type fonts, he saw the printing press as the answer.

2. Chevalier de Mère's passion for gambling led him to approach Pascal, who married several mathematical principles to come up with the theory of probability. Later innovators saw the possibility of using it as the foundation of the modern insurance business.

3. As a young patent attorney, Chester Carlson saw the need for a device to copy abstracts and met that need by combining his knowledge of the phenomenon of photoconductivity and of the physics of electrostatics to discover xerography. (But thousands of other bisociative acts were then required from John Dessauer and Xerox research and engineering staffs to refine the concept until it led to a marketable product.)

4. A former consulting colleague of mine, while product manager with Scott Paper, saw a problem of excess capacity in his company's

wax paper production line. At the same time he was worried about the limited success of one of his own new products, a tampon called Confidets. By including a waxed paper bag to dispose of each used tampon, he increased the unit volume of his product as well as the waxed paper, bringing both to profitability.

5. DuPont created Teflon and marketed it for years as insulation for copper wires. It was unfortunately not until a few years before the expiration of the patents that its usefulness as a nonstick coating for cookware was "bisociated" and linked to a market need to generate a new product line with explosive market impact.

6. The origins of zero-base budgeting are no different. While many of its initiates wonder why they didn't think of it before, its originator, Peter Pyhrr, will readily admit that it contains nothing new. Rather, he drew on a number of concepts including "starting from scratch," problem solving, cost/benefit analysis, and systems analysis to "create" this powerful tool.

All well and good, you say, but these discoveries were obviously the products of exceptionally creative people. How can such creativity be possible among rank-and-file employees?

The experience of several organizations pioneering in zero-base budgeting suggests that bright ideas are in fact *not* the exclusive preserve of "eggheads." For instance, in Georgia, one civil servant wondered why state policemen were trained, uniformed, and provided a car at heavy expense when every tenth day each officer was required to man the radio dispatch desk and handle administrative paperwork. During the zero-base budgeting process, he suggested that all troopers be placed on the road and the station chores be handled by the handicapped. Here, a need to save money led to an innovative solution based on the bisociation of two ideas: to increase the level of service of the highway patrol and to provide a productive job for someone perceived as otherwise unemployable. That civil servant, incidentally, was not a bright young M.B.A. but a corporal in the state police force.

In a state university system, a custodian wondered why he seemed to be picking up a large amount of test tubes from the chemistry labs every night. This led to a suggestion during the zero-base budgeting process that the test tubes be cleaned and reused. As it happened, the test tubes were being discarded because the lab budget was already fat and the administrator was using lab supplies as a contingency to cover possible future expense overruns in other areas.

Also in Georgia, a state highway department employee wondered why the grass along the right of way was cut in two passes of fifteen feet each. If the need was to save money, satisfy environmental needs, and prevent accidents in the ditches, why wouldn't one pass be sufficient? Another innovative idea accepted!

The incidents are not isolated and suggest that what the rank and file may lack in formal training is more than made up for by hands-on, in-depth understanding of the situation, gained through many years' experience. By placing the burden of budget formulation at the lowest practicable level, zero-base budgeting serves as a vehicle to foster and surface ideas—from the most knowledgeable sources—for improving operations. If you've had any experience with a suggestion system, you can appreciate the importance of this point.

Closer to the day-to-day world of your own organization's operations, constant change will require constant reassessment of the type described earlier. The needs that produced the organization's present structure, staffing levels, weekly meetings, performance reports, and monthly analyses have a way of becoming ossified into bureaucratic systems. As the needs change (and they inevitably will), so should all these management trappings. But they rarely will unless someone creatively challenges the way things are. Zero-base budgeting's structure and philosophy are designed to facilitate just this process—regularly and systematically.

What all this means is that innovation need *not* be a black art solely within the charter of the research or planning staff. The creative act is not an act of creation in the sense of the formation of the universe. Fortunately for our civilization, only in rare instances does it spring from the depths of genius; in the vast majority of cases it is a logical process that can be undertaken by anyone, executive or clerk, foreman or production worker. It merely requires questioning, shuffling, uncovering, selecting, combining, and synthesizing available concepts, facts, principles, or skills. "It is obvious," says Hadamard, "that invention or discovery . . . *takes place by combining ideas.* . . . The Latin verb *cogito* for 'to think' etymologically means 'to shake together.' St. Augustine had already noticed that and also observed that *intelligo* means 'to select among.' "

WHY IT IS A PROBLEM

Fostering innovation in a zero-base budgeting environment is a serious challenge for two reasons. First, zero-base budgeting as presently employed most frequently finds its best applications in larger, well-structured organizations—generally those with annual sales exceeding $25 million. Second, the larger the organization grows—

whether business, government, or not-for-profit—the more it hungers for new streams of income, products, or services, but the weaker is its ability to innovate. This latter fact is no mere coincidence: The larger an organization grows, the more important it becomes to establish a firm structure and unified systems and policies if it is to avoid floundering in confusion. Concentration on planning—often previously non-existent—emerges, and it is a brand of planning that is minute, exhaustive, and time-consuming. At the same time, a "healthy conservatism" develops with regard to change.

By contrast, innovation is a creative process in which flexibility, imagination, curiosity, a sense of urgency, and a certain streak of tempered insanity are all essential. To carelessly plant the seeds of such a potentially disruptive power in a rigid environment is to invite upheaval, and for highly structured and ossified organizations, it becomes impossible to rock the boat without capsizing it. Thus, imperial China fell in 1911 in the face of radically innovative ideas on the nature of government and society, and so did its successor government 38 years later. Failure to grasp the implications of the innovative marriage of armor and fighter aircraft for blitzkrieg tactics caused the French army no end of upheaval and embarrassment in 1940. In the contemporary business world, Richard Goodwin's problems in trying to reorient Johns-Manville (eventually resulting in his own demise) or Westinghouse's back-to-basics retrenchment into the electricity business come to mind. But where innovative ideas are nurtured, focused, and controlled, there have been many obvious successes, including Meiji Japan, Bell Laboratories' transistor, IBM's 360 computer, the moon shot, or Xerox' 914 copier.

Conventional wisdom holds that innovation is next to impossible through normal channels inside a public corporation that has passed beyond its own entrepreneurial phase. Exceptions do exist, but corporate salary structures, bonus systems, career paths, and organizational delineations are generally too rigid to accommodate the rewards entrepreneurial innovators demand, to justify sticking their necks out if they're already on a healthy career path, or to respond to the immediate needs of the infant idea fast enough to keep it afloat. Moreover, the bigger the parent, the easier it is for the innovative decision package (be it an idea for a new product, process, sales approach, or word processing system) to disappear. After all, what's even a half-million-dollar item in a billion-dollar enterprise? Hardly two hours' revenue!

This problem is recognized by many larger organizations, and increasingly the established line-and-block chart is being circumvented. Figure 30 arrays the range of alternatives now in use for surfacing and managing new ideas; the range shows a progressive decline in corporate involvement in the start-up phase. At some point, the thoughtful company tends to use all alternatives, including zero-base budgeting in the broadest sense. In that form, zero-base budgeting calls for assigning the most creative and innovative members to

Figure 30. Eight ways to manage innovation.

Product Managers	Taking the product out of the lab and giving it to a manager for coordination to the market.
Project Teams	Nurturing entrepreneurial teams inside the corporation. (3M has this down to an art.) Just being a team member is a reward because it's fun, but there may still be a problem of inadequate incentives.
Spinoffs	Taking a product already developed for internal use and "going public." This is an entirely internal way to innovate, perhaps least painful because so many questions are already resolved.
Corporate Venture Groups	Creating a separate group whose sole purpose is to start up ventures and bring them to a point of stability.
Cooperative Agreements	Ideally, combining small-company inventions with big-company dollars and marketing. Agreements between large companies often run into problems.
Contract Entrepreneurs	Managing the start-up phase of a venture until it has become stable enough to attract a professional manager.
Acquisition	If you can't make it, buy it. This often leads to castration of the acquired company. Eventually, it must end because parents can't handle too many children.
Venture Capital Lending	Exxon, for instance, funds small start-up ventures in return for equity.

Adapted from *Management Practice*, Fall 1976, by permission of Main, Jackson & Garfield, Inc., management consultants.

the ranking committees (or, in the long-range planning mode, perhaps the Delphi panel) and disciplining their efforts with a forceful but inspiring chairman, then letting them run rampant to come up with bold but practical new ideas on how to run the business.

In addition to problems caused by the organization's size, innovators cite another principal obstruction: lack of funds, or conversely, high start-up costs. These are real problems, and in no way would I attempt to belittle them. However, as I noted in Chapter 5, zero-base budgeting's greatest appeal to the innovative likes of Sherman Newthought or even Sterling Brightman is the opportunity it provides them to compete on equal footing with current programs for scarce resources.

But difficulties in funding have existed for many decades, and while they no doubt have contributed to the slowdown in innovation as organizations grow, they have not caused it. The causal factors, displayed in Figure 31, lie far deeper. In brief, they are: (1) lack of a clear understanding of market or organization needs; (2) ignorance of the management processes required to innovate, that is, to translate these needs into goals, product concepts, action plans, decision packages, or whatever; and (3) fear not only of failure but of change itself. Let's look at each of these.

Failure to understand market or organization needs. The discovery of abstract mathematical theorems excepted, most innovations begin with a clear statement of market or organization needs. We may all marvel at the intellects of William Shockley, Walter Brittain, and John Bardeen and wonder how we could duplicate the deep thought processes that went into discovering the transistor at Bell Laboratories. Shockley himself ascribes the discovery to receiving, early in the game, a clear-cut statement of need from Mervin Kelly, his research director and later president of Bell Labs. To Shockley it meant pursuing "the objective of an electronic telephone exchange; that is, where everything is done electronically, with no relays."

Failure to understand how to manage innovation. Many seasoned executives say that inept management of the innovative process—to the extent that it is possible to isolate the management aspect of innovation from all others—is the single most important barrier to success. One proponent of this viewpoint, William Foster of Resource Management Systems, argues quite effectively that failure to innovate within large corporations can in part be blamed on the increase of financially oriented chief executives. "New ideas [or innovative decision packages, if you will] are fragile," he says. "They must be treated gently through a continual process of balancing the past against the future." [Remem-

Figure 31.   Chief culprits in the innovation logjam.

1. *Much of what makes a line manager good is diametrically opposed to what makes an innovator good.* The innovator marches to a different drum. He questions the system rather than obeying it. He is a freewheeler to whom organizational security is less a comfort than a straitjacket.

2. *Many managers are ignorant of the process and structure required to manage innovation.* The bulk of the innovative process consists of cycles of testing, evaluation, development—and testing again. Unless one person or team is constantly aware of the entire picture emerging, the significance of new data is distorted by whoever is in charge at the moment.

3. *It is more profitable to follow the leader than to be it.* Although profits on new technological products, like Xerox, can be spectacular, they are also relatively rare: Failure rates for new products in new markets push 95 percent, while "Me-too" introductions are almost sure winners. Moreover, any truly innovative effort appears as cost for many years before it can begin returning profits.

4. *Those companies best equipped materially to innovate are least capable of doing so.* The larger the company, the more rigid its structure and decision-making processes. Separated by layer upon layer of intermediaries, chief executives typically lose what understanding they might have had of what it takes to give birth to a business.

5. *Smaller companies in closer touch with such gritty matters—and thus better at innovating—find it difficult or impossible to obtain funds for start-ups.* Risk capital is controlled by a shrinking group of investment managers, both in industry and in the financial community, with a uniform disinclination for risk taking.

6. *Decision makers at all levels suffer from fear, not only of failure, but of change of any kind.* A National Science Foundation study indicates corporations' innovative capabilities are falling victim to insecurity: (a) high individual fear of being blamed for failure; (b) sense of threat to one's hierarchical position; and (c) reluctance to enter new, unfamiliar theory.

Adapted from *Management Practice*, Fall 1976, by permission of Main, Jackson & Garfield, Inc., management consultants.

ber our point about new programs competing against old for scarce resources!] "The cold analytical feasibility data [must be balanced] against the excitement generated by the idea's potential. Potential is something numbers can't nail down precisely, but the financial man, who heads more than a third of our major corporations, tries to do just that. He is by nature and training concerned more with what has been and what is than with what could be. He is a conservative, low-risk oriented, and focused primarily on the short-term bottom line." *

A big company also tends to overstaff a new project (captured and approved in a major decision package) as if it were a perfect miniature of the parent. The problem is not only the number of people but the fact that each additional person is one more player who often doesn't know what game he's in and is either ignorant of or insensitive to the management processes necessary to foster innovation.

Fear of change. There are also fear of failure and fear of change itself. In this regard, Foster discusses the problems created by consensus management:

> Consensus management is death to innovation because it tends to be too careful. To innovate, you must be bullheaded and at least somewhat naive. . . . That's why the most ingenious developments usually come from outside the established companies in the industry. Burlington Mills didn't invent nylon, Kodak didn't pioneer instant photography, and Detroit won't produce the first economical nongasoline engine for cars—they already know why it can't work. But the guy who'll make it work fortunately doesn't. †

Eat your hearts out, Kodak, IBM, and General Electric, for politely declining a guy named Chester Carlson and his funny ideas on xerography.

For these reasons, innovation will never be an orderly process or a safe one—which is why venture capitalists select so few opportunities and ask for an arm and a leg when they do.

But the alternative to learning how to manage innovation—particularly during and following a zero-base budgeting process—is slow death. In an economy based on finite resources, innovation isn't an option, it's an imperative. For individual businesses, industries, public organizations, and nations it is a survival factor.

To successfully embark on zero-base budgeting, the executives

* From "Innovation: Circumventing the Corporate Logjam," *Management Practice,* Fall 1976. Reprinted by permission of Main, Jackson & Garfield, Inc., management consultants.
† *Ibid.* Reprinted by permission.

responsible for it will have to learn how to structure and manage an innovative organization, at the grass roots to create clever decision packages, in the ranking committees to fine-tune them, and at the top level to nurture those that are approved. Some key ideas on how to do this are summarized in the following list.

THE FIVE STEPS IN THE INNOVATION PROCESS	CORRESPONDING ELEMENTS IN ZERO-BASE BUDGETING
Create a sense of urgency.	Gain top management's commitment and involvement.
Understand and clearly define your *needs* and translate them into *objectives* and *goals*.	State your objectives in the decision packages.
Bisociate two known concepts.	Think up alternative *ways* and describe them along with the recommended approach in the decision package.
Refine the idea into a practical approach that meets and supports your goals and objectives.	Describe alternative *levels* of effort, conduct a feasibility assessment, and describe the intangibles of the proposed approach.
Ensure a responsive environment that will embrace the idea and facilitate its implementation.	Employ selling skills to see your packages through the implementation state.

What's required, in sum, is not so much basic creativity as clearly defined goals, effective management processes, and an open environment. The following points were originally formulated as guidelines for managing a start-up venture,* but they apply equally to starting a zero-base budgeting process, and particularly to handling innovative proposals introduced by some decision packages.

1. The top executive (CEO, group, division, or department executive) must appreciate that approved decision packages must be *managed* continuously by one person or team throughout their entire development, that is, from their inception in the research and planning stages to their operational launch.

2. Each decision package, if approved, must be able to command support within the key corporate power structures if it is to prove feasible. While objections are possible from some of the power holders,

---

* Adapted by permission from "Innovation: Circumventing the Corporate Logjam," *loc. cit.*

support by the top executive's own circle is imperative: In any confrontation, these people will carry at least 51 percent of the vote.

3. The top man (and his superior, often right up to the board) have to move aggressively to effect the change in mental attitudes that the proposed approach requires. They must learn to work with a new technology, product, market, or business approach, whether or not the effort succeeds.

4. The top executive must have an appreciation of the intuitive aspect of managing creative, inventive people. He needs to know that the innovator is a bit like a three-year-old—not necessarily impelled by logic or even reasonable forces but at times terribly shrewd and incisive—and that he needs to put up with it, much like Sloan with Kettering in General Motors' formative years.

5. The corporation must cross a major "cultural barrier" and understand the implications of this. It must recognize and acknowledge both its own ignorance and its predisposition to respond in ways that may not be appropriate for the new approach. Zero-base budgeting's requirement to shift the burden of proof for spending decisions from the top man to the first-line supervisor is an example of crossing a major cultural barrier. Both old dogs must learn new tricks.

6. The top executive must have an appreciation of the threat any new approach poses to the established hierarchy. Unless he makes it clear to company executives that the approach does not threaten them and that it's to their advantage to cooperate and contribute, warfare between the lords and their barons will scuttle the ship of state before it's launched.

7. The top executive must know how to test the managers responsible for implementing the innovative decision package, and once he has ascertained their competence, he must be able to trust them as he would trust the people who are reporting directly to him. This holds whether we're talking about a new product or analytical approach, a new field sales office, a word processing pool, or an industrial security effort. Unless this trust is cemented during the earliest stages, the strain of mushrooming responsibilities, inevitable minor day-to-day implementation problems, and in some cases unforeseen cost overruns will jeopardize the whole effort.

SOME SPECIFIC GUIDELINES

To foster innovation, management must understand four of its key ingredients and must commit itself to making each happen.

1. There must be a *need* to create ideas for new products or im-

proved operations. It must be coupled with a *sense of urgency.* Innovation—and zero-base budgeting for that matter—is no job for faint-hearted country clubbers. Necessity remains the mother of invention.

2. This need must be translated into one or more *objectives* that are explicitly communicated as *organization goals* to all participants in the zero-base budgeting process, particularly to those assigned to the ranking committees.

3. There must be an *appreciation of the concept of bisociation*— the ability to take two seemingly unrelated principles or concepts and meld them into a practical solution that meets the needs or supports the goals.

4. The *environment of the organization must be ready* to embrace and implement the new approach aggressively, either because of market or profit exigencies, a will to manage on the part of the top brass, or pressures from public agencies, interest groups, or the employees—or better yet, all of these.

Several specific pointers come to mind in pulling all this together. In order of importance, they are:

Define your organization's needs and goals and communicate them to all participants in the zero-base budgeting process. I cannot emphasize this enough. Most mature business organizations do have a planning process, but few take the time or effort to communicate the findings and goals developed out of it to the rank and file. As a result, if the rank-and-file managers possess any spark of creativity, it is unfocused and without purpose. But with goals, their energies can be channeled toward constructive problem solving—and creative decision packages.

Stick with the basic elements of your zero-base budgeting decision packages. Figure 9 in Chapter 2 depicts the "bare bones" elements of a decision package. This format requires an explicit statement of what's to be accomplished, how it's to be accomplished, the costs and benefits, the alternatives not chosen, and the consequences of disapproval. These questions are incorporated into virtually all successful zero-base budgeting systems. During the second or third year, someone in the organization will inevitably suggest that some of these elements be eliminated. Reasons vary, but the common ones include "to cut out paperwork," "to simplify the system," or "nobody seems to come up with an acceptable alternative after a year or so anyway." This is unfortunate, for these five questions are the essence of the problem-solving process. While it is unreasonable to expect every manager to conceive a creative alternative every year for every spend-

ing need, keeping those elements in the form will keep the heat on—
and the challenge—to innovate. And even if only in one of a hundred
cases it produces a significant improvement, the results will be more
than worth the effort. Such low success rates are not much different
from the chances of success of a new product or venture, and the cost
is far less. What if one of those packages were an Ivory soap or a
Xerox 914 copier?

*Hire talented people and assign your best to the ranking commit-
tees.* As "Adam Smith" says, if you can do that, you can forget a lot
of the other rules of business. As noted above, they do not have to be
blessed with super-high IQs. All they need is sufficient open-
mindedness and informed judgment to be able to bisociate two and
two to make four—or maybe five! All well and good, you say, for a
Texas Instruments, or Ford or Procter & Gamble, who are hip-high in
talent. But what of the rest of us, who, when faced with the departure
of a particularly talented manager, agonize with our personnel manager for days over a possible replacement, only to reach for the telephone in frustration to call our old college roommate who left the
organization rat race years ago to found a highly successful executive
search practice? That's where the next rule comes in.

Have all the facts at hand and make sure that everyone is informed.
The major need here is to keep informed on new opportunities to
improve your market position or internal operations. It may require
instituting a competitive intelligence program or a management development program, or perhaps an executive reading program. It might
even require beefing up the corporate library or the subscription budget for professional literature. In zero-base budgeting, as in innovation
generally, it's not absolutely necessary to be smart (although it does
help), *but it's indispensable to be well-read and informed.* If you
aren't, you won't have anything to bisociate. No bisociation, no
innovation. No innovation, no creative decision packages.

Use your talented people. As particularly talented people surface
during the zero-base budgeting process, as indeed they will, reward
them with public recognition and cash incentives where possible.
Stretch their fertile minds by reassigning them to problem areas that
perhaps aren't so innovative in their zero-base budgeting submissions.
There is only one greater danger to the organization and to zero-base
budgeting than a dull manager: a bright manager who is left un-
challenged.

Maintain records of all decision packages, including those approaches that are rejected. Since new ideas are threatening, many will
be efficiently screened out as they move upward through the ranking

committee. But because ultimate power rests at the top, support of the top brass is a necessity if a good idea (or decision package) is to be enacted and become an innovation. How is this accomplished? Quite simply, those responsible for the administration of the zero-base budgeting process should keep aside all decision packages that appear to be of unique merit but have been rejected for whatever reason. Acting in the role of the "devil's advocate" or, better still, the "conscience of the organization," they should review these packages directly with the top decision maker to determine if they merit further consideration.

Keep people communicating. Setting up managers, task forces, committees, or ranking groups *against* one another does *not* foster innovation. Competition *is* in order when it comes to implementing approved programs; but nothing is more detrimental to creativeness than putting your key people at loggerheads with one another. The minute one feels another will one-up him with a bright idea, everybody dummies up. Again, no communication, no ideas to bisociate. No bisociation, no innovation. In discussing the development of the transistor at Bell Laboratories, William Shockley noted that the last thing needed was an *individual* incentive system, for it was liable to work at cross-purposes with the need to exchange ideas. (Team incentives to foster innovation may, however, be an entirely different matter. Perhaps the success of the Scanlon Plan in union-management cooperation can be attributed to this element.) What's required, then, is a climate of mutual support and openness in which differences can be discussed frankly and worked out, an environment in which all view one another as resources and not competitive threats and in which there is general feedback on performance so that all can contribute better.

This is obviously at variance with classic management doctrine. But a clear distinction is necessary between the requirements of an environment to foster innovation and those of an environment to implement results. If we appreciate that difference and adjust our management styles accordingly, successful zero-base budgeting will follow.

One final thought: Profitable translation of innovative ideas into bottom-line results is by no means inevitable. It was almost 120 years between Jenner's discovery of the principle of smallpox vaccination and Pasteur's discovery that the same principle could be applied to cholera, rabies, and a host of other ills. Hero of Alexandria invented the steam engine in 200 A.D., but 1,500 years passed until James Watt harnessed the idea. Hero also invented an ingenious device for dispensing holy water—1,700 years before the invention of vending machines! The discovery of turbine movement we owe to the Tibetans, who promptly used it to drive their prayer wheels and nothing else. Galilei astonished the world when he turned the telescopic toys of Dutch craftsmen toward the skies. The Chinese invented gunpowder and used it for little more than fireworks. Univac launched the first successful commercial computer, but IBM rapidly gained market dominance.

In modern times, the link between the innovative discovery and its practical application for the advancement of society (whether as customers, managers, employees, or shareholders) is usually the business organization, and within that organization, it is either a smart individual or team that uncovers that opportunity. In a zero-base budgeting environment, the tools for generating ideas are the decision packages and the intensive thought processes behind each, as well as the ranking-committee sessions and their open, freewheeling discussions that synthesize known ideas and principles and marry them with goals and needs to produce improved operations. If you can link a principle like xerography or microprocessors or glass fiber optics or satellite communications with a market need, couple it with a hard-nosed set of organizational goals, and hammer it out in a creative ranking committee armed with well-thought-out decision packages, you don't have to worry about bureaucratic inertia in the rest of the organization or about not being blessed with a legion of smart people.

All you have to do is make sure your decision packages for customer order forms and sales office switchboards are funded to the maximum level.

7

Top Management's Role

A prince, therefore, [ought to be] both the fox and the lion; because the lion cannot defend himself against snares and the fox cannot defend himself against wolves. Therefore, it is necessary to be a fox to discover the snares and a lion to terrify the wolves. Those who rely simply on the lion do not understand what they are about.
Machiavelli, *The Art of War*

SEVERAL months ago, I was boarding an airplane for a return flight from a state capital to my home. As I was stowing my luggage under the seat, a friend, booked on the same flight, came down the aisle. After we exchanged greetings, I inquired as to the reason for his trip. He proudly noted that his district had just elected him a representative to the state legislature. I extended my congratulations, and he asked about the purpose of my trip. I stated that I was returning from a seminar on zero-base budgeting that I had given earlier that day to a group of professional managers. The conversation then went something like this:

"Say, can we sit together on this flight? I've got something to discuss with you," he said.

"Oh? What's that?" I asked.

"Well, one of my key campaign planks in my recent election was a promise to push for zero-base budgeting in our state government. Now that I've been elected, I guess I'll have to deliver. But I haven't the foggiest notion of what it's all about, except that it sure gets votes! Could you give me a quick one-hour cram course on the subject?"

My friend's question was indicative of an attitude shared by most key executives—whether public administrators, elected legislators, or businessmen—about zero-base budgeting. If they know nothing else about it, its name alone has a tremendous intrinsic appeal. (No doubt a few voters even believe it is the magic touchstone that will automatically deliver a horn of plenty of public services, at zero cost!) What these executives lack, though, is a thorough appreciation, not so much of what it is, but of its subtleties and the requirements on them to make it work. In other words, my friend's dilemma was quite simple: He had learned how to be quite an effective Machiavellian lion but was grasping for the necessary insights and knowledge that would make him a clever fox.

Zero-base budgeting's successes can be attributed in no small part to the critical role played by top managers who can balance both roles. This chapter discusses (1) who top management is, (2) why they're important in making the zero-base budgeting process happen and their role in it, and (3) some thoughts, based on observations provided by a number of executives, on how they can help the process along.

WHO IS TOP MANAGEMENT?

Top management is a term of many definitions. In its narrowest extreme, it incorporates only the chief executive officer and possibly the individuals reporting directly to him. In a broader sense, it has been used to encompass the entire executive cadre, comprising perhaps the top 2 percent of the organization's total payroll. For zero-base budgeting, I'd like to use a somewhat different definition that includes the organization's top man, his key lieutenants, his controller, and selected individuals on the budget staff or task force who will administer the process. While the last group may not be all that involved in central decisions on the organization's strategies or policies and certainly isn't all that well paid, it is nonetheless critical to the success of the zero-base budgeting process.

Of all these individuals, the top man (whether he's the chief executive who elects to implement the process in his entire organization or a department head who decides to "go it alone" within his own smaller entity) will play a cardinal role. The reason is more basic than just rank. It rests on the following premise: Although zero-base budgeting is perceived—due to its name—as a budgeting technique, it is more accurately regarded as a planning and decision-making tool. And since the ultimate authority and accountability for decisions in any organization rest with the key executives, it is they and not the controller's staff who must shoulder ultimate responsibility to make the process happen. I know of no organization that has successfully pulled off zero-base budgeting without a high degree of support from the top echelon. In a similar vein, I know a few that have indeed pulled it off successfully with personal initiative from the top, only to drop it after a few years with the departure of the key person.

TOP MANAGEMENT'S IMPORTANCE AND ROLE

In a nutshell, successful zero-base budgeting requires the *commitment* and *involvement* of an executive cadre possessed by a *will to manage*. Let's examine each of these needs and discuss why they're important.

Commitment. The top executives may or may not be among the first in the organization to become aware of the need for zero-base budgeting. But until they do, not much is likely to happen, and after they do, whether or not anything happens will depend primarily on them. Zero-base budgeting in itself will be a trying process, particularly during the first year, and will generate many, many ideas for improved operations. Top management bears the main responsibility for deciding whether the proposed changes are practical and wise, whether the organization should in fact accept them or whether they carry unacceptable risks, and at what pace they can be safely introduced. The zero-base budgeting process, as well as the proposed changes that are crystallized in the rankings of decision packages, must truly reflect a strategy, an action plan, and operational goals with which the top people are comfortable, for as we saw in the last chapter, the changes cannot be successfully implemented unless the team at the top is willing to work very hard to put them across. Commitment means quite a bit more than a pen scratch to a memorandum from the chief executive to the troops to implement zero-base budgeting. Rather, the commitment required is a solid determination to implement and manage change for the better, with acceptance of all the risks implied for the organization, its short- and long-term performance, its people and their careers.

Involvement. Zero-base budgeting's decision orientation will require the key executives to frequently take personal stands on important and controversial problems. Since those decisions will of necessity be ones they will have to live with, implement, and quite often defend before directors, employees, shareholders, or voters, the key executives must participate actively in finalizing them. Final budget reviews under the traditional approaches typically focus on the issues of "How much is that department going to cost next year?" or "Why is their proposed spending rising so sharply?" On the other hand, final executive reviews of a zero-base budget will commonly focus on such questions as "Why are we doing this effort?" or "How is it going to be implemented?" or, most importantly, "How does this tie to our strategic goals?" These are not issues or decisions that can be delegated to a support staff. To be sure, that staff can play an invaluable role in ensuring the analytical integrity of the packages, but it cannot make the final decisions. That will require considerable, albeit rewarding, time on the part of the key executives.

Will to manage. Zero-base budgeting requires decisive leadership. Few of the decision packages being submitted for approval will be completely new to top management: Most represent a continuation of business-as-usual approaches (although some imply a slight change in focus). And even most of the remaining packages have usually been debated by the staffs for some time. But because many have implications for individual careers, discussions soon become quite subjective and too often never lead to action. Proposals to liquidate a product line are often debated endlessly for months or even years. Often the missing link to success is a will to manage at the top.

Sometimes (although infrequently) the process stalls because of a lack of backbone. More frequently, priorities that conflict with zero-base budgeting play a role. A senior executive approaching retirement may set his priorities so as to have more time for other pursuits. The changes and efforts required by zero-base budgeting may just be too much for him. Similarly, an elected public official getting his card punched prior to running for higher office may not wish to bare all the skeletons in the spending closet that zero-base budgeting will inevitably uncover.

To be sure, these examples may seem overdrawn, but there are countless cases where other pressing and urgent priorities may well dictate that an organization not embark on zero-base budgeting, even where possessed with the sturdiest of backbones. Several examples come to mind. If the company is tottering on the verge of bankruptcy and the top men are spending all their waking hours with the bankers; if it is the subject of an unfriendly tender offer or shareholders' suit or is faced with an upheaval in a core department that requires the termination of several key people; if its sales force is demoralized by the introduction of a competitive new product, requiring the top men to spend a lot of time giving pep talks in the field sales offices, then the timing is obviously not right for zero-base budgeting. The same observations would apply to a school board having to deal with a court-mandated busing order or a city manager faced with a unionization drive. Although a simplistic view would hold that a strong dose of tough-minded planning and decision making (as encompassed by zero-base budgeting) might be just what the doctor would order to get the organization's operational house in order, the quality of the process will invariably suffer unless the top executives can spend a lot of time on it and are not restrained in implementing their decisions.

As we have seen in this chapter and the previous one, switching from the traditional management approach to a zero-base budgeting mode and translating the results into effective decisions is an entrepreneurial innovative art that cannot be reduced to a systematic cookbook procedure. It works best with a management team that prefers to operate openly and makes thoughtful, deliberate, and deliberative decisions so as to avoid unpleasant surprises, continuous crises, and constant flail and confusion. Other teams are more attuned to a management style characterized by seat-of-the pants decisions (or avoidance of decisions) and moving on hunches and gut feelings. They enjoy making the fur fly after letting intrigue, country-club politics, and hallway agreements run their course. Zero-base budgeting is clearly inappropriate for them. My own preference in management styles is the former. In any case, top management clearly should make a careful, objective, introspective assessment of the organization's environment and management styles before deciding to embark on an approach such as zero-base budgeting.

ARE YOU READY FOR ZERO-BASE BUDGETING?

In sum, making zero-base budgeting happen is essentially an educational, attitudinal task in which the key executives will be the prime movers. But some concrete steps can be taken to facilitate the process.

Provide leadership. Sound simple? Normally it is, but zero-base budgeting offers some unique challenges. Forceful leadership by a tenacious and determined top executive team is absolutely essential for successful zero-base budgeting. The top people, in turn, must have the solid support of middle managers who are able and willing to follow their lead. A newly appointed chief executive or one who for any of the reasons outlined earlier doubts his ability to effectively control the organization's thrust should refuse to even consider zero-base budgeting unless driven against the wall by economic imperatives.

Although zero-base budgeting can be applied to one or two selected departments, its full impact will be felt only when it is applied to all staffs. That requires leaders who are willing to focus on much more than just a profit improvement snipe hunt. Although I do not mean to minimize the importance of cost savings, it is only when zero-base budgeting is implemented on a broad basis that decision packages can be coherently tied to the organization's overall objectives and strategies and innovation can be fostered through the exchange of ideas between the various staffs.

The commitment to provide the required leadership should not be taken lightly. Before undertaking zero-base budgeting, a careful self-appraisal is in order to determine whether you'll be able to do what is necessary. Several specific subissues must be addressed. Here are some of them:

♦ Will you insist on nothing but the best? The top management team will need to review, often in some detail, many decision packages. The standards required must be nothing less than those demanded by generals Scharnhorst and Gneisenau of the Prussian army: "I cannot . . . be bound by a battle order that provides less firepower than is possible." If a particular decision package or array of alternatives is less than the best, would you insist that it be reworked? And would you repeatedly insist on improvements until you're fully satisfied?

♦ Are you prepared to make decisions under uncertainty, despite lack of hard data, and reverse them forcefully if they don't meet expectations? Approval or rejection of each decision package will be the result of a systematic, but admittedly subjective, process of balancing all savings and benefits against costs and consequences; and legal, technical, and operational imperatives must be considered as well. Of necessity, most assessments will require your judgment based on data that are incomplete or less than accurate. The top executives must be prepared to trust the discipline of the zero-base budgeting process and of their subordinates; they must be in a position to assume that the recommendations that have made their way through the ranking committees have been adequately thought out. To insist on elaborate quantification invites the syndrome of "paralysis through analysis."

♦ Will you assign your best talents to launch and administer the process? Zero-base budgeting must be one of the organization's leading priorities, particularly during the first cycle in which it is used, if it is to work properly. The caliber of the key people on the budget or planning staff (or the special task force) who will quarterback the process must be exceptional. But despite zero-base budgeting's large potential rewards, to assign four or five of your most qualified and credible managers away from their regular duties for the start-up phase will be a difficult decision, particularly if the organization is on shaky economic grounds.

Prepare to spend time. This is particularly true in the first year, when everything will require a thorough assessment that has often not been made for many years, if ever. For those packages that address fundamental and complex strategic issues facing the organization, just sifting the data and understanding the alternatives is a monumental task. More important, once the packages have been formulated, the real task begins: sorting them out and relating them to strategic goals and objectives. As discussed in the preceding chapter, this is in a real sense an innovative process. It cannot be programmed according to a ready-made procedure but will demand good judgment and perspective.

Many top executives will find the job an uncomfortable one and may well prefer the old ways with their admitted simplicity. But you get what you pay for. Those willing to spend the time will find the results most rewarding in terms of their confidence factor, if nothing else.

Leave your side arms outside the executive suite. Being an analytical, fact-founded approach, zero-base budgeting is not for gunslingers. Its inherent structure and framework will in large part minimize shooting from the hip. Those who insist on a showdown at high noon will probably find themselves gunned down when confronted by an adversary well briefed by his subordinates on their decision packages, or they'll be disarmed by the CEO in the boardroom.

Elicit and solicit ideas from all sources. Since the top executives will be physically unable to create the decision packages and come up with innovative alternatives in every last case, they must rely on their subordinates and not infrequently on outsiders. Maximizing the sources of input will serve to increase the number of alternative ways, highlight the strengths and weaknesses of those formally proposed, and above all bring to light relevant information that will help decide which packages are best pursued.

The style required for elicitation is one of *self-restraint*. It is a trait that characterizes most successful television interviewers, but it applies no less to top executives. Consider the following:

> Mike Wallace began as a hard-edged, on-camera prosecutor, but has since developed an effective backhand—a disarming, disbelieving smile when confronted with obviously unpersuasive answers. The thoughtful Edwin Newman is so self-effacing that at times he seems to be turning away from the camera. Barbara Walters offers a quickstep apology for asking a sharp question, then zeros right in. Bill Moyers is a moralizer whose imponderable "big" questions sometimes drive his hapless subjects to embarrassingly hasty profundities. *But all of these interviewers know that their job is to draw out a person.* [emphasis added] It is not, as in the quite different *Firing Line* assignment of William F. Buckley, Jr., to debate as an equal.*

So, too, it is with soliciting ideas and scrutinizing packages in a zero-base budgeting environment. Lions debate in loud roars, only to terrify the lesser beasts of the jungle into passive submission. Foxes cleverly listen to discover the snares—and opportunities.

Prepare to make the organization's value system known and provide rewards. This involves a willingness to communicate objectives, strategies, and problems with the rank and file—in short, involving them while recognizing the inherent risks to inadvertent disclosure of proprietary information—as well as rewarding talent. Let's examine each of these points.

The great advantage of a strong and clear signal from the top on goals, objectives, and approaches is that even quiet junior managers, when tuned in, can conduct a focused assessment of alternative courses of action and formulate thoughtful and realistic decision packages without worry or unnecessary confusion. All managers involved in the process can conduct their analyses, pose questions, reach decisions, and trade off resources sensibly and decisively rather than timidly and evasively, because they appreciate the big picture and know what the business is all about and what's expected of them. If the signal is transmitted strongly enough from the top, much time will be saved that would otherwise be wasted pursuing impractical and unrealistic decision packages or alternatives, since everyone knows what the verdict will be. Questions like "Why are we launching this

---

* Thomas Griffith, "You Have to Be Neutral to Ask the Questions," *Time,* September 13, 1976. Reprinted by permission from *Time* The Weekly Newsmagazine; Copyright Time Inc., 1976.

product?" or "Why are we pursuing this technology?" or "Why do we build rather than buy this part?" require proper and full explanations that lead to a two-way discussion. Such dialogue fosters the spread of the goals and vision of the top throughout the organization—or perhaps prompts a realization by the top that there is indeed a better way. This is certainly a very basic departure from the management style implied by an answer like "Because that's the way we always cast engine blocks—now get on with it."

If zero-base budgeting does nothing else, it will surely uncover talent previously unrecognized as well as confirm hunches about other assets and weaknesses in the workforce. Although I know of no organization that has taken full advantage of this aspect for its formal personnel planning and executive career development system, there are many that keep informal records of the bright stars discovered through the zero-base budgeting process, recognize and reward them, and employ that most powerful of all incentives, namely a promotion into a challenging assignment—often itself identified by the zero-base budgeting process.

In sum, a key factor for a successful zero-base budgeting effort is the commitment and involvement of the top executives. They must fully recognize and appreciate the need for the process and the changes it will inevitably require. They must be prepared to spend considerable time and effort with their lieutenants and in executive conference on honing and approving the final plan. Although they will not be required to work out the details of every decision package and its alternatives, they must be willing to lay out clear and consistent business objectives and strategies to those who are, work with them in thinking them out, and maintain a close relationship with the people in the controller's staff who will administer the process. In turn, the success of the administrative team will hinge on developing an effective rapport with the people at the top, as well as on their skills in eliciting the cooperation of the rank-and-file management cadre. In the final analysis, developing the attitude that everyone in the organization is in the same boat is top management's most important strategy for successful zero-base budgeting.

8

Overcoming
Common Concerns

*Illegitimum non carborundum.**
Motto of General George S. Patton, Jr.

IN general, traditional budgets merely address the issue of *how much* and say nothing of the considerations that led to the spending proposal. By contrast, zero-base budgeting expands the effort to focus on the more critical and substantive issues of *what* is going to be done, *how* it is to be accomplished, and *why* it's important—as well as how much it will cost. The common approach required for all cases is outlined in Chapter 5: simply stated, you must employ the best of your weapons from your arsenal of persuasion skills. Nonetheless, there will be legitimate concerns regarding what it is all about. Some questions will reflect such concern, but others will be a thin disguise for deeper objections. This chapter discusses some of the most frequently cited areas of concern.

* "Don't let the bastards wear you down."

155

Management Skills

It would seem, then, that one of the prerequisites for successful zero-base budgeting is a cadre of managers astute in business analysis and with a fundamental appreciation of the subtleties of the zero-base approach. There is no reason, however, why the necessary skills cannot be developed in the course of preparing the zero-base system and implementing it. If both the preliminaries and the follow-through are seen as learning experiences, managers who work on zero-base budgeting require only the skills needed for any other budgeting approach.

To be sure, building all the required skills will be a long and tough process, but it will be rewarding. The zero-base budgeting process may often bring to light faulty analyses and thereby create opportunities for their correction, thus improving the effectiveness of the organization and the quality of management.

Zero-Base Budgeting versus Tough-Minded Management

Several months ago, I was specifically asked what was so unique about zero-base budgeting that couldn't be accomplished by a strong dose of good old-fashioned tough-minded management. My answer remains the same now as it was then: reduced to its essentials, nothing. But if you ask yourself what skills and techniques a tough-minded management team might employ, in the absence of zero-base budgeting, your laundry list might include: careful scrutiny of what's going on, a fact-founded development of goals and strategies, systematic analysis of alternative courses of action, cost/benefit analysis of the chosen alternatives, problem solving, soliciting from your rank and file ideas for improved operations, a decentralized, participative, and open management style, and approval and funding of only those efforts that are affordable and necessary and sufficient to achieve your goals. As it happens, zero-base budgeting incorporates all of these concepts! All zero-base budgeting does, then, is to tie them together into one neat integrated system.

One advantage of zero-base budgeting that isn't easily duplicated by other approaches, no matter how tough-minded, is the flexibility it affords management in adjusting budgets during the budget cycle. If the assumptions made in preparing the decision packages and rankings are invalidated by experience, it is an easy matter for management to identify the elements that need revision. Similarly, if the affordable levels of expenditure differ from those that were anticipated when the budget was first put together, the ranked set of priorities enables management to add or cut whole levels of decision packages around the decision point. In short, zero-base budgeting automatically creates a contingency plan. This, incidentally, ties in directly with the concern raised above over the time required for zero-base budgeting: how much time do you spend during the year reworking budgets or creating a contingency plan with your traditional approach? In zero-base budgeting, contingency plans are generated automatically!

The Minimum Level of Effort

Two rules come to mind for determining the appropriate "minimum level of effort." The first is to specify that the minimum level must equal approximately 70 percent of the present year's level of spending for an ongoing program. Unfortunately, some will in fact be closer to 100 percent—and for good reasons—while many others may well be several increments of 10 to 20 percent each from the zero base. I'd therefore prefer a different rule requiring each manager to submit *at least two packages, the sum of which equals the current year's level of spending.* The first would represent a minimum level, but greater than zero. The second would be the recommended increment. Both together would equal this year's spending. Exceptions can, of course, be permitted in those cases where such an approach is obviously unrealistic.

As a corollary to this, the word "base" is frequently misinterpreted. If management decides to set the minimum level for an activity at 70 percent of the current year's level, many staff managers might claim that they're dealing with a "70 percent base budgeting" concept rather than a true zero-base approach. This view, however, is fundamentally incorrect. Mandating a 70 percent level as the minimum for decision packages doesn't imply that this minimum will be automatically approved. Management may in fact elect to eliminate the effort—that is, reduce it to the zero base. But more commonly, it will approve something else—perhaps between zero and 70, or 80, 90, 100, or even 120 percent of the current spending level.

Avoiding Gamesmanship

Several business periodicals have documented the fact that in Georgia, many managers assigned a low rank to programs of obvious merit or appeal to their superiors and placed their own pet items toward the top. How can such games be avoided?

As with other budgeting approaches, nothing in zero-base budgeting eliminates the need for informed review by higher-level management. With that informed review, playing such games becomes extremely difficult. During the ranking sessions, higher management will have available the entire spectrum of decision packages, and it will very likely question certain priorities and change some of the rankings. Gamesmanship is more common in the traditional approach, in which everything is buried within the current level of expense. Herein lies a key built-in control aspect of zero-base budgeting: *if subjected to an informed review,* staff managers tend to put together good packages and rank them reasonably, because, in Peter Pyhrr's words, "they do not like to look stupid."

Frequency of Zero-Base Budgeting

Once zero-base budgeting has been implemented, it might not be necessary to conduct a complete zero-base process every year. The procedure might be done every second or third year. Basically, there is no reason why zero-base budgeting cannot be modified in this way. Once you've done the job thoroughly and are comfortable with the results, the organization may for a couple of years prepare detailed packages only to justify new programs or revise old ones where the assumptions have obviously changed. My personal preference, however, is to pursue the process regularly every year. Perhaps this is because I've always worked in organizations with fast-changing environments, where packages are rapidly outdated. More positively, I'd like to believe that the disciplined thought process demanded by zero-base budgeting is a good thing: It *does* foster innovation.

The Scope of Zero-Base Budgeting

Some managers remain confused about which areas zero-base budgeting can be properly applied to. As we have seen, the approach is intended for that fuzzy domain called "staff." It is not intended for line operations, such as production operations in the manufacturing plants. In these cases, standard factors are usually available, and the budget is put together by multiplying the projected volume by labor rates and standard costs.

But zero-base budgeting will have an indirect effect on these costs. For example, an effort under development by the sales staff (to increase unit volume) or by the manufacturing engineering staff (to improve rates or reduce standard costs, be it through a new plant layout or piece of capital equipment) will be the subject of decision packages. Its justification will hinge on improved productivity in the line operations. So in this sense, zero-base budgeting can have a very pervasive effect on the entire organization, both line and staff.

The Need to Specify Alternative Ways and Levels

The requirement of specifying alternative ways and levels of accomplishing the same objective may seem to involve unnecessary paperwork. To simply detail the preferred approach is an easy way out, and it may not be a bad approach for the first year when many people will have a difficult enough time grasping the basic concepts of zero-base budgeting and learning how to employ them skillfully. Indeed, I opted for just that solution in my first try at it!

During subsequent years, though, a couple of things drove me to incorporating a requirement to state alternative ways and levels.

First, not requiring an explicit statement of alternatives leaves the key decision maker in the dark and puts the burden of proof back on him as to whether the preferred approach is in fact the best approach. But more important, as noted earlier, the discipline of putting down on paper the alternative ways and levels is good in that it stimulates innovation.

The Threatening Connotations of "Zero-Base Budgeting"

In its early years (and to a degree even today) "zero-base budgeting" had a negative connotation to rank-and-file managers. Indeed, its increased use is explained by its appeal to those chief executives and chief financial officers who latched on to it for its name, but were then quick to see it for what it really was: something more than merely "starting from scratch" every year. Many of them elected to call it by a different name just to avoid prejudice among the rank and file.

However, whether it was called "integrated planning and control," "program-based budgeting," or "budgeting to objectives," the substance was still the same. Such rechristening did indeed make the concept more palatable and help defuse resistance. More recently, though, as the concept has come to be more widely applied, I find that this has become less of a need.

Handling Other Negative Aspects

There is a widespread perception that zero-base budgeting is a ready tool for layoffs, transfers, or cutbacks. How does one get around the problems caused by that attitude?

In a way, we're dealing here with a superficial misconception. If the organization has its back to the wall, cutbacks will be inevitable, with or without zero-base budgeting. The alternative will be bankruptcy, which will mean layoffs for everyone.

The problem should, however, be approached positively and with the full support of your personnel staff. If zero-base budgeting is properly integrated with the personnel department's workforce planning effort, there is (except in the extraordinary circumstances described earlier) no reason why the savings cannot be captured through normal attrition coupled with an aggressive in-house transfer effort. For those with unique skills, help in finding employment elsewhere is in order.

In addition, the compensation staff can play a key role. Where new ideas for improved operations are approved, a bonus can be offered. This approach was taken in Georgia, where civil servants were given bonuses of up to 10 percent of the first-year savings.

What's more important, though, is to continually stress that zero-base budgeting never implies that everyone's budget will be reduced to zero. Cost-effective proposals for improved operations or of obvious merit will be approved. Thus, zero-base budgeting may well mean that an individual's operation will grow rather than be cut.

Integrating the Approach with Your Accounting System

This issue has two aspects: short-term and long-term. For the short term, the final budget can be rolled up and for overall control purposes be fed into the current accounting system, using the account-level detail contained on each decision package. To facilitate specific control on packages of obvious merit, they should be so identified (as illustrated in the last block of Figure 11b on page 44), copied, and placed in a suspense file for follow-up. You may also wish to invite your audit staff to conduct a performance audit on selected packages.

For longer-term purposes, you may well choose to rewrite your chart of accounts and the entire accounting system to track along program (or decision package) lines as well as functional lines. Those organizations doing extensive government contract or construction work are already in a position to do this, because their control systems are often set up to track programs. But I do not suggest that this be done if the system isn't already in place in the first year—it's simply unnecessary and risky. Imagine the reaction of a chief executive being asked by his budget staff to embark on zero-base budgeting. Even if he wholeheartedly signs off on the concept, can you guess his response to getting a bill of $100,000 or more for resources required to rewrite the accounting system and for all the one-shot training and staff efforts to implement zero-base budgeting?

Of course, if you want to try this approach, by my guest. But make sure you've got your résumé dusted off.

Minimizing the Paperwork

Paperwork can be minimized in three ways. First, the job of those who create the decision packages can be simplified by careful attention to the design of the forms. They should incorporate only elements that will serve some valid and useful purpose. This is why it's important to sit down well in advance and figure out specifically what information you will need as final output, why that information is necessary, and what you'll use it for. This is also why it's important not to adopt some other organization's forms and procedures thoughtlessly.

Second, the job of those who must rank the decision packages can be facilitated by instructing them to focus their efforts on the score of packages around the "decision point" or "level of affordability." It is simply a waste of time to have them review and critique in detail packages of obvious merit or required by law (which will be approved and funded anyway) or those at the bottom of the list.

Third, for very large organizations, you may elect to set a minimum size on decision packages. Let's suppose you're responsible for a $1 billion budget. Further, you decide that you can reasonably cope with 1,000 decision packages, which is quite possible if some of the more sophisticated ranking techniques described in Chapter 3 are used. Whether you realize it or not, you're almost at a solution: by dividing the preferred number of packages into the total budget, you can set a preferred minimum size to your packages of $1 million each. You must understand, however, that there is a tradeoff here. With larger packages, you get less paperwork, but they will bring you closer to the traditional approach and make it difficult to understand what's really going on. With smaller packages, you get more paperwork and greater insight into your organization's operation. In either case, you have to make the choice, based on your own personal assessment of what your needs are and what your organization can reasonably tolerate.

In the final analysis, some paperwork is inevitable. What's important is to approach the problem in a positive frame of mind. If the packages are carefully constructed and well thought out, the quality of resource allocation decisions will be markedly improved. And if you want better decisions and improved profitability, the paperwork is a small price to pay.

Most organizations that have used zero-base budgeting for several cycles agree that the front-end paperwork (although not necessarily the total time required) has increased. But even if they cannot quantify the benefits of zero-base budgeting (and most can), virtually all agree that their comfort over the quality of their decisions as well as their ability to develop responsible and responsive budgets has improved substantially. Not surprisingly, only a few have returned to their former ways.

Common First-Year Problems

Even if you put together and follow a careful implementation plan, you should expect to encounter a number of common problems during the first budget cycle. No system or plan is perfect, and even if it were, it would be no better than the people who use and manage it. So there are many potential problems. Those cited by the greatest number of organizations are:

> Senior management doesn't get involved enough.
> Management expects too much and tries to move too fast.
> A number of decision packages will be received incomplete or poorly completed—and usually submitted at the last minute.
> Feedback to managers preparing the packages is insufficient.
> Economic or planning assumptions underlying the budget proposals are not specified clearly and concisely.

Notice that all these are issues more of management focus and direction and less of the procedural mechanics of the system itself. As such they are shared with traditional budget approaches.

Guidelines to Avoid These Problems

Bill Phelps of Combustion Engineering's Power Systems Group, one of the early successful users of zero-base budgeting, developed a set of principles for implementing zero-base budgeting that he calls "Phelps' Fifteen." * Here they are:

1. Obtain the endorsement, cooperation, and participation of senior management.
2. Set your goals—both for your organization and the zero-base budgeting process—and get to them.
3. Before starting, review your organization.
4. Obtain adequate staff to start up the zero-base budgeting process.
5. Set up contacts throughout the organization.
6. Establish clear review procedures for the decision packages.
7. Get off to a good start.
8. Reevaluate the program after a trial period.
9. Beware of self-appointed experts.
10. Expect to spend a lot of time.
11. Beware of shortcuts. Zero-base budgeting is not easy. You get what you pay for.
12. Maintain your local contacts.
13. Follow up with feedback to all participants on what happened to their decision packages or ideas.
14. Do not expect immediate ROI.
15. Do not expect miracles.

Other Guidelines

I would add three other principles to the "Phelp's Fifteen." "Cheek's Sixteenth" goes like this: If you're the controller or manager in charge of the zero-base budgeting process in your organization keep your cool. As Robert Townsend says, the controller "must never lose his head—that's what managements do, not controllers. . . . There abideth accuracy, timeliness, understanding, and unflappability in the controller's office—and the greatest of these is all four of them." †

"Cheek's Seventeenth" applies to everyone involved in the process, whether they're developing decision packages, reviewing them, or ranking them, and even to those developing the basic procedures and forms. It states that *anything* connected with the zero-base budgeting

* William W. Phelps, "Zero Base Budgeting: Practical Implementation," *Managerial Planning* (Oxford, Ohio: Planning Executives Institute), July-August 1977.

† *Up the Organization*, New York: Alfred A. Knopf, 1970.

process must be challenged with three questions. The three questions are: "So what"? "What else?" and "Why?"

Finally, "Cheek's Eighteenth" is a reminder that zero-base budgeting is a means to an end and not an end in itself. It is very easy to become trapped in analyzing all the information that zero-base budgeting will invariably produce. While much of the analysis will be provocative and will indeed in many cases lead to innovative ideas for improving operations, the information contained in the decision packages is above all a *means to make informed decisions quickly* on better resource allocation. In other words, don't be trapped in the "paralysis through analysis" syndrome.

These, then, are what I feel are the questions most commonly raised about zero-base budgeting and how they can be fielded. If you decide to use it in your organization, you will no doubt hear many more. How should they be handled? Aside from remembering General Patton's motto, Thomas Jefferson's statement in his second inaugural address may be appropriate: "Error of opinion may be tolerated where reason is left free to combat it."

The same principle applies to those embarking on zero-base budgeting. Reduced to its essentials, the simplest, most effective approach to dealing with any objection to zero-base budgeting is the one that gives zero-base budgeting its cutting edge over traditional techniques. That approach is *logic*.

9

A Final Word

*The American challenge is not ruthless.
. . . Its weapons are the use and systematic perfection of all the instruments of
reason. Not simply in the field of science,
where it is the only tool, but also in
organization and management.*
Jean Jacques Servan-Schreiber, *The American Challenge*

SEVERAL circumstances prompted the writing of this book, but one was overriding. Although the zero-base concept has enjoyed widespread and increasing use in business and government, experience suggests that planning and budgeting executives often encounter great difficulties in using it. Even if they've mastered its basic concepts—"starting from scratch," capturing all proposed activities in decision packages, and ranking them—achieving the bottom-line benefits claimed for it too often remains an elusive hope.

Usually, what's lacking is either an in-depth appreciation of zero-base budgeting techniques or, more commonly, the art of handling the behavioral subtleties of the organization. If management fails on either of these counts, zero-base budgeting may well generate more heat than light. Unfortunately, the two crucial topics—what zero-base budgeting is and what it takes to make it work—are not adequately covered in the existing management literature. Having been involved with the approach in both line and staff roles and having observed its use in scores of other organizations, I developed and tested several hypotheses, which were presented here.

The purpose of this book, then, is to help current or potential users of zero-base budgeting to overcome the difficulties most commonly encountered. There are an increasing number of line and staff executives in both private and public life who share a common need to formulate plans and budgets that are practical and achievable and represent the best use of their organizations' scarce resources. In order to make this book a useful tool for them, I have employed the simplest possible conceptual framework, starting from a systematic discussion of the concept of zero-base budgeting and its mechanics and proceeding to a review of several behavioral techniques required for bottom-line success.

Taking a cue from a classic definition of economics, we could say that zero-base budgeting's objective is to compare alternative uses of scarce resources. This is just what any smart manager does when he asks whether a new plant should be built or several older ones used to greater capacity; whether a new technology should be pursued and exploited for a new product or the available resources applied to improving an old one; or whether the revenue from gasoline taxes should be used for building new or improving old highways, or be re-channeled into urban mass transit. In a real sense, the basic job of a business executive as he goes about his daily chores is to compare alternative uses of scarce resources in order to decide how best to exploit them, then to move out smartly and implement the best alternatives. In this book, I've attempted to show how the zero-base concept can be combined with other proven techniques to force such comparisons on a regular, systematic basis, evaluate alternative solutions, and quickly select and implement the most feasible ones.

But in a broader sense, the goals and strategic objectives of the organization (or, in the case of public agencies, its constituents) must be considered. A decision package to make the organization's employment function more cost-effective may indeed make eminent sense for the personnel staff but be totally irrelevant if the organization's hiring is to be drastically curtailed. Effective zero-base budgeting therefore dictates considering the broader long-range needs of the whole organization if it is to be of practical use. On this score, those organizations losing sight of the forest for the trees have found zero-base budgeting an exercise in academic futility.

A full understanding of all the ramifications of zero-base budgeting might well leave one overwhelmed with a feeling of discouragement. For effective zero-base budgeting demands more than an appreciation of the mechanics of "starting from scratch." Indeed, it dictates incorporating time-tested principles drawn from many wide-ranging management disciplines:

◊ Conceiving and synthesizing new ideas involves well-known principles of problem solving.
◊ Evaluating the decision packages incorporates established techniques of systems analysis and cost/benefit analysis.
◊ Tying the decision packages to the organization's long-range goals is not unlike management by objectives.
◊ And finally, implementing approved packages to achieve results requires careful attention to age-old persuasion skills, as well as harnessing the chain of command by getting top management on board.

These demanding aspects of zero-base budgeting inject a sobering element into our high aspirations for it. Considering the broad skills required to implement the process successfully, it may well seem amusing that budget staffs go through elaborate gymnastics to install zero-base budgeting procedures. On the one hand, if we fail to pay attention to these management basics, we risk failure by oversimplification; on the other hand, with proper attention to the basics we may well create an unmanageable leviathan. Given this "damned if you do, damned if you don't" dilemma, should we then conclude that zero-base budgeting had best be abandoned? Or should we pursue the beast, fully expecting to be overwhelmed by it like Laocoön by the snakes?

Neither need occur. An objective look at how resource allocation decisions are made suggests the reason. In the final analysis, all management decisions will be colored by our personalities, backgrounds, and mutual relationships, by our abilities to innovate, analyze, and synthesize. Innovative bold plans are rarely made in a flash but result from careful studies and lengthy discussions. Several alternatives must often be pursued until the best strategy is apparent to all or until economic or organizational imperatives dictate that some decision be made. And for all the objectivity and analytical thoroughness captured in a series of decision packages, a final "go/no-go" resolution often requires several meetings of committees, task forces, or working groups, each clouded by political intrigue and attacks and counterattacks by different pressure groups. It is in this long, complex, potentially destructive process leading to major decisions that zero-base budgeting has in fact won its spurs as an aid to informed judgment. There are good reasons for this.

First, it is a disciplined technique for arraying the possible alternative decisions, analyzing the costs, benefits, and risks of each, and revealing their broad impact on the *entire* organization rather than merely on one functional part of it. But in addition to honing the insights of individual managers, both the format of the packages and the proper use of persuasion skills disciplines the collective discussions during ranking meetings. At the outset, each participant may well champion the merits of particular packages over others, drawing on his intellect, training, and personal prejudices and fighting for the interests he represents. Arguments ensue, often ignoring factual evidence. But zero-base budgeting in its broadest sense refocuses the discussion away from tangential political issues by imposing its logical fact-based framework. That framework helps distinguish phony arguments from fair criticisms. More important, the framework provides a means for the members of the management team to gain a clear understanding of the problem, identify and evaluate alternative solutions, and select an appropriate and affordable level of effort.

This is where the essential importance of zero-base budgeting lies and why rigorous exposition of alternative ways and levels of achieving the same objective is necessary. If only the costs of a given approach were important, then traditional budgeting techniques (or more probably simple cost/benefit analyses) would suffice to grasp the packages' economic implications. The characteristic strength of zero-base budgeting derives from its subtler aspect: the analytic discipline it requires from its users, who must assess the assumptions of each package, how it ties to the organization's objectives and strategies, and what its legal, technical, and operational ramifications are. This characteristic of zero-base budgeting, substantially missing in other techniques, makes it the exciting valued new management tool it is, and has made it come of age.

Notwithstanding its demonstrated value in business, one might argue that applying it to government programs represents an impossible task. This might be answered by simply pointing out that the system has in fact worked for hundreds of thousands of civil servants in the dozen or so state governments and municipalities that have successfully installed zero-base budgeting. Still, one could argue that elevating the concept to the federal level for national policy planning and budgeting would create a paperwork nightmare.

This objection is not to be taken lightly, for if the entire federal budget were captured in one-page decision packages averaging $1,000 each, we would indeed create a stack of paper 28 miles high! But the real challenge of zero-base budgeting in the government arena rests in a far more complex problem: Unlike business enterprises, whose primary objective is profit, government programs typically must meet multiple objectives. And as if that were not enough, the various agencies' programs not infrequently work at cross-purposes. For instance, a public housing program may be embarked on with the high-minded objectives of integrating the neighborhoods, raising housing and public health standards, and improving the schools. But the sudden arrival of the low-income high-rise buildings may prompt a flight to the suburbs by the higher-income groups, thus defeating the objectives of improving the schools and compounding the problems of an over-burdened commuter transit system while stretching already scarce energy resources and threatening the weakened property-tax base to boot.

To analyze all these ramifications thoroughly would simply require more time and resources than are available. In such situations, I find it best to enumerate in broad terms all the possible impacts of each program and incorporate those findings into the program's technical and operational feasibility assessment. An intensive analysis should then be conducted only for the one or two aspects of greatest economic impact. This, in my experience, not only simplifies the analytic task but, incidentally, overcomes much of the paperwork problem blamed for the death of the Program Planning and Budgeting (PPB) system. Finally, aggregating packages into large amounts—with minimum sizes at the national level in the seven- or eight-figure range—should nail the coffin shut on the paperwork problem.*

A little over three years ago, I found myself writing the concluding remarks to a paper describing my first attempt at zero-base budgeting in one department of Xerox. At that time, I wrote, "Quite conceivably, the same concepts may very well be applied in future years in other functional areas. But whether or not that happens, using it . . . has brought about better resource allocation and, in so doing, helped crystallize our overall strategy. I believe this approach is applicable to a great many organizations, particularly larger ones, in industry, the services, and government. In addition, incorporating it would permit many organizations to move away from 'gut feel' approaches

---

* For a discussion of zero-base budgeting applications in the public sector see, for example, David L. Leininger and Ronald C. Wong, "Zero Base Budgeting in Garland, Texas," *Management Information Report,* Vol. 8, No. 4A (Washington, D.C.: International City Management Association, April 1976), as well as Appendix C.

and, worse yet, the intrigue and politics characteristic of budgeting and resource allocation decisions. In a more positive vein, given the profit and productivity improvements that can be achieved from revelant staff programs that are targeted on results, I hope that it will be widely applied in the future." That this future would arrive in only three years never ceases to amaze me. Yet, given the rapid refinement and chain reaction of acceptance of the concept in even this short period, I can, in all humility, regard its successes with satisfaction and its future with confidence.

For those who persist in decrying how complicated it is: It need only be as cumbersome as you make it. And to those still faint-hearted at the challenge of zero-base budgeting. I offer this final thought: To make tough decisions isn't easy, but that's what good managers are paid to do.

APPENDIX A

Zero-Base Budgeting Procedure

The procedure that follows is intended for managers who will be developing decision packages as well as for those who will rank them. It was synthesized from procedures actually in use in several leading organizations and draws on what was felt were the best features of each. While I feel it is the basis for a sound manual, it should not be considered a model. Rather, it should be modified on the basis of your answers to the issues raised in Chapter 2.

As mentioned in that chapter, a good zero-base budgeting procedure will incorporate most, if not all, of the following six elements:

1. A letter of transmittal from top management.
2. A discussion of the purpose, objective, and basic concepts of zero-base budgeting.
3. An economic overview of the organization and its industry, as an introduction to the organization's objectives, planning assumptions, and spending guidelines.
4. A discussion of decision packages and how they're developed.
5. A discussion of the ranking process.
6. A detailed schedule or calendar for the zero-base budgeting cycle.

To preclude an overly detailed package, however, some organizations, particularly larger ones, choose to split the procedure two ways. First, a basic procedure is developed that focuses strictly on the needs of those developing the decision packages and incorporates all the above elements except the fifth. The ranking process is then explained in a second guideline, which is prepared exclusively for those responsible for ranking.

My personal preference is to have only one procedure. This approach allows everyone to understand quite specifically how the entire process will work and defuses any uncomfortable feelings of being threatened among the rank-and-file managers.

What follows, then, is an outline of how to prepare a zero-base budgeting manual for internal use by the managers involved in the process. Where appropriate I will refer back to illustrations in the text.

While there are no universal rules for organizing such a manual, a section breakdown such as the following appears natural:

Letter of Introduction
1. Zero-Base Budgeting: Its Purpose, Objectives, and Concepts
2. The Economic Outlook for Our Company and Its Industry
3. Instructions for and Examples of Decision Packages
4. Instructions for the Ranking Process
5. Calendar for the Budgeting Cycle
6. Standard Factors and Assumptions

LETTER OF INTRODUCTION

As we discussed in Chapters 2 and 7, the chief executive's full and explicit support is essential if the zero-base budgeting process is to be implemented successfully. The manual should therefore start with a letter of introduction from the chief executive, such as the one depicted in Figure 7 in Chapter 2, expressing his firm personal commitment to and intent to be involved in the zero-base budgeting effort.

SECTION 1: ZERO-BASE BUDGETING—
ITS PURPOSE, OBJECTIVES, AND CONCEPTS

The objective of this section is to briefly describe the zero-base approach and sell its benefits. Specific details of how to construct the decision packages or rank them are reserved for later sections of the manual. A text such as the following is probably appropriate for most situations.

Zero-base budgeting is a powerful general management tool that will provide our organization with a systematic way to evaluate operations and programs and allow management to shift resources into high-priority efforts. Through the proper use of the process, managers of activities will be able to specify the amount, quality, and cost of the service that will be provided to the organization and gain their supervisors' agreement to their proposed projects. In addition, the approach offers several other advantages.

♦ Thorough examination of every function ensures that managers have evaluated the need for every program and considered different levels of effort and alternative ways to perform it.

♦ Zero-base budgeting provides a cost/benefit basis for departmental budget decisions, eliminating the necessity for arbitrary across-the-board reductions of budget requests.

♦ Once activities are identified in "decision packages" and given a priority ranking, subsequent budget cycles do not require a complete recycling of budget inputs ("Decision packages" are discussed further in Section 3.) Instead, the ranked decision packages identify the expenditures that should be added or deleted. (Ranking packages will be discussed in detail in Section 4.)

♦ The list of ranked decision packages can be used during the budget year to identify functions to be reduced or expanded if available resources vary from the budgeted estimate.

♦ If it becomes necessary during the budget year to add new work not contemplated by the approved budget, the decision packages will help identify the other expenditures that must be reduced or eliminated to free the necessary resources.

♦ Zero-base budgeting links long-range goals and plans with budgets; strengthens higher-management awareness of what is proposed; clarifies each unit's role in the organization and identifies appropriate measures for evaluating performance; and assists in aligning management's expectations with reality by associating service levels with costs. In addition to specifying costs and benefits, it communicates problems and opportunities to higher management and shifts the focus to *making decisions.*

♦ Finally, managers can be measured against the activities and benefits to which they committed themselves in each approved decision package, as well as against their budget.

The zero-base budgeting process has proven its value in a number of organizations in improving management development, strengthening communications, fostering innovative ideas for improved operations, and resolving key issues in business policy and strategy.

Zero-base budgeting is based on the premise that service and cost levels for overhead activities can be changed without reducing the level of business activity. Managers do have discretion about the level of service that can be provided, and zero-base budgeting is an appropriate tool to help determine, communicate, agree upon, and commit to the proper level of service and cost.

There are six major activities in preparing our zero-base budget:

1. During the long-range planning cycle, we conduct an intensive assessment of our company and industry and of the economic, competitive, marketing, and regulatory environment we face. Out of this, our growth goals and objectives are established, as well as the broad strategies through which we will accomplish them.

2. "Decision units" are then identified by segmenting the organization into discrete functions, operations, or activities for analysis.

3. An analysis and documentation of each decision unit is made by the responsible manager. The goals of this step are to:

♦ Outline the current operations and performance of the decision unit, and tie its activities to our organization's strategic goals.

♦ Establish tactical objectives to support these strategic goals.

♦ Develop alternatives to the current way of achieving the objectives.

♦ Select the best alternative and document the various levels of effort that can be used to accomplish that alternative.

4. These incremental levels of effort are ranked in order of priority.

5. The budget staff then compiles and finalizes the operating expense budget, based on the packages approved by the various department heads.

6. After preparation of the zero-base operating plan, the performance of the decision units is monitored during the budget year.

One important point: In spite of its name, zero-base budgeting is primarily a *planning and decision-making technique*. One of its end products, if it's properly done, happens to be a budget, but its primary purpose is to help us determine *what* we're going to do, *how* we're going to do it (or do it better), and *why* we're doing it. If we can answer these questions convincingly, the issue of how much it will cost will be resolved in a simple, mechanical, unemotional way.

SECTION 2: SUMMARY OF THE ECONOMIC OUTLOOK FOR THE COMPANY AND ITS INDUSTRY

The purpose of this section of your manual is to relate the proposed zero-base budgeting system to the organization's long-range plans. Obviously, information about such plans must be treated as

confidential. A text along the following lines can serve as an introduction.

> Any practical operational budget—zero-based or otherwise—should
> be tied to our organization's long-range business plans and market
> goals. In turn, these goals must be based on a realistic assessment
> of our industry's economic situation and the emerging technologies.
> Accordingly, this section summarizes the results of our company's
> recent long-range planning effort, including (1) an evaluation of
> our industry and our competitive position in it, (2) how each of
> our staff departments can influence company profits and help in
> achieving our goals, and (3) our organization's specific objectives
> for the next five years. *The information contained in this section is
> confidential. It should be discussed outside the company under no
> circumstances, and with fellow employees only on a strict "need
> to know" basis.*

The natural order of presentation for the body of this chapter
would be to start with a broad assessment of the industry, translate
this evaluation into long-range objectives to be pursued by the organization, and finally discuss the specific strategies for achieving them.
To illustrate this, I will use a specific example involving a hypothetical
company, the Cosmotronex Corporation. After the introduction to
Section 2, this company's zero-base budgeting manual might read as
follows.

OUR INDUSTRY ECONOMICS

Cosmotronex Corporation and its industry have faced several
significant business challenges over the past five years.

The domestic market for our mainline products has essentially
reached maturity. While the growth rate for our industry varied
from year to year, its overall average was only 5 percent per year,
about the same as the gross national product. Neither we nor any
of our competitors have gained a significant edge during that period: All enjoy about the same market share today as they did five
years ago.

The overseas markets, however, are an entirely different matter.
We have been able to significantly increase our export volumes to
Western Europe at 20 percent per year, compounded through
1975, although that growth moderated to 8 percent last year. Also,
last year saw our exports to the Middle East and Asia jump by 50
percent (from an admittedly small base), and they should continue to grow significantly for at least the next three years.

Our marketing and engineering staffs have recently identified a

$50 million potential market for the ZEPHYR program. As many of you know, we have invested significantly in the development of this effort and expect to launch it in four product configurations between March and November of next year. Our competitive planning staff assures us that we have a 30-month technical lead in this product, and this lead is supported by a fairly strong patent position.

Our controller's staff and industrial engineers indicate that our unit costs have increased at about 4.2 percent per year for the past five years whereas productivity has increased only 1.7 percent in the same period. In some cases, we've offset this problem with pricing actions, but in others, where we face severe competition, we've had to hold the line and suffer some deterioration to our profit margins.

Finally, a task force composed of members of our manufacturing, public relations, legal, and personnel staffs recently assessed the impact of the spiraling public regulation we face in such areas as employee safety, product liability, affirmative action, environmental quality, and employee benefits. They concluded that, with all due respects for the fine intentions of the regulatory agencies, the costs of staff, outside counsel, and attendant paperwork now exceed $500,000 per year. This figure is up from $50,000 five years ago and is projected to rise to $1.2 million by the early 1980s.

COSMOTRONEX'S KEY SUCCESS FACTORS

These findings indicate that (1) our profit sensitivities for our "business as usual" activities will not change significantly in the next five years, and (2) capturing several new business opportunities and markets can significantly increase our profits and position us as the acknowledged industry leader. *We intend to do just that.* Figure A-1 summarizes those profit sensitivities and indicates their bottom-line impact on our earnings per share (EPS), both for next year and for 1983.

Based on this analysis, the key factors for success in our business in the near future are as follows:

- Aggressively exploit overseas market potential for both current and new products.
- Tightly control costs of manufacturing labor, materials, and purchased services for all current products.
- Increase productivity of the sales force and headquarters staff for all current products.
- Successfully launch our ZEPHYR product line and its subsequent refinements.

Figure A-1. Profit sensitivities and their impacts on earnings.

A 1% improvement in these areas...	results in these profit impacts...	with these EPS impacts	
		1978	1983
Overseas unit volumes	$10.6 ▨▨▨ $21.2	19¢	38¢
Current products	$10.6 ▨▨▨ $11.7	19¢	21¢
New products	$9.5	0¢	17¢
Cost of materials and services	$6.4 ▨▨ $10.5	11¢	18¢
Domestic	$5.2 ▨▨ $6.3	9¢	11¢
Overseas	$1.1 ▨ $3.9	2¢	7¢
Sales and distribution productivity	$3.0 ▨ $4.8	5¢	8¢
Administrative productivity	$1.7 ▨ $5.0	2¢	6¢
Manufacturing productivity	$4.1 ▨ $6.6	5¢	8¢
Goods-in-process inventory	$2.2 ▨ $3.9	4¢	7¢
Finished inventory	$2.1 ▨ $3.7	4¢	7¢
Collection of accounts receivable	$1.8 ▨ $2.4	3¢	4¢
Tax reduction	$1.3 ▨ $2.0	2¢	3¢
Domestic unit volumes	$1.2 ▨ $13.2	2¢	22¢
Current products	$1.2 ▨ $4.8	2¢	8¢
New products	$8.4	0¢	14¢
Recovery of uncollected receivables	$1.1 ▨	0.1¢	0.1¢

▨▨▨ 1978 impact (in millions of dollars)

☐ 1983 impact (in millions of dollars)

♦ Intelligently manage and control our destiny in the regulatory arena.

Our organization's objectives and strategies are based on these five ingredients.

Cosmotronex's Five-Year Objectives and Strategies

Accordingly, our objectives for the long-range planning horizon are as follows:

1. Increase unit volume for current products 10 percent per year, primarily in overseas markets:
   (a) Maintain domestic market share at 15 percent by growing unit volume 5 percent per year.
   (b) Reverse growth trend in Western Europe to 12 percent next year and hold it to 15 percent thereafter.
   (c) Maintain Middle East and Asian market growth at 25 percent per year for the next five years.
2. Make current products more cost-effective throughout our worldwide operations:
   (a) In domestic markets, increase line productivity (manufacturing and sales) 5 percent per year through 1982 and cut staff expenses 3 percent per year in each of the next two years.
   (b) Bring overseas expense-to-revenue ratios (exclusive of depreciation, product development costs, amortization, and taxes) into line with current domestic rates by 1980.
3. Launch the ZEPHYR line of products and their refinements, with two objectives:
   (a) Achieve a $25 million sales volume in domestic markets by 1982.
   (b) Achieve a $15 million sales volume in overseas markets by 1983.
4. Manage regulatory challenges with a positive, aggressive stance through institutional advertising and appropriate policies in the areas of employee relations, environmental protection, and safety. Full efforts of our executive group, headquarters staffs, and the trade associations of which we're members will be directed toward this end. In this regard, we intend to comply fully with the letter and spirit of the law and act as a socially responsible corporation.

NOTE: *All zero-base budgeting submissions must be tied to one or more of these four objectives.*

SECTION 3: INSTRUCTIONS FOR AND EXAMPLES OF DECISION PACKAGES

Having explained (and hopefully sold) the benefits of zero-base budgeting and summarized its basic concepts in the first section of the manual, and having identified your organization's business objectives in the second, you're now ready to discuss the mechanics of the system. This may be achieved with a text along the following lines.

In essence, zero-base budgeting requires each manager to (1) establish tactical objectives for each function within his area of responsibility; (2) consider *alternative ways* of achieving each objective; (3) briefly assess the benefits and costs (both explicit and implicit) associated with each alternative way of performing the same function; and (4) select the best alternative, breaking it up into different increments, or *levels of effort,* and costing out and documenting each level.

Each of these steps is summarized in Figure A-2 and discussed in detail in the following pages.

Figure A-2. Zero-base budgeting work flow.

Steps	*Supporting Forms*
1a. Define your tactical objectives for your unit and tie them to our company's strategic goals.	Prepare worksheet as shown in Figure A4 in this chapter [= Figure 13 in the text].
1b. Think up and describe alternative ways to accomplish these objectives.	
1c. Describe alternative levels of effort, starting with the most important and adding incremental levels.	
2. Capture your one (and only one) recommended *way* in a decision package and evaluate its feasibility.	Prepare decision package ("bare bones" elements and supplemental elements) as shown in A5 and A6 in this chapter [= Figures 11a and 11b in the text].
3. Detail your alternative *levels* of effort (or increments of service) for your chosen alternative on the decision cards.	Prepare decision cards as shown in Figure A7 in this chapter [= Figure 19 in the text].
4. Rank all the cards (each representing activities in your organization) and copy them as a ranking sheet.	Prepare a ranking summary as shown in Figure A8 [= Figure 21 in the text].

1. Defining Objectives

Developing an objective (or objectives) for your area of responsibility is the first step in putting together your zero-base budgeting submission. As in other management and planning systems, the word objective means *what* you're proposing to do, and not necessarily *how* you're going to do it. (The *how* is developed later when you define alternative ways.)

The distinction is important. Often, we fall into a trap of describing our purpose in terms of how we do it or what approach we take, rather than in terms of our outputs, end products, or services delivered. The three examples developed below contrast the difference between a results-oriented objectives statement; one which merely lists throughputs or activities; and a third which is too fuzzy and vague to be of any use at all.

A Results-Oriented Objectives Statement

"To repair and return to inventory all defective spare parts (from either field service or manufacturing) at a reliability level exceeding their newly built equivalent, and at a return on investment of at least 50 percent."

Notice how the performance indicators are crisp and quantified, or at least quantifiable. The manager's effectiveness can be readily assessed by measuring his products' reliability and his organization's profit against its capital asset base.

But too often, budget center objectives statements are not so well defined.

A Throughput Statement

"First we receive material, then we fix and test it. Our work is coordinated with inventory control and production planning during the monthly interface meeting. Our liaison manager troubleshoots periodic problems with the field on credits."

This statement focuses on activities rather than results. And peculiar activities at that! What's being described is how the work is done rather than what happens when it is done.

A Vague Objectives Statement

"This section supports the field and manufacturing production lines at an appropriate level of service and provides information derived from our efforts to the quality control and engineering staffs in line with budgeted resources."

This sort of statement supplies no relevant information. We can't even be sure which division or department it is in. It prompts questions like "So what?" "What else can you say?" or, more appropriately, "I don't understand."

Stating objectives well is no easy task, but is very important in zero-base budgeting. If it's well done, you'll find that putting together the rest of your decision packages will flow quickly and easily. If it's poorly done, you'll probably have to rework them, with all sorts of unnecessary paperwork.

One way of putting together a good objectives statement is to sketch out an "input-output" diagram. It might look something like that depicted in Figure A-3. Put yourself inside the center square. Then try to describe your operations and responsibilities in terms of outputs and inputs. The outputs, properly described and quantified where possible, will be your objectives.

Figure A-3. Input-output model.

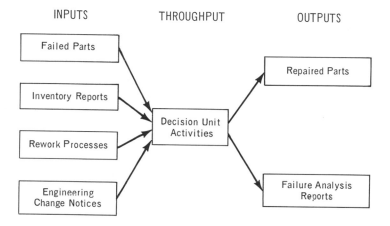

The objectives statement for Figure A-3 could be much like the results-oriented example described above. As it turns out, the operation depicted above is the same for *all three* of the examples cited above.

Once you have nailed down the objective (or objectives) for your budget center, you should write each down on a separate sheet of the form shown in Figure A-4.

Insert here a sample decision package worksheet such as Figure 13 on page 50.

Figure A-4 is intended as a simple and informal *working* document to help you in breaking down your program proposals into alternative ways and levels as required by zero-base budgeting. If you feel you should expand on it, you are encouraged to do so, but this is not mandatory.

2. DESCRIBING ALTERNATIVE WAYS

The development of sound alternatives is one of the most difficult and challenging aspects of the zero-base budgeting process.

When the word "alternative" is used in zero-base budgeting, it means finding a different way of accomplishing the budget center's objective. For example, if the current method of operating involves doing the functions internally, one alternative might be to engage an outside service to accomplish the job. Examples of types of alternatives which frequently are suggested are:

Perform function internally.

Purchase outside service.

Substitute machine for manual effort.

Combine with another unit.

Eliminate function.

Transfer function to another budget center.

This emphasis on alternatives is a departure from normal thinking, which usually focuses not on finding different ways to do the job but on finding ways to improve the current process. Please don't be shy about suggesting a totally different approach. Experience has shown that new alternative ideas frequently stimulate the thinking of others during the ranking process.

A real effort should be made to support the new alternative with an estimate of what benefits and risks might be associated with it. In some cases, there is not enough time to capitalize on the new idea in the upcoming year. By all means list it anyway. Perhaps a feasibility study can be initiated to move the idea along toward eventual acceptance.

3. Choosing the Best Alternative

Out of all the alternatives you come up with, one will probably stand out as the best, most logical way to accomplish your objective. Obviously, this is the one you will choose. It should be described in detail in a decision package such as the one shown in Figures A-5 and A-6.

Insert here a sample decision package, designed for your organization. For an example of such a package, see Figures 11a and 11h on pages 43–44.

In describing the chosen alternative, you are asked to assess its feasibility from six aspects. Let's review each of these.

Is the program legally required? This calls for a simple yes or no answer. If the program is legally required, it will be accorded highest priority when later ranked against all others. Examples of legally required efforts are our environmental protection program, affirmative action, collective bargaining, and SEC reporting. Most packages, though, will get a no answer to this question.

The material on pages 180–182 was derived from a manual prepared for a client of MAC, Inc.

Does the package pay back immediately? Again, this requires a simple yes or no answer. If it will pay back in the next year, it makes obvious business sense to approve it, no matter how small the dollar savings. In this regard, you are reminded of our recent announcement that all such programs, if approved, will result in a special payment of up to 10 percent of the first-year savings to the originator.

Is the package technically feasible? To assess the technical feasibility of a package, ask yourself whether it will involve new or unfamiliar elements requiring major staff efforts and developmental costs.

For instance, assigning our office typing operations to word processing stations involves no terribly unfamiliar effort. Therefore, its technical feasibility is quite high. On the other hand, some of the research effort resulting in our patents for the ZEPHYR product line did indeed involve unfamiliar effort. That's why we were awarded the patents. Prior to embarking on that effort, though, the technical feasibility of that effort was "low."

Our standards for evaluating technical feasibility follow.

- Evaluate technical feasibility as *high* if the program appears simple, skilled personnel is currently available within the company, and EDP programming, if required, is simple and hardware available within the company.
- Evaluate technical feasibility as *medium* if the program appears complex, skilled personnel is not available in the company but available outside, or EDP programming, if required, is difficult or hardware is not available within the company but is on the market.
- Evaluate technical feasibility as *low* if the program involves a major state-of-the-art effort, personnel is not available on staff or outside, or EDP programming, if required, is very complex or hardware is not available.

Is the package operationally feasible? To assess the operational feasibility of a decision package, ask yourself whether the effort will involve a major change in our traditional way of doing things. Does it imply a significant departure from our policies and practices and the philosophies of both our customers and management? For instance, when we first tried word processing in the customer relations department, some managers were reluctant to give up their private secretaries. The operational feasibility here was therefore "medium." It was important, though, that we were aware of this so we could anticipate any potential problems and prepare to handle them.

On the other hand, market tests of our ZEPHYR product line in

Denver and Atlanta indicate a very positive customer reception. Operational feasibility in this case therefore is clearly "high."

Our standards for evaluating operational feasibility follow.

♦ Evaluate operational feasibility as *high* if implementing the program requires *little or no effort* to effect a change in line organization attitudes, policies, structure, operating environment, or management styles, or in customer purchasing habits, and *does not imply a radical departure* from historic company or market practices.

♦ Evaluate operational feasibility as *medium* if implementing the program appears to require *moderate efforts* to effect a change in line organization attitudes, policies, structure, operating environment, or management styles, or in customer purchasing habits, and *implies some departure* from historic company or market practices.

♦ Evaluate operational feasibility as *low* if implementing the program appears to require *substantial efforts* to effect a change in line organization attitudes, policies, structure, operating environment, or management styles, or in customer purchasing habits, and implies a *radical departure* from historic company or market practices.

Is the package economically feasible? This involves a simple question: Can we make money on this approach, and if so, how much? Assessing the economics of a decision package requires intelligent evaluation of *all* its costs and benefits, both to your organization and others. Standard factors and assumptions described in Section 6 of this manual must be used consistently by all budget center managers in developing their cost/benefit assessments, and must be projected over the five-year planning horizon. After developing all the benefits (whether increased revenue, unit volume, productivity, decreased turnover, or decreased costs to your own or other organizations), the costs of your approach must be described, detailed, and subtracted from the benefits. The *net five-year benefit figure* is then assessed using the following standards:

♦ Evaluate the proposal's net benefits as *high* if they exceed $600,000.

♦ Evaluate the proposal's net benefits as *medium* if they exceed $100,000 but are less than $600,000.

♦ Evaluate the proposal's net benefits as *low* if they are less than $100,000.°

What are the risks of not acting? Finally, a similar assessment is made of what will happen if we fail to approve this decision pack-

---

° These dollar figures will vary depending on the organization, as will the figures for evaluating risks of not acting.

age. The same approach as in the last step is used, although not to that level of detail. Once the consequences are established, the risks of not acting are assessed using the following standards:

♦ Evaluate risks of not acting on the proposal as *high* if they exceed $1,000,000.

♦ Evaluate risks of not acting as *medium* if they exceed $100,000 but are less than $1,000,000.

♦ Evaluate risks of not acting as *low* if they are less than $100,000.

One important point: A natural risk of not approving a package is that we will have to forgo the benefits identified. This will be obvious and assumed by all who will review and rank the packages. So to save time and effort, it is not necessary to restate benefits in the negative form in this section.

Other data requested in the decision packages are explained in the sample package depicted in figures A-5 and A-6 [*Figures 11a and 11b*] earlier in this appendix.

4. Describing Different Levels of Effort

The final step is to describe in detail several incremental levels of effort for accomplishing your objective through the alternative you chose. You've already done most of the work as you completed your matrix in Figure A-4 [*Figure 13*].

♦ Going across the matrix from left to right, you described any of a number of alternative ways to achieve your objectives and selected one of those alternatives as the best way.

♦ For each alternative, you then built up—from a "zero base"— several incremental levels of effort. Normally, you would start with the most urgent (in some cases, legally mandated) effort. For instance, your level-one effort may represent the legally required minimum OSHA compliance review and reporting. To that base you then add logical increments, starting with the next most important (or profitable) effort and culminating in the last increment that is desirable but less essential than the others.

Above all, the increments, including the minimum level, must be practical. Budget center managers should avoid writing up increments that are impractical or do not support the basic objective described at the top of the matrix. Also, for ongoing efforts, *the sum of the first two increments proposed should equal this year's spending level.*

You are now ready for the final step of describing in hard copy *each* of the increments of your chosen alternative.

The index card (or decision card) depicted in Figure A-7 is a convenient tool to accomplish this. You should have one card for *each* of your chosen increments. For instance, if you have identified five incremental levels for your chosen alternative, you will require five decision cards.

Insert here a figure such as Figure 19 on page 83, showing the front and back sides of a decision card.

Remember, the card has two sides: don't forget to complete the account-level detail on the back side of each decision card to indicate the resources required for that increment—but *only that increment.*

SECTION 4: INSTRUCTIONS FOR THE RANKING PROCESS

As discussed earlier, management may decide to issue two separate guidelines, one for those who will design the decision packages and another for those who must rank them. If this approach is chosen, the section outlined in the following will of course be prepared as a separate manual. In either case, a text like the following will be appropriate.

The ranking process will allow our company to allocate scarce resources by answering three questions:

1. Which of the proposed decision packages best support our organization's goals, as established during the long-range planning cycle and described in Section 2?
2. How much are we willing to spend in pursuing these goals?
3. For the packages we don't approve, what are the consequences of not implementing them? How can we anticipate those problems, and how do we manage around them?

These questions are answered by taking the decision cards and ranking them in order of importance to the organization as shown in Figure A-8.

Insert here a figure such as Figure 21 on page 88, showing a ranking sheet created from decision cards. Also, a figure along the lines of Figure 20, which shows how the cards are used, may be inserted here.

The initial ranking of the decision cards should occur within the organization in which they were developed. This allows each manager to evaluate the relative importance of his own activities or operations. Each manager will be responsible for ranking the decision cards from all units reporting to him. They are then reviewed with his superior. In turn, the superior consolidates all those from the people reporting to him and ranks them. Finally, all decision cards are reviewed and consolidated by the department's vice president, who presents the final results to the executive committee for approval.

Several specific suggestions for ranking will be presented by the budget staff just prior to the ranking process. However, here are some helpful pointers that will apply to most ranking situations.

♦ Most packages will have an associated dollar benefit. But many others—often very basic to supporting the business—will not. Examples include the accounts payable, auditing, or personnel records. Rather than ranking everything strictly on its economic merit, some flexibility will be necessary. Some call this judgment, others call it common sense.

♦ The first important job during the ranking process is to ensure that *the feasibility standards described in Section 3 have been applied consistently* and that programs that are legally mandated (or that pay for themselves) are just that and nothing more.

♦ Each program should be assigned to one of the following six categories:
   1. Legally required efforts
   2. Immediate payback (regardless of how much)
   3. Highly desirable
   4. Moderately desirable
   5. Marginal but desirable
   6. Not worthwhile

The appropriate category should be checked in the lower right hand section of each decision card. The first two categories are self-explanatory. Where appropriate, block 1 or 2 of the decision card is checked. The other four are handled using the decision table depicted in Figure A-9.

Insert here a figure such as Figure 17 on page 76.

Using this table for *each* decision package increment will yield one of four overall feasibility categories:
   Highly desirable (check block 3 of the decision card).
   Moderately desirable (check block 4).
   Marginal but desirable (check block 5).
   Not worthwhile (check block 6).

Decision cards can then be ranked within each of these six categories.

♦ The task of ranking increments can be shortened and simplified if managers do not concentrate on ranking those that have high priority or are "requirements" and are well within the expenditure guidelines. In these cases, efforts should be limited to ensuring that all alternatives, cost reduction opportunities, and operating improvements have been explored and incorporated as appropriate. Managers should concentrate on discretionary functions and levels of service, and on ranking those increments that fall within the cumulative range of, say, 80 percent to 120 percent of the previous year's budget. These will normally fall in categories 4, 5, or 6. If pressed for time, you may ignore category 6 altogether.

♦ Once the decision cards are ranked, conduct an "eyeball check" of the levels appearing in the top margin of the cards. Generally, they should descend, starting with a series of "level 1 of n" cards down to a series of "level 4 of 4" or "level 5 of 5" cards. There will, of course, be occasional exceptions to this rule.

♦ Once the final ranking is agreed upon, we can enter the rank, or priority, in the space in the middle of the top margin of each decision card.

♦ We must also conduct a thorough check to make sure that we have laid in sufficient tactical programs (or decision cards) to guarantee achievement of each of our strategic goals. This is done by rearranging the cards into piles, each of which supports one of the major strategic objectives discussed in Chapter 2. If we don't have sufficient support behind each goal, additional proposals may be entertained and resources to fund them either drawn from low-priority efforts supporting other goals or added as an increment to expenses.

♦ Once an acceptable ranking has been achieved, the final set of prioritized decision packages should be copied in two "cuts": by priority for each strategic goal (this is for planning purposes); and by priority for each department (this is for control purposes).

The cards for all approved efforts are then turned over to the budget staff for consolidation.

SECTION 5: CALENDAR FOR THE BUDGETING CYCLE

To ensure timely completion of the budgeting process, the manual should incorporate a detailed schedule for the zero-base budgeting effort. An example of such a calendar appears on the following page.

1978–1979 Zero-Base Budget Calendar

Task	Prime Mover(s)	Due Date	Audience
1. Set up procedures and forms.	Budget Staff	Done	
2. Kick off process and conduct training sessions.	CEO/Budget Staff	6/1–6/14	H.Q. Managers
3. Recast 1977 budget into decision packages for "live" training.	H.Q. Managers	6/15–7/6	Budget Staff/ H.Q. Managers
4. Critique process and conduct checkpoint with executive committee.	Budget Staff	7/7–7/14	Exec. Comm.
5. Develop 1978–1979 budget and rank at section level.	H.Q. Managers	7/14–8/4	Dept. Heads
6. Review and conduct initial ranking at department level.	Dept. Heads	8/4–8/11	Staff VPs
7. Refine packages and conduct final ranking.	Dept. Heads	8/11–8/18	Staff VPs
8. Present findings and recommended 1978–1979 budget.	Staff VPs	8/18–9/1	Exec. Comm.
9. Approve final budget.	CEO/Exec. Comm.	9/1–9/8	—
10. Consolidate submissions for control.	Budget Staff	9/8–9/22	VP Finance
11. Critique process with staff managers and department heads.	Budget Staff	9/22–10/6	Dept. Heads/ Staff Managers
12. Conduct checkpoint review on system, refine approach for 1979–1980.	Controller	10/6–10/13	Exec. Comm.
13. Implement recommended changes.	Budget Staff	Open	—

SECTION 6: STANDARD FACTORS AND ASSUMPTIONS

As discussed in Section 2, any successful management system will require a common set of ground rules for cost factors and assumptions. This is particularly critical for a zero-base budgeting system, where many, many rank-and-file managers will be involved—often for the first time—in the planning process. Unless all use the same values for such things as revenue growth, labor rates, or productivity improvements, the ranking and decision-making process will become hopelessly confused.

The factors and assumptions will, of course, be unique for any

Cost Factors	Profit Improvement over 1977				
	1978	1979	1980	1981	1982
Economic Assumptions					
Labor (Cost Increase)	5.8%	11.6%	17.2%	22.7%	28.1%
Materials (Cost Increase)	2.9%	6.0%	9.3%	12.6%	15.5%
1% Increase in Productivity					
Sales	$2.5	$2.8	$3.2	$3.6	$3.8
Distribution	$0.5	$0.6	$0.8	$0.9	$1.0
Administration	$1.7	$2.5	$3.3	$4.1	$5.0
Manufacturing *					
1 Point Decrease in Turnover	$3.9	$4.9	$6.1	$7.2	$8.4
Sales	$1.9	$2.3	$2.7	$3.1	$3.5
Distribution	$0.3	$0.3	$0.4	$0.4	$0.5
Administration	$1.1	$1.7	$2.3	$2.9	$3.5
Manufacturing	$0.3	$0.3	$0.4	$0.4	$0.5
Other	$0.3	$0.3	$0.3	$0.4	$0.4
Other Factors					
1% Change in Local Tax Rates	$1.3	$1.5	$1.7	$1.8	$2.0
1% Speedup in Receivables	$1.8	$2.0	$2.3	$2.3	$2.4
1% Reduction in Inventory	$4.6	$5.0	$5.4	$6.9	$8.1
Finished	$2.1	$2.1	$2.5	$3.1	$3.7
On Consignment	$0.3	$0.3	$0.4	$0.4	$0.5
Work in Process	$2.2	$2.6	$2.5	$3.4	$3.9

* Available only from Corporate Director of Industrial Relations.

organization undertaking zero-base budgeting and will have to be updated for every new budgeting cycle. They should be detailed enough to permit developing intelligent, reasonably accurate decision packages, but not so overly complicated as to invite the "paralysis through analysis" syndrome mentioned in Chapter 8.

An example of standard factors and assumptions appears on these two pages. Notice how they tie directly to Cosmotronex's long-range objectives described in Section 2 of this appendix.

A statement instructing managers to use the assumptions (in millions of dollars) in the tables when putting together zero-base budgeting decision packages should accompany the tables.

	PROFIT IMPROVEMENT OVER 1977				
REVENUE FACTORS	1978	1979	1980	1981	1982
1% Increase in Unit Volume	$11.8	$14.4	$19.5	$27.0	$34.4
Domestic Markets *	$ 1.2	$ 3.1	$ 5.9	$ 9.6	$13.2
Current Products *	$ 1.2	$ 2.3	$ 3.1	$ 4.0	$ 4.8
Forward Products	0	$ 0.8	$ 2.8	$ 5.6	$ 8.4
Overseas Markets †	$10.6	$11.3	$13.6	$17.4	$21.2
Current Products †	$10.6	$10.9	$11.4	$11.6	$11.7
Forward Products	0	$ 0.4	$ 2.2	$ 5.8	$ 9.5
1% Increase in Prices	$ 3.9	$ 6.7	$ 8.7	$10.9	$12.2
Domestic Markets	$ 0.6	$ 1.5	$ 2.9	$ 4.8	$ 6.6
Current Products	$ 0.6	$ 1.1	$ 1.5	$ 2.0	$ 2.4
Forward Products	0	$ 0.4	$ 1.4	$ 2.8	$ 4.2
Overseas Markets	$ 3.3	$ 5.2	$ 5.8	$ 6.1	$ 5.6
Current Products	$ 3.3	$ 3.4	$ 3.6	$ 3.7	$ 3.7
Forward Products	0	$ 1.8	$ 2.2	$ 2.4	$ 1.9

* Divide number for each year by 5.6 to get the short-term market share equivalent.

† Divide number for each year by 2.8 to get the short-term market share equivalent.

APPENDIX B

Sample Forms, Decision Packages, and Ranking Summaries

Several different formats for decision packages and ranking summaries were depicted in Chapters 2 and 3. Neither those nor the ones shown on the following pages should be considered "ideal" or "model" formats. They can, however, be characterized as follows:

◇ All seek to identify what service is being delivered and at what cost. Thus, they focus on resolving the "what's going on" and "how much" issues.

◇ Many, but not all, also require detailing the approach proposed, alternatives considered, different levels of effort, and the consequences of disapproval. In this sense, they address the issues of "how" and "why."

◇ Finally, all incorporate some requirements—sometimes on separate forms—that are unique to the organizations using them. Such requirements are usually intended to ease the administrative chores as well as to facilitate the consolidation of analysis, ranking, and budgeting.

Perhaps the best word to describe all of them is *prototype*. Should you decide to employ zero-base budgeting in your organization, the formats must be structured to fit *your* needs, *your* objectives, and *your* style.

I wish to thank the organizations whose forms and worksheets are included in this appendix for granting permission to reproduce them.

Companies and Forms

Combustion Engineering Inc. (Windsor, Conn.)

DECISION PACKAGE FORM

C-E POWER SYSTEMS		DECISION PACKAGE		PERIOD:	
DIVISION: DEPARTMENT: SECTION:	NO. NO.	ACTIVITY NAME: ACTIVITY NO. LEVEL:		OF	RANK

ACTIVITY PURPOSE:	ACTIVITY RESOURCE REQUIREMENTS		
	– COST ANALYSIS* –		
	CLASSIFICATION	PRIOR PERIOD	BUDGET PERIOD
ACTIVITY DESCRIPTION:	SALARIES & WAGES		
	OTHER CONTROL.		
	OTHER DIR. CONT.		
	DIR. MAT'L & SVC.		
	DIRECT TRAVEL		
	DIRECT COMPUTER		
	INDIRECT CONT.		
	TRANSFER OUT		
	ACTIVITY COST		

RELATED ACTIVITIES:

– FUNDING FROM OUTSIDE SOURCES –

ADVANTAGES OF RETAINING ACTIVITY:

– RESOURCE ANALYSIS –

PERIOD	TOTAL COST	EXEMPT	NON-EXEMPT
BUDGET PERIOD			

CONSEQUENCES IF ACTIVITY IS ELIMINATED:

ALTERNATIVE METHODS OF PERFORMING ACTIVITY, COSTS, AND STAFFING

PREPARED BY: DATE:	APPROVED BY: DATE:	APPROVED BY: DATE:

Combustion Engineering Inc. (Windsor, Conn.)

RANKING SUMMARY FORM

Dillingham Corporation (Honolulu, Hawaii)

DECISION PACKAGE FORM

Date: _____

PACKAGE NAME		DEPARTMENT		PREPARED:		RANK
				APPROVED:		

STATEMENT OF PROGRAM AND GOALS

RESOURCES REQUIRED	1974	1975	▲ 1975–1974
People			
Current Salaries			
Salary Increases			
Total Package Cost			

ALTERNATIVES AND CONSEQUENCES

	PEOPLE	1975 COST

Total Cost All Levels of Effort

BENEFITS

QUANTITATIVE MEASURES	1974	1975

Dillingham Corporation (Honolulu, Hawaii)

RANKING SUMMARY FORM

R A N K	PACKAGE NAME	CURRENT YEAR		PLAN YEAR		Cumulative Expense
		EXPENSE	PEOPLE	EXPENSE	PEOPLE	

Group _____ Department _____ Prepared By _____ Date _____

Florida Power & Light Co. (Miami, Fla.)

DECISION PACKAGE FORM

This form was used for a three-year period prior to 1977 when zero-base budgeting was formally introduced, and for all *new* spending proposals. Using this approach, this organization's rank-and-file managers became knowledgeable of the concept and technique of zero-base budgeting in advance of its use for the entire budget.

DATE PREPARED	BUDGET DECISION ANALYSIS		BDA NUMBER
1. MANAGEMENT ACTION NAME		PREPARED BY	
CHARGE LOCATION NAME	LOCATION CODE	APPROVED BY	
2. MANAGEMENT ACTION OBJECTIVE			
3. HOW WILL YOU ATTAIN OBJECTIVES (Programs/Projects)			
4. BENEFITS OF MANAGEMENT ACTION (What will it do for FPL)			

Florida Power & Light Co. (Miami, Fla.)

DECISION PACKAGE FORM (continued)

5. METHOD OF MEASURING BENEFITS

6. QUANTITATIVE BUDGET ANALYSIS MEASURES

CAPITAL EXPENDITURES REQUIRED	THIS BUDGET YEAR	TOTAL PROJECT COST	ESTIMATED ANNUALIZED FUTURE YEARS
IPC BI # _____	$ _____	$ _____	
OPERATING EXPENSES			
A. SAVINGS	$ _____	$ _____	$ _____
B. COST	$ _____	$ _____	$ _____
C. NET	$ _____	$ _____	$ _____

D. ADDITIONS/REDUCTIONS — PERSONNEL

NUMBER	CLASSIFICATION
_____	_____
_____	_____
_____	_____
_____	_____
TOTAL _____	_____

E. ADDITIONS/REDUCTIONS BY MONTH

Jan.	_____	July	_____
Feb.	_____	Aug.	_____
March	_____	Sept.	_____
April	_____	Oct.	_____
May	_____	Nov.	_____
June	_____	Dec.	_____

7. WHAT ALTERNATIVES EXIST

8. WHAT ARE THE CONSEQUENCES OF NOT APPROVING THIS ACTION

Fox Grocery Company (Belle Vernon, Pa.)

DECISION PACKAGE FORM

	Department (2)	Prepared	DATE:	
Level Of	Division (2)	Approved		Rank(3)

Objective (1)						
Purpose/Results (4)	(7) Resources Required	Current Year	Budget Year			
	Personnel					
Activity Description (5)	Supervision $					
	Clerical $					
	Other Labor $					
	Other $					
	TOTAL $					
Options (8)						
Advantages/Benefits (9)						
Consequences (6)						

Fox Grocery Company (Belle Vernon, Pa.)

RANKING SUMMARY FORM

Department Name: _____   Manager: _____

Rank	Objective - Activity	Level of Effort	People		Gross Spending			Recommendation
			Number	Cum. No.	$	Cum. $	%	

MANAGER'S CHECKLIST
(Fox Grocery requires this checklist for self-audit purposes)

Detailed Analysis of Zero-Base Budget

1. Is priority listing sound? Does the display of organization activities permit meaningful evaluation and operational decision making by senior management?

2. Does personnel/cost data appear reasonable?

3. Do high-priority packages contain low-priority activities?

4. Do reasonable alternatives appear to have been investigated?

5. What "hidden savings" were made, if any?

6. What is your overall evaluation of the ZBB budget?

   _____ Excellent _____ Good _____ Poor

7. Comments:

   _____   _____
   Date   Analyst

Greece Central School District (Greece, N.Y.)

DECISION PACKAGE FORM

PACKAGE NAME

STATEMENT OF PROGRAM AND GOALS

RESOURCES REQUIRED	CODE A = LEGAL REQUIRE. B = CONTRACT REQUIRE. C = BOARD POLICY	CURRENT YEAR	NEXT YEAR	CHANGE
DIRECT COSTS – SALARIES FRINGE BENEFITS EQUIPMENT SUPPLIES & MATERIALS CONTRACT SERVICES BOCES				
TOTAL				
SPECIAL FUNDING – SOURCE ___ YES ___ NO				

SERVICE REQUIREMENTS

QUANTITATIVE MEASURES	CURRENT YEAR	NEXT YEAR

BENEFITS

ALTERNATIVES ATTACHED ☐ YES ☐ NO

PREPARED BY

DATE

Greece Central School District (Greece, N.Y.)

DECISION PACKAGE GROUPINGS

Most organizations allow their managers free rein in picking the subjects for decision packages. In contrast to this approach, the Greece Central School District predefines the subject of decision packages. This is partly due to state-mandated reporting requirements and partly to time pressures. This chart depicts the major groupings of those packages. Any one of these items (such as "Junior High Programs") was the subject of several decision packages.

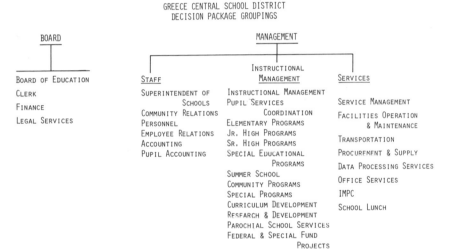

GREECE CENTRAL SCHOOL DISTRICT
DECISION PACKAGE GROUPINGS

BOARD

MANAGEMENT

BOARD OF EDUCATION

CLERK

FINANCE

LEGAL SERVICES

STAFF

SUPERINTENDENT OF
          SCHOOLS
COMMUNITY RELATIONS
PERSONNEL
EMPLOYEE RELATIONS
ACCOUNTING
PUPIL ACCOUNTING

INSTRUCTIONAL
MANAGEMENT

INSTRUCTIONAL MANAGEMENT
PUPIL SERVICES
          COORDINATION
ELEMENTARY PROGRAMS
JR. HIGH PROGRAMS
SR. HIGH PROGRAMS
SPECIAL EDUCATIONAL
          PROGRAMS
SUMMER SCHOOL
COMMUNITY PROGRAMS
SPECIAL PROGRAMS
CURRICULUM DEVELOPMENT
RESEARCH & DEVELOPMENT
PAROCHIAL SCHOOL SERVICES
FEDERAL & SPECIAL FUND
          PROJECTS

SERVICES

SERVICE MANAGEMENT
FACILITIES OPERATION
          & MAINTENANCE
TRANSPORTATION
PROCUREMENT & SUPPLY
DATA PROCESSING SERVICES
OFFICE SERVICES
IMPC
SCHOOL LUNCH

Greece Central School District (Greece, N.Y.)

DECISION PACKAGE CODING STRUCTURE FOR CHART OF ACCOUNTS

In implementing zero-base budgeting, the Greece Central School District found it necessary to completely rewrite its accounting system. The coding structure and the specific chart of accounts shown here are designed to accommodate state reporting requirements and to provide the basis for follow-up control on the decision packages.

Shown below is a summary of the general coding structure to be used for Decision Package accounting. The following pages provide the detail application of the structure.

FUND	DIV	FUNC/LVL	LOC	SEC	PGM	OBJ
XX	X	XXX-X	XX	X	XXX	XXX

Fund — Used to insure separation of various funds and to distinguish between expenditures and receipts

Division — Used to classify and aggregate expenses by major organizational components

Function/Level — Function element is used to identify expenditures by broad purposes - Level is used primarily within the Instructional function to identify grade level grouping and specific purposes. Level is also used in accounting for specific fiscal years with federally funded projects

Location — Used to identify specific school locations

Section — Used primarily in non-instructional areas to provide accounting by specific decision package

Program — Used primarily within the Instructional function to provide accounting by specific Decision Package (i.e. program)

Object Code — Used to identify specific type of expenditure (attached are specific explanations of each object code to insure consistent accounting around Decision Packages.)

Greece Central School District (Greece, N.Y.)

CHART OF ACCOUNTS

DECISION PACKAGES - STANDARD TITLES

Group	Code	Package Name
Board of Education	A1-1-010-0-00-0-000	Board of Education - Operation
	A1-1-020-0-00-1-000	Clerk - District Meeting
	A1-1-020-0-00-2-000	Clerk - Records
	A1-1-030-0-00-1-000	Finance - Treasurer
	A1-1-030-0-00-2-000	Finance - Auditing
	A1-1-030-0-00-3-000	Finance - Tax Collection
	A1-1-030-0-00-4-000	Finance - Insurance
	A1-1-030-0-00-5-000	Finance - BOCES Administration
	A1-1-030-0-00-6-000	Finance - Assessments, Claims, Etc.
	A1-1-030-0-00-7-000	Finance - Inter-Fund Transfer
	A1-1-030-0-00-8-000	Finance - Debt Services
	A1-1-040-0-00-0-000	Legal Services
Staff	A1-2-100-0-00-0-000	Superintendent of Schools
	A1-5-110-0-00-0-000	Community Relations
	A1-6-120-1-00-0-000	Personnel
	A1-6-120-2-00-0-000	Employee Relations
	A1-4-130-0-00-1-000	Accounting - Budget & Management
	A1-4-130-0-00-2-000	Accounting - General Accounting & Control
	A1-4-130-0-00-3-000	Accounting - Cash Control
	A1-4-130-0-00-4-000	Accounting - Accounts Payable
	A1-4-130-0-00-5-000	Accounting - Payroll
	A1-4-140-0-00-1-000	Pupil Accounting - Census
	A1-4-140-0-00-2-000	Pupil Accounting - Attendance
Instruction	A1-3-200-1-00-0-000	Instructional Management
	A1-3-200-2-00-0-000	Pupil Services Coordination
	A1-3-200-2-00-0-040	Pupil Services - Nurses
	A1-3-200-2-00-0-680	Pupil Services - Tutors
	A1-3-220-0-00-0-000	Instruction - F.S.D.
	A1-3-220-1-bb-0-010	Elementary Programs - Building Administration
	A1-3-220-1-bb-0-040	Elementary Programs - Nurses
	A1-3-220-1-bb-0-060	Elementary Programs - Lunchroom Monitors
	A1-3-220-1-bb-0-100	Elementary Programs - K-6
		- Language Arts
		- Math
		- Social Studies
		- Science
		- Family Living
	A1-3-220-1-bb-0-410	Elementary Programs - Art
	A1-3-220-1-bb-0-460	Elementary Programs - Music/Vocal
	A1-3-220-1-bb-0-480	Elementary Programs - Music/Instrumental
	A1-3-220-1-bb-0-510	Elementary Programs - Physical Education
	A1-3-220-1-bb-0-610	Elementary Programs - Library/A.V.
	A1-3-220-1-bb-0-640	Elementary Programs - Psychologists
	A1-3-220-1-bb-0-660	Elementary Programs - Speech
	A1-3-220-1-bb-0-680	Elementary Programs - Tutors
	A1-3-220-1-bb-0-710	Elementary Programs - Learning Centers
	A1-3-220-2-bb-0-010	Junior High Programs - Building Administration
	A1-3-220-2-bb-0-030	Junior High Programs - Undistributed
	A1-3-220-2-bb-0-040	Junior High Programs - Nurses
	A1-3-220-2-bb-0-210	Junior High Programs - Language Arts
	A1-3-220-2-bb-0-230	Junior High Programs - Social Studies
	A1-3-220-2-bb-0-260	Junior High Programs - Math
	A1-3-220-2-bb-0-280	Junior High Programs - Science
	A1-3-220-2-bb-0-310	Junior High Programs - Industrial Arts
	A1-3-220-2-bb-0-330	Junior High Programs - Home Economics

Greece Central School District (Greece, N.Y.)

CHART OF ACCOUNTS (continued)

DECISION PACKAGES - STANDARD TITLES

Group	Code	Package Name
Instruction (Continued)	A1-3-220-2-bb-0-410	Junior High Programs - Art
	A1-3-220-2-bb-0-460	Junior High Programs - Music/Vocal
	A1-3-220-2-bb-0-480	Junior High Programs - Music/Instrumental
	A1-3-220-2-bb-0-510	Junior High Programs - Physical Education
	A1-3-220-2-bb-0-530	Junior High Programs - Health
	A1-3-220-2-bb-0-560	Junior High Programs - Interscholastics
	A1-3-220-2-bb-0-610	Junior High Programs - Library/A.V.
	A1-3-220-2-bb-0-620	Junior High Programs - Guidance
	A1-3-220-2-bb-0-640	Junior High Programs - Psychologists
	A1-3-220-2-bb-0-680	Junior High Programs - Tutoring
	A1-3-220-2-bb-0-710	Junior High Programs - Learning Centers
	A1-3-220-3-bb-0-010	Senior High Programs - Building Administation
	A1-3-220-3-bb-0-030	Senior High Programs - Undistributed
	A1-3-220-3-bb-0-040	Senior High Programs - Nurses
	A1-3-220-3-bb-0-080	Senior High Programs - Student Activities
	A1-3-220-3-bb-0-210	Senior High Programs - Language Arts (English & Reading)
	A1-3-220-3-bb-0-230	Senior High Programs - Social Studies
	A1-3-220-3-bb-0-260	Senior High Programs - Math
	A1-3-220-3-bb-0-280	Senior High Programs - Science
	A1-3-220-3-bb-0-290	Senior High Programs - College Courses
	A1-3-220-3-bb-0-310	Senior High Programs - Industrial Arts
	A1-3-220-3-bb-0-330	Senior High Programs - Home Economics
	A1-3-220-3-bb-0-360	Senior High Programs - Business Education
	A1-3-220-3-bb-0-380	Senior High Programs - Cooperative Education
	A1-3-220-3-bb-0-410	Senior High Programs - Art
	A1-3-220-3-bb-0-430	Senior High Programs - Foreign Language
	A1-3-220-3-bb-0-460	Senior High Programs - Music/Vocal
	A1-3-220-3-bb-0-480	Senior High Programs - Music/Instrumental
	A1-3-220-3-bb-0-510	Senior High Programs - Physical Education
	A1-3-220-3-bb-0-530	Senior High Programs - Health
	A1-3-220-3-bb-0-560	Senior High Programs - Interscholastics
	A1-3-220-3-bb-0-610	Senior High Programs - Library/A.V.
	A1-3-220-3-bb-0-620	Senior High Programs - Guidance
	A1-3-220-3-bb-0-640	Senior High Programs - Psychologists
	A1-3-220-3-bb-0-680	Senior High Programs - Tutoring
	A1-3-220-3-bb-0-710	Senior High Programs - Learning Centers
	A1-3-220-3-bb-0-720	Senior High Programs - Occupational Education
	A1-3-220-4-00-0-000	Special Education Programs - State Handicapped School
	A1-3-220-4-00-0-730	Special Education Programs - Learning Disabilities
	A1-3-220-4-00-0-740	Special Education Programs - Mentally Retarded
	A1-3-220-4-00-0-750	Special Education Programs - Physically Handicapped
	A1-3-220-5-00-0-000	Summer School
	A1-3-220-6-00-0-800	Community Programs - Management
	A1-3-220-6-00-0-810	Community Programs - Continuing Education
	A1-3-220-6-00-0-820	Community Programs - Board Supported Programs
	A1-3-220-6-00-0-830	Community Programs - Driver Education
	A1-3-220-6-00-0-850	Community Programs - Swim Programs
	A1-3-220-6-00-0-860	Community Programs - High School Equivalency
	A1-3-230-0-00-0-901	Special Programs - F.M. Station
	A1-3-230-0-00-0-910	Special Programs - Staff Development
	A1-3-230-0-00-0-920	Special Programs - Mini-Grants - Teachers
	A1-5-230-0-00-0-921	Special Programs - Mini-Grants - Community
	A1-3-230-0-00-0-930	Special Programs - Performing Arts
	A1-3-240-0-00-0-000	Curriculum Development - Improvement of Curriculum
	A1-3-240-0-00-0-010	Curriculum Development - Management
	A1-3-240-0-00-0-210	Curriculum Development - Language Arts
	A1-3-240-0-00-0-230	Curriculum Development - Social Studies
	A1-3-240-0-00-0-260	Curriculum Development - Math/Science
	A1-3-240-0-00-0-300	Curriculum Development - Vocational Technology
	A1-3-240-0-00-0-380	Curriculum Development - Co-op Coordination
	A1-3-240-0-00-0-400	Curriculum Development - Music/Art
	A1-3-240-0-00-0-510	Curriculum Development - Physical Education
	A1-3-240-0-00-0-560	Curriculum Development - Interscholastics
	A1-3-240-0-00-0-610	Curriculum Development - Library/A.V.
	A1-3-240-0-00-0-620	Curriculum Development - Guidance
	A1-3-240-0-00-0-700	Curriculum Development - Special Education

Greece Central School District (Greece, N.Y.)

CHART OF ACCOUNTS (continued)

DECISION PACKAGES - STANDARD TITLES

Group	Code	Package
Instruction (Continued)	A1-3-250-0-00-0-000	Research & Evaluation
	A1-3-260-0-00-0-040	Parochial School Services - Nurses
	A1-3-260-0-00-0-000	Parochial School Services - Textbooks
	A1-3-260-0-00-0-680	Parochial School Services - Tutors
Services	A1-4-300-0-00-0-000	Services Management
	A1-4-310-0-00-1-000	Facilities Operation & Maintenance - Management
	A1-3-310-0-00-2-000	Facilities Operation & Maint. - Cust. Serv./Dist. Wide
	A1-3-310-1-00-2-000	Facilities Operation & Maint. - Cust. Serv./Elementary
	A1-3-310-2-00-2-000	Facilities Operation & Maint. - Cust. Serv./Jr. High
	A1-3-310-3-00-2-000	Facilities Operation & Maint. - Cust. Serv./Sr. High
	A1-4-310-0-00-3-000	Facilities Operation & Maintenance - Utilities
	A1-4-310-0-00-4-000	Facilities Operation & Maintenance - Buildings
	A1-4-310-0-00-5-000	Facilities Operation & Maintenance - Roads & Grounds
	A1-4-320-0-00-1-000	Transportation - Management
	A1-4-320-0-00-2-000	Transportation of Pupils - Regular
	A1-4-320-0-00-3-000	Transportation of Pupils - Vehicle Maintenance
	A1-4-320-0-00-4-000	Nonpupil Carrying Vehicles
	A1-4-330-0-00-1-000	Procurement & Supply - Management
	A1-4-330-0-00-2-000	Procurement & Supply - Purchasing
	A1-4-330-0-00-3-000	Procurement & Supply - Warehouse
	A1-4-330-0-00-4-000	Procurement & Supply - Distribution
	A1-4-330-0-00-5-000	Procurement & Supply - A.V. Repairs
	A1-4-330-0-00-6-000	Procurement & Supply - Stock
	A1-4-340-0-00-1-000	Data Processing Services - Operations
	A1-4-340-0-00-2-000	Data Processing Services - Systems & Programming
	A1-4-350-0-00-1-000	Office Services - Printing
	A1-4-350-0-00-2-000	Office Services - Mail & Duplicating
	A1-4-360-0-00-1-000	IMPC - Management
	A1-4-360-0-00-2-000	IMPC - Library Processing
	A1-4-360-0-00-3-000	IMPC - Instructional Kits & Training
	A1-4-360-0-00-4-000	IMPC - Film & A.V. Services
	A1-4-360-0-00-5-000	IMPC - Reading & Math Support
	A1-9-600-0-00-0-000	Fringe Benefits Control
	A1-1-700-0-00-0-000	Planned Balance
School Lunch	C1-4-370-0-00-1-000	School Lunch - Management
	C1-4-370-0-00-2-000	School Lunch - Preparation & Selling
Federal Funds	F1-3-910-6-00-0-000	ESEA I - Greece
	F1-3-910-6-64-0-000	ESEA I - St. Joseph's Villa
	F1-3-930-3-00-1-000	ESEA III - Redesign
	F1-3-930-3-00-2-000	ESEA III - Pre-School
	F1-3-930-4-00-1-000	ESEA III - Redesign
	F1-3-930-4-00-2-000	ESEA III - Pre-School
	F1-3-930-5-00-0-000	ESEA III - Project Search
	F1-3-940-6-00-1-000	ESEA IV-B - Career Awareness
	F1-3-940-6-65-0-000	ESEA IV-B
	F1-3-940-6-65-1-000	ESEA IV-B - Career Awareness
	F1-3-945-7-00-1-000	ESEA IV-C
	F1-3-950-7-00-0-000	Drug Abuse
	F1-3-970-6-00-0-000	Adult Basic Education
	F1-3-980-7-64-0-000	BOCES Mini-Grant
Trust & Agency	T1-0-000-0-00-0-000	T&A - Nonpayroll
	T1-0-000-0-00-1-000	T&A - Payroll
	Z1-0-000-0-00-0-000	Cash Clearing

New York Telephone Co. (New York, N.Y.)

DECISION PACKAGE (INSTRUCTIONS)

(1) Package Name	(2) Organization	(3) Ranking by

Descriptive title suggesting nature of the subject (also identify level of effort)

Use of Division level title from organization chart is suggested (if appropriate)

Div.	Dept.

(4) Purpose: Expected Benefits (Describe)

Indicate what this package will accomplish; i.e., what will happen as a result of these efforts or what service will the effort provide. Describe what benefit the Company will get from it. Avoid description of what will be <u>done</u>, concentrating on what will be <u>accomplished</u>, the end result. Think in terms of goals/objectives/expectations.

Include quantifiable accomplishment when possible; e.g., 10 training courses; 1,500 employees covered; 85% accomplishment; 12 reports issued.

(5) How This Will Be Accomplished (Describe)

Describe what will be done (and how) to achieve the purpose described above. This might include:

- Action (e.g., develop; maintain; extend; reduce; provide)
- Method (e.g., mechanize; go to outside contractor; reorganize)
- Period (e.g., full year; part time; quarterly)
- Number and types of people required (e.g., 5 Grade 22; 3 Grade 10; 8 non-management)

(6) Consequences Of Not Approving This Package

Suggest the probable effect if this is not done. Think in terms of specific consequences. If there will be problems, state as clearly as possible what they will be. If consequences are quantifiable (e.g., revenue loss), estimate approximate magnitude. Consequences will frequently be introduced by phrases such as:

- Elimination would...........,..
- Reduction would.............
- Failure to approve would.....

(7) Resources Required ($ In Thousands)		This Package	Cum. 1976	Funded Total 1975	Percent Cum. 76/75
Wages/Salaries					
Data Processing					
Other (Non Computer)					
Total					
Employees (Management/Non-Management)					

DISTRICT HEAD _____ PREPARED BY _____ DATE _____

New York Telephone Co. (New York, N.Y.)

DECISION PACKAGE SUMMARY FORM

Decision Package Summary

Function	Organization

Decision Packages
(Alternative Levels Of Effort And Cost To Perform This Function)　　Expense　　Employees
($000 Omitted)

Approaches Considered But Not Recommended

New York Telephone Co. (New York, N.Y.)

DECISION PACKAGE LEVEL 1
This completed package reflects level one of five incremental levels that will provide corporate safety services. The remaining levels and a summary sheet are given on successive pages.

Decision Package - Year 1976
(FOR ILLUSTRATIVE PURPOSES ONLY)

(1) Package Name	(2) Organization	(3)Ranking by:	
		Div.	Dept:
Corporate Level Safety Services (1 of 5)	Safety and Personnel Policies and Practices		6

(4) Purpose; Expected Benefits (Describe)

Provide the minimum level of required safety services at the company level. Basic liaison with AT&T and Occupational Safety and Health Administration (OSHA) will be maintained.

(5) How This Will Be Accomplished (Describe)

Issue monthly/quarterly accident results reports. Review accident reports from field (occupational and non-occupational). Maintain file on injury reports. Liaison with AT&T on environmental health problem. Coordinate and interpret OSHA regulation for Company (health and work standards).

1 third level, 3 second level, 2 Grade 2's and 1 Grade 3.

(6) Consequences of Not Approving This Package

Failure to meet Company commitments and obligations to OSHA and AT&T, and the inability to meet the absolute minimum requirements of a company-wide safety program.

(7) Resources Required ($ In Thousands)		This Package	Cum. 1976	Funded Total 1975	Percent Cum. 76/75
Wages/Salaries		$142.0	$142.0	$180.0	(21.1)
Data Processing		18.0	18.0	24.0	(25.0)
Other (Non Computer)		58.0	58.0	64.0	(9.4)
Total		218.0	218.0	268.0	(18.7)
Employees (Management/Non-Management)	/	7 / 0	7 / 0	10 / 0	(33)/ 0

DISTRICT HEAD＿＿＿＿＿＿＿＿＿ PREPARED BY ＿＿＿＿＿＿＿＿＿ DATE ＿＿＿＿＿

New York Telephone Co. (New York, N.Y.)

DECISION PACKAGE LEVEL 2

Decision Package - Year 1976
(FOR ILLUSTRATIVE PURPOSES ONLY)

(1) Package Name	(2) Organization	(3) Ranking by:	
		Div.	Dept:
Corporate Level Safety Services (2 of 5)	Safety and Personnel Policies and Practices		15

(4) Purpose; Expected Benefits (Describe)

Obtain an ongoing corporate assessment of the safety-consciousness of Company personnel and the quality of accident prevention activities throughout the Company.

(5) How This Will Be Accomplished (Describe)

Company level Operational Reviews will be conducted at least once a year in each Area and Department. Additional field visits to assist local safety staffs and line forces will be made as necessary.

1 second level supervisor

(6) Consequences of Not Approving This Package

The accident rate and the associated cost of accidents would probably rise above present levels. A lack of uniformity in the safety program would result and the emphasis on safety would decline in the Regions and Departments as the reduction of Company support for the safety program became evident.

(7) Resources Required ($ In Thousands)		This Package	Cum. 1976	Funded Total 1975	Percent Cum. 76/75
Wages/Salaries		$25.0	$167.0	$180.0	(7.2)
Data Processing		–	18.0	24.0	(25.0)
Other (Non Computer)		6.0	64.0	64.0	0
Total		31.0	249.0	268.0	(7.1)
Employees (Management/Non-Management)	/	1/0	8/0	10/0	(20)/0

DISTRICT HEAD _____ PREPARED BY _____ DATE _____

New York Telephone Co. (New York, N.Y.)

DECISION PACKAGE LEVEL 3

Decision Package - Year 1976
(FOR ILLUSTRATIVE PURPOSES ONLY)

(1) Package Name	(2) Organization	(3) Ranking by:	
Corporate Level Safety Services (3 of 5)	Safety and Personnel Policies and Practices	Div.	Dept: 26

(4) Purpose; Expected Benefits (Describe)

Provide an extensive and in-depth safety advice and consultation service to assist field in accident prevention activities.

(5) How This Will Be Accomplished (Describe)

Provide a broad range of safety services at the Company level including: safety information and programs to Regions and Departments; periodic analysis of Company safety results; and a number of OSHA related activities including improved liaison with OSHA officials and AT&T, reviewing and commenting on proposed legislative changes, and providing the field with information and guidance on OSHA problems.

1 second level supervisor

(6) Consequences of Not Approving This Package

An increase in safety oriented labor relations problems with OSHA could be expected. The accident rate and the associated cost of accidents would probably rise. New safety legislation adversely affecting company might be passed because of insufficient attention by the Company.

(7) Resources Required ($ In Thousands)		This Package	Cum. 1976	Funded Total 1975	Percent Cum. 76/75
Wages/Salaries		$25.0	$192.0	$180.0	6.7
Data Processing		6.0	24.0	24.0	0
Other (Non Computer)		8.0	72.0	64.0	12.5
Total		39.0	288.0	268.0	7.5
Employees (Management/Non-Management)	/	1/ 0	9/ 0	10 / 0	(10)/ 0

DISTRICT HEAD⎯⎯⎯⎯⎯⎯ PREPARED BY ⎯⎯⎯⎯⎯⎯ DATE⎯⎯⎯⎯

New York Telephone Co. (New York, N.Y.)

DECISION PACKAGE LEVEL 4

Decision Package - Year 1976
(FOR ILLUSTRATIVE PURPOSES ONLY)

(1) Package Name	(2) Organization	(3)Ranking by:	
		Div.	Dept:
Corporate Level Safety Services (4 of 5)	Safety and Personnel Policies and Practices		34

(4) Purpose; Expected Benefits (Describe)

Establish an ongoing accident analysis program to identify major causes of accidents and promptly report developing trends to field.

(5) How This Will Be Accomplished (Describe)

Prepare special computer studies showing trends that have developed. Analyze trends by areas, departments, etc. Identify common causes of accidents by area. Prepare reports for supervisor on recommended corrective action.

1 Grade 2

(6) Consequences of Not Approving This Package

A less than optimum utilization of mechanized procedures which are presently available. Could adversely affect the overall accident reduction program.

(7) Resources Required ($ In Thousands)		This Package	Cum. 1976	Funded Total 1975	Percent Cum. 76/75
Wages/Salaries		$11.0	$203.0	$180.0	12.8
Data Processing		3.0	27.0	24.0	12.5
Other (Non Computer)		2.0	74.0	64.0	15.5
Total		16.0	304.0	268.0	13.5
Employees (Management/Non-Management)	/	1/0	10/0	10/0	0/0

DISTRICT HEAD_____ PREPARED BY_____ DATE_____

New York Telephone Co. (New York, N.Y.)
DECISION PACKAGE LEVEL 5

Decision Package - Year 1976
(FOR ILLUSTRATIVE PURPOSES ONLY)

(1) Package Name	(2) Organization	(3)Ranking by:	
Corporate Level Safety Services (5 of 5)	Safety and Personnel Policies and Practices	Div.	Dept:
			36

(4) Purpose; Expected Benefits (Describe)

Increase the safety-consciousness of field personnel beyond current levels, with an undefined but probable reduction in accidents.

(5) How This Will Be Accomplished (Describe)

Conduct field and training center safety reviews throughout the Company on a full time basis. In addition, this package would include the preparation and distribution of a monthly "Tail-Gate" bulletin for all Plant management and would provide for the distribution of the National Safety Council seasonal safety booklets to all employees.

1 second level

(6) Consequences of Not Approving This Package

Safety services and results will continue at current levels.

(7) Resources Required ($ In Thousands)		This Package	Cum. 1976	Funded Total 1975	Percent Cum. 76/75
Wages/Salaries		$25.0	$228.0	$180.0	27.0
Data Processing		-	27.0	24.0	12.5
Other (Non Computer)		34.0	108.0	64.0	69.0
Total		59.0	363.0	268.0	35.5
Employees (Management/Non-Management)		1 / 0	11 / 0	10 / 0	10 / 0

DISTRICT HEAD_____ PREPARED BY _____ DATE _____

New York Telephone Co. (New York, N.Y.)

DECISION PACKAGE SUMMARY

1976 Decision Package Summary

Function	Organization
Corporate Level Safety Services	Safety & Personnel Policies & Practices

(FOR ILLUSTRATIVE PURPOSES ONLY)

Decision Packages (Alternative Levels Of Effort And Cost To Perform This Function)	($000) Expense	Employees
o Corporate Level Safety Services (1 of 5) Provide the minimum level of required safety services at the Company level. Basic liaison with AT&T and Occupational Safety and Health Administration (OSHA) will be maintained.	$218,000	7
o Corporate Level Safety Services (2 of 5) Obtain an ongoing corporate assessment of the safety-consciousness of Company personnel and the quality of accident prevention activities throughout the Company.	$ 31,000	1
o Corporate Level Safety Services (3 of 5) Provide an extensive and in-depth safety advice and consultation service to assist field in accident prevention activities.	$ 39,000	1
o Corporate Level Safety Services (4 of 5) Establish an ongoing accident analysis program to identify major causes of accidents and promptly report developing trends to field.	$ 16,000	1
o Corporate Level Safety Services (5 of 5) Increase the safety-consciousness of field personnel beyond current levels, with an undefined but probable reduction in accidents.	$ 59,000	1

Approaches Considered But Not Recommended

Transfer of activities to Regions or Departments was considered. That alternative would cause duplication and would result in our company trying to operate without a group to establish and support uniform company safety policies. (The distribution of National Safety Council bulletins per package 5-5 would be an exception. The cost to the company, however, would be the same or somewhat higher.)

DISTRICT HEAD _____ PREPARED BY _____ DATE _____

New York Telephone Co. (New York, N.Y.)

DECISION PACKAGE LEVEL 1

This completed package reflects level one of four incremental levels that will provide nonexempt employment services. The remaining levels and a summary sheet are given on successive pages.

Decision Package - Year 1976
(FOR ILLUSTRATIVE PURPOSES ONLY)

(1) Package Name	(2) Organization	(3)Ranking by:	
		Div.	Dept:
Downstate Non-Management Hiring (1 of 4)	General Employment	8	8

(4) Purpose; Expected Benefits (Describe)

Provide the capability to hire for the estimated 1500 job openings projected for Downstate in 1975. Meet EEO targets for minorities in clerical and operator. Miss EEO targets for minorities in craft, and for females in non-traditional jobs.

(5) How This Will Be Accomplished (Describe)

Maintain an employment office in New York City with 29 employees, an employment office in Hempstead with 5 people, and an office in White Plains with 5 people. Screen, test and interview applicants. Maintain and up-date wait-lists of qualified applicants. Place as job openings occur.

The 39 employees consist of a third level, 2 second level, 7 supervisors (Salary Grade 1B), 15 interviewers (Salary Grade 1C), 7 testers (Salary Grade 1F), and 7 non-management.

(6) Consequences of Not Approving This Package

Those job openings for which there are no qualified UTP candidates, and which would not be filled by new hires, would remain vacant with an impact on service and revenue.

(7) Resources Required ($ In Thousands)		This Package	Cum. 1976	Funded Total 1975	Percent Cum. 76/75
Wages/Salaries		$550.0	$550.0	$1111.0	(50)
Data Processing		-	-	-	-
Other (Non Computer)		132.0	132.0	308.0	(57)
Total		682.0	682.0	1419.0	(52)
Employees (Management/Non-Management)	/	32/7	32/7	61/16	(48)/(56)

DISTRICT HEAD_____ PREPARED BY _____ DATE_____

New York Telephone Co. (New York, N.Y.)

DECISION PACKAGE LEVEL 2

Decision Package - Year 1976
(FOR ILLUSTRATIVE PURPOSES ONLY)

(1) Package Name	(2) Organization	(3)Ranking by:	
		Div.	Dept:
Downstate Non-Management Hiring (2 of 4)	General Employment	18	20

(4) Purpose; Expected Benefits (Describe)

Provide <u>part-time</u> employment facilities accessible to the heavily-minority population in Harlem, South Bronx and Bedford-Stuyvesant. The proximity to these areas will enable employment to meet more EEO targets for minorities in craft. We will continue to miss some targets for females in non-traditional jobs.

(5) How This Will Be Accomplished (Describe)

Maintain a 3 day per week employment office in Brooklyn with 10 people and a 2 day per week office in Harlem with 2 people. Screen, test and interview "walk-in" applicants. Maintain wait-lists of qualified applicants. Place as job openings occur. During the remainder of the week, the people would be processing new hires, conducting scheduled tests and interviews, and performing clerical duties.

The 12 people consist of a supervisor (Salary Grade 1B), 5 interviewers (Salary Grade 1C), 2 testers (Salary Grade 1F) and 4 non-management.

(6) Consequences of Not Approving This Package

The lack of these minimal employment facilities near the minority centers will make our efforts to hire qualified minority people into craft very difficult; cause us to miss some EEO targets in these jobs; and downgrade our Company image in the eyes of the minority community.

(7) Resources Required ($ In Thousands)		This Package	Cum. 1976	Funded Total 1975	Percent Cum. 76/75
Wages/Salaries		$203.0	$753.0	$1111.0	(32)
Data Processing		–	–	–	–
Other (Non Computer)		81.0	213.0	308.0	(31)
Total		284.0	966.0	1419.0	(32)
Employees (Management/Non-Management)	/	8 / 4	40 / 11	61 / 16	(34)/(31)

DISTRICT HEAD_____ PREPARED BY _____ DATE_____

New York Telephone Co. (New York, N.Y.)

DECISION PACKAGE LEVEL 3

Decision Package - Year 1976
(FOR ILLUSTRATIVE PURPOSES ONLY)

(1) Package Name Downstate Non-Management Hiring (3 of 4)	(2) Organization General Employment	(3) Ranking by:	
		Div.	Dept:
		25	29

(4) Purpose; Expected Benefits (Describe)

Provide full-time employment service accessible to the heavily-minority population centers of Harlem, South Bronx and Bedford-Stuyvesant. The full-time availability of employment services to these areas will enable us to meet all EEO targets for minorities in craft, and meet most targets for females in non-traditional jobs.

(5) How This Will Be Accomplished (Describe)

Maintain a full-time employment office in Brooklyn with 11 additional people, and in Harlem with 1 additional person. Screen, test and interview more applicants. Maintain more extensive wait-lists of qualified minority applicants. Place as job openings occur.

The 12 people consist of a supervisor (Salary Grade 1B), 5 interviewers (Salary Grade 1C), 2 testers (Salary Grade 1F) and 4 non-management.

(6) Consequences of Not Approving This Package

The lack of full-time employment facilities near these minority centers will make our efforts to hire qualified minority people into craft jobs more difficult; cause us to miss targets for minorities in these jobs and females in non-traditional jobs.

(7) Resources Required ($ In Thousands)		This Package	Cum. 1976	Funded Total 1975	Percent Cum. 76/75
Wages/Salaries		$187.0	$ 940.0	$1111.0	(15)
Data Processing		-	-	-	-
Other (Non Computer)		71.0	284.0	308.0	(16)
Total		258.0	1224.0	1419.0	(14)
Employees (Management/Non-Management)	/	8 / 4	48 / 15	61 / 16	(21)/(6)

DISTRICT HEAD_____ PREPARED BY _____ DATE_____

New York Telephone Co. (New York, N.Y.)

DECISION PACKAGE LEVEL 4

Decision Package - Year 1976
(FOR ILLUSTRATIVE PURPOSES ONLY)

(1) Package Name	(2) Organization	(3)Ranking by:	
		Div.	Dept:
Downstate Non-Management Hiring (4 of 4)	General Employment	28	38

(4) Purpose; Expected Benefits (Describe)

Provide an employment service for non-management hiring in Bronx and Mt. Vernon (Westchester). This will enable us to meet EEO targets in these areas for women in non-traditional jobs, and will provide an employment presence in heavily minority population centers.

(5) How This Will Be Accomplished (Describe)

Maintain an employment office in the Bronx with 10 people, and in Mt. Vernon with 5 people. Screen, test and interview applicants. Maintain and up-date wait-lists of qualified candidates. Place as job openings occur.

The 15 people consist of 2 supervisors (Salary Grade 1B), 9 interviewers (Salary Grade 1C), 3 testers (Salary Grade 1F) and 1 non-management.

(6) Consequences of Not Approving This Package

The lack of these employment services in the heavily minority centers of Bronx and Mt. Vernon will impair our Company image, and cause us to miss some targets for women in non-traditional jobs.

(7) Resources Required ($ In Thousands)		This Package	Cum. 1976	Funded Total 1975	Percent Cum. 76/75
Wages/Salaries		$194.0	$1134.0	$1111.0	2
Data Processing		-	-	-	-
Other (Non Computer)		43.0	327.0	308.0	6
Total		237.0	1461.0	1419.0	3
Employees (Management/Non-Management)	14 / 1	14 / 0	62 / 16	61 / 16	(2)/0

DISTRICT HEAD_____ PREPARED BY _____ DATE_____

New York Telephone Co. (New York, N.Y.)
DECISION PACKAGE SUMMARY

1976 Decision Package Summary

Function	Organization
Downstate Non-Management	General Employment

(FOR ILLUSTRATIVE PURPOSES ONLY)

Decision Packages (Alternative Levels Of Effort And Cost To Perform This Function)	($000) Expense	Employees
o Downstate Non-Management Hiring (1 of 4) Provide the capability to hire for the estimated 1500 job openings projected for Downstate in 1975. Meet EEO targets for minorities in clerical and operator. Miss EEO targets for minorities in craft and for females in non-traditional jobs.	$682,000	39
o Downstate Non-Management Hiring (2 of 4) Provide part-time employment facilities accessible to the heavily minority population in Harlem, South Bronx and Bedford-Stuyvesant. The proximity to these areas will enable employment to meet more EEO targets for minorities in craft. We will continue to miss some targets for females in non-traditional jobs.	$284,000	12
o Downstate Non-Management Hiring (3 of 4) Provide full-time employment service accessible to the heavily minority population centers of Harlem, South Bronx and Bedford-Stuyvesant. The full-time availability of employment services to these areas will enable us to meet all EEO targets for minorities in craft and meet targets for females in non-traditional jobs.	$258,000	12
o Downstate Non-Management Hiring (4 of 4) Provide an employment service for non-management hiring in the Bronx and Mt. Vernon (Westchester). This will enable us to meet EEO targets in these areas for women in non-traditional jobs and will provide an employment presence in heavily minority population centers.	$237,000	15

Approaches Considered But Not Recommended

o The alternative of transferring this hiring to the Regions would incur the same Company expense, would result in non-uniformity and duplication; and a lack of emphasis on EEO targets.

o The alternative of obtaining new hires from outside agencies would entail fees, and require relinquishing our concept of a System-qualified applicant by placing selection process and decision in outside hands.

DISTRICT HEAD _____ PREPARED BY _____ DATE _____

New York Telephone Co. (New York, N.Y.)

DECISION PACKAGE LEVEL 1

This completed package reflects level one of four incremental levels that will provide long-range planning services. The remaining levels and a summary sheet are given on successive pages.

Decision Package - Year 1976
(FOR ILLUSTRATIVE PURPOSES ONLY)

(1) Package Name	(2) Organization	(3) Ranking by:	
		Div.	Dept:
Six Year Plan (1 of 4)	Corporate Planning	1	1

(4) Purpose; Expected Benefits (Describe)

An approximation of a six year corporate strategic plan will be devised and proposed to the EPC.

Staff services will be provided for the EVP-Corporate Development.

(5) How This Will Be Accomplished (Describe)

Iteration 2 1/2 and the 1974 SYP will be examined as presented, without detailed comparison and analysis. Insights will be translated to corporate strategies. Ad hoc committees formed by Corporate Planning will explore the cross-regional potentials and search for additional strategies to close the corporate earnings gap.

A high proportion of staff time will be devoted to staff services for the EVP-Corporate Development.

Requires 7 employees (1 fourth level; 1 third level; 3 second level; 2 first level).

(6) Consequences of Not Approving This Package

The only unifying force for integrated long range planning will be disbanded. It is unlikely that a comprehensive corporate (and perhaps Regional) long range plan will be prepared and followed through other means.

(7) Resources Required ($ In Thousands)		This Package	Cum. 1976	Funded Total 1975	Percent Cum. 76/75
Wages/Salaries		$186.0	$186.0	$262.1	(29.1)
Data Processing		10.0	10.0	23.9	(58.2)
Other (Non Computer)		18.0	18.0	32.1	(43.9)
Total		214.0	214.0	318.1	(32.7)
Employees (Management/Non-Management)	/	7 / 0	7 / 0	11 / 0	(36)/0

DISTRICT HEAD_____ PREPARED BY _____ DATE_____

New York Telephone Co. (New York, N.Y.)

DECISION PACKAGE LEVEL 2

Decision Package - Year 1976
(FOR ILLUSTRATIVE PURPOSES ONLY)

(1) Package Name	(2) Organization	(3)Ranking by:	
		Div.	Dept:
Six Year Plan (2 of 4)	Corporate Planning	2	2

(4) Purpose; Expected Benefits (Describe)

A viable six year corporate strategic plan will be supported by sufficient detail to permit immediate implementation and tracking of strategic recommendations.

Corporate long range goals will be revised to make them entirely suitable for planning purposes, and subsidiary goals will be recommended to the Regions and HQ organizations.

(5) How This Will Be Accomplished (Describe)

1974 SYP and Iteration 2 1/2 data will be studied for (1) information re. viable strategies already contemplated and (2) probable opportunities for improved earnings. Corporate Planning will form Ad Hoc committees to explore strategies to reduce corporate earnings shortfall. Final strategic recommendations will have substantial supporting data.

Corporate, Regional and HQ goals will be derived from analysis of Iteration 2 1/2 and final strategic recommendations, reviewed and validated with key management people.

Adds 3 Managers (Grade 23).

(6) Consequences of Not Approving This Package

Proposal for corporate strategic plan will be based upon readily available data. Back-up detail will tend to be superficial.

Long range goals will not be suggested for Regions and HQ organizations, thereby weakening the linkage between corporate and subsidiary goals and plans.

(7) Resources Required ($ In Thousands)		This Package	Cum. 1976	Funded Total 1975	Percent Cum. 76/75
Wages/Salaries		$69.0	$255.0	$262.1	(2.8)
Data Processing		7.0	17.0	23.9	(28.9)
Other (Non Computer)		8.0	26.0	32.1	(19.0)
Total		84.0	298.0	318.1	(6.3)
Employees (Management/Non-Management)	/	3/0	10/0	11/0	(9)/0

DISTRICT HEAD_____ PREPARED BY _____ DATE_____

New York Telephone Co. (New York, N.Y.)

DECISION PACKAGE LEVEL 3

Decision Package - Year 1976
(FOR ILLUSTRATIVE PURPOSES ONLY)

(1) Package Name	(2) Organization	(3)Ranking by:	
		Div.	Dept:
Six Year Plan (3 of 4)	Corporate Planning	3	6

(4) Purpose; Expected Benefits (Describe)

Undertake a pilot project and do the requisite preliminary work to test and demonstrate the linkages between environmental analysis and long range planning.

(5) How This Will Be Accomplished (Describe)

The environmental linkage project will make extensive use of questionnaires to key management people to identify specific relationships between the environment and the business. Appropriate environmental data will be gathered into a functional data base, and then applied to business decisions and plans for some organizational unit on a "show-and-tell" basis.

Adds one third level employee (Grade 26).

(6) Consequences of Not Approving This Package

Continuing acknowledgement that environmental analysis is important, and after-the-fact recognition of the impact of environmental changes; but also, a continuing low level of success in anticipating and acting to control the effects of environmental change.

Corporate Planning staff reduced below 1974 level, jeopardizing ability to undertake a complete planning cycle in 1976.

(7) Resources Required ($ In Thousands)		This Package	Cum. 1976	Funded Total 1975	Percent Cum. 76/75
Wages/Salaries		$34.0	$289.0	$262.1	10.3
Data Processing		5.0	22.0	23.9	(7.9)
Other (Non Computer)		1.0	27.0	32.1	(15.9)
Total		40.0	338.0	318.1	6.3
Employees (Management/Non-Management)	/	1/0	11/0	11/0	0/0

DISTRICT HEAD_____ PREPARED BY_____ DATE_____

New York Telephone Co. (New York, N.Y.)
DECISION PACKAGE LEVEL 4

Decision Package - Year 1976
(FOR ILLUSTRATIVE PURPOSES ONLY)

(1) Package Name	(2) Organization	(3)Ranking by:	
		Div.	Dept:
Six Year Plan (4 of 4)	Corporate Planning	4	12

(4) Purpose; Expected Benefits (Describe)

Study total factor and other productivity measurements, seeking to recommend by 4Q 1975 a viable process whereby Regions can (1) measure the effect of long range plans on regional productivity and (2) regional contributions to corporate productivity.

Develop and conduct (as required) a training program and manual for Regional and HQ personnel.

(5) How This Will Be Accomplished (Describe)

Draw upon Business Research, AT&T, Regional personnel and current literature to establish the current status of productivity measurement. Undertake additional research and testing to develop the methodology for plan-related productivity measurement.

Consult with planning coordinators to establish problems and training needs, and devise suitable course material.

Adds one second level employee (Grade 23)

(6) Consequences of Not Approving This Package

It will continue to be virtually impossible to discern the relationships between long range plans and productivity claims.

Time and effectiveness will be lost every planning cycle while newly assigned planners try to figure out what to do and how to do it.

(7) Resources Required ($ In Thousands)		This Package	Cum. 1976	Funded Total 1975	Percent Cum. 76/75
Wages/Salaries		$25.0	$314.0	$262.1	19.8
Data Processing		0	22.0	23.9	0
Other (Non Computer)		1.0	28.0	32.1	(12.8)
Total		26.0	364.0	318.1	12.8
Employees (Management/Non-Management)	/	1 / 0	12 / 0	12 / 0	9.1 / 0

DISTRICT HEAD ————————— PREPARED BY ————————— DATE —————

New York Telephone Co. (New York, N.Y.)

DECISION PACKAGE SUMMARY

1976 Decision Package Summary

Function	Organization
Six Year Plan	Corporate Planning

(FOR ILLUSTRATIVE PURPOSES ONLY)

Decision Packages (Alternative Levels Of Effort And Cost To Perform This Function)	($000) Expense	Employees
• Six Year Plan (1 of 4) Minimum Package: Devise and propose an approximation of a six year corporate strategic plan, and provide staff services for EVP-Corporate Development.	$214,000	7
• Six Year Plan (2 of 4) Devise a viable six year corporate strategic plan, with sufficient supporting detail to permit immediate implementation and tracking of strategic recommendations. Revise corporate long range goals and recommend subsidiary goals for Regions and HQ organizations.	$ 84,000	3
• Six Year Plan (3 of 4) Test and demonstrate the linkages between environmental analysis and long range planning.	$ 40,000	1
• Six Year Plan (4 of 4) Develop a process whereby Regions can measure the effect of long range plans on regional productivity, and the contributions of Regions to corporate productivity.	$ 26,000	1

Approaches Considered But Not Recommended

1. Combine long range planning with other regular business activities. O.P.&E. provide nominal coordination and Accounting periodically summarize financial results. Could save approx. $110,000 in CPD expense. O.P.&E. and Accounting expense would increase. Planning effort would deteriorate substantially because of (1) inadequate coordination and direction and (2) inability to devote sufficient time (within framework of normal O.P.&E. and Accounting organizations) to corporate level analysis and evaluation.

2. Confine strategic planning efforts to HQ staff organizations, with Regional participation only for advice and consultation. No CPD savings and undefined but probably minor Regional savings (no dedicated planning organizations at present). Cuts off the single best source of ideas - the Regions. Removes the planning one step further from reality, and makes it questionable whether strategies would be accepted by Regions and converted to funded implementation plans.

3. Corporate Planning do the entire strategic planning job. Has all the problems of (2), and would probably require a buildup of expertise (i.e., force expense) in Corporate Planning.

DISTRICT HEAD _____ PREPARED BY _____ DATE _____

New York Telephone Co. (New York, N.Y.)
RANKING SUMMARY

(FOR ILLUSTRATIVE PURPOSES ONLY)
1976 Decision Package Ranking
($000)

R A N K	Package Name	1976 Resources		Cumulative 1976		Cumulative % '76 Vs '75	
		$	Emps	$	Emps	$	Emps
1	Workmen's Compensation (1 of 4)	154	11	154	11	9.8	14.7
2	Unemployment Insurance (1 of 4)	59	4	213	15	13.6	20.0
3	Salary Administration (1 of 3)	71	2	284	17	18.1	22.7
4	Employees Benefit Committee (1 of 2)	277	10	561	27	35.7	36.0
5	Personnel Policies and Practices (1 of 3)	51	2	612	29	39.0	38.7
6	Corporate Level Safety Practices (1 of 5)	218	7	830	36	52.9	48.0
7	Personnel Services - Headquarters (1 of 2)	76	4	906	40	57.7	53.3
8	Management Job Evaluation (1 of 3)	62	2	968	42	61.7	56.0
9	Other Benefit Services (1 of 3)	51	3	1019	45	64.9	60.0
10	Budget and Expense Control (1 of 1)	17	1	1036	46	66.0	61.3
11	Unemployment Insurance (2 of 4)	132	5	1168	51	74.4	68.0
12	Workmen's Compensation (2 of 4)	112	7	1280	58	81.5	77.3
13	Pioneer Activities (1 of 2)	89	3	1369	61	87.2	81.3
14	Home Sale Plan (1 of 3)	3	1	1372	62	87.4	82.7
15	Corporate Level Safety Practices (2 of 5)	31	1	1403	63	89.4	84.0
16	Salary Administration (2 of 3)	24	1	1427	64	90.9	85.3
17	Employees Benefit Committee (2 of 2)	22	1	1449	65	92.3	86.6
18	Personnel Policies and Practices (2 of 3)	33	1	1482	66	94.4	88.0
19	Personnel Services - Headquarters (2 of 2)	21	0	1503	66	95.8	88.0
20	Management Job Evaluation (2 of 3)	90	4	1593	70	101.5	93.3
21	Other Benefit Services (2 of 3)	11	1	1604	71	102.2	94.7
22	Workmen's Compensation (3 of 4)	23	1	1627	72	103.7	96.0
23	Unemployment Insurance (3 of 4)	20	1	1647	73	104.9	97.3

Organization Ranked	Prepared By	Date	Page 1 of 2
Personnel Administration			

New York Telephone Co. (New York, N.Y.)

RANKING SUMMARY (continued)

(FOR ILLUSTRATIVE PURPOSES ONLY)
1976 Decision Package Ranking
($000)

R A N K	Package Name	1976 Resources $	Emps	Cumulative 1976 $	Emps	Cumulative % '76 Vs '75 $	Emps
24	Salary Administration (3 of 3)	1	0	1648	73	105.0	97.3
25	Home Sale Plan (2 of 3)	5	0	1653	73	105.3	·97.3
26	Corporate Level Safety Practices (3 of 5)	39	1	1692	74	107.8	98.7
27	Pioneer Activities (2 of 2)	23	0	1715	74	109.3	98.7
28	Homes Sale Plan. (3 of 3) ##	7	0	1722	74	109.7	98.7
29	Class "A" Discounted Service (1 of 1)	46	0	1768	74	112.6	98.7
30	Personnel Policies and Practices (3 of 3)	35	1	1803	75	114.9	100.0
31	Management Job Evaluation (3 of 3)	113	4	1916	79	122.1	105.3
32	Workmen's Compensation (4 of 4)	24	1	1940	80	123.6	106.7
33	Unemployment Insurance (4 of 4)	21	1	1961	81	124.9	108.0
34	Corporate Level Safety Practices (4 of 5)	16	1	1977	82	126.0	109.3
35	Other Benefits (3 of 3)	18	1	1995	83	127.1	110.6
36	Corporate Level Safety Practices (5 of 5)	59	1	2054	84	130.9	112.0
	1975 $1569.6 75 People						
	## Current Level of Operations						

Organization Ranked	Prepared By	Date	Page 2 of 2
Personnel Administration			

Owens-Illinois, Inc. (Toledo, Ohio)

DECISION PACKAGE FORM (Front)

Date _____

Activity Name	Dept: Name, No. & Mgr.	Staff Function	Staff Area

Level ____ of ____	Does this proposed plan represent the current level of effort as indicated by latest plan? ☐ Yes ☐ No

ACTIVITY PURPOSE

DESCRIPTION AND SCOPE OF ACTIVITY (Operations)

COST/BENEFIT ANALYSIS

ACTIVITY COSTS	Percent	1976	1977	% Change
Gross Spending				
Direct Billing				
Service Cross Charge				
Allocated and Retained				
Man-Years				

ACTIVITY BENEFITS

ACTIVITY SCHEDULE

CONSEQUENCES OF NON-APPROVAL

Legally Required? ☐ Yes ☐ No   Is this the Minimum Level Required? ☐ Yes ☐ No

Cost/Service Levels discussed with Customer/User Organizations? ☐ Yes   ☐ No

Owens-Illinois, Inc. (*Toledo, Ohio*)

DECISION PACKAGE FORM (Back)

Used to summarize expense data for each decision package by account-level detail. It is printed on the reverse side of each decision package.

G/L ACCOUNT NAME	G/L ACCOUNT NUMBER	AMOUNT $ (M)
Salaries & Wages	_ _ 13	
Wage Increments	_ _ 96 · 0040	
Special Fees	_ _ 38	
Moving Expenses	_ _ 14	
Expense & Supplies	_ _ 40	
Travel & Entertainment	_ _ 47	
Telephone	_ _ 96 · 0006	
General Office Facilities	_ _ 96 · 0041	
Data Processing, Systems, Programming	_ _ 96 · 0001, 0005, 0026	
All Other		

	TOTAL	

Owens-Illinois, Inc. (Toledo, Ohio)

ACTIVITY DETAIL
Used to cross reference to other supporting decision packages.

DEPARTMENT NAME _____

DEPARTMENT MANAGER _____

ACTIVITY DESC.	PRIORITY	SERVICES DIV/CORP	BUDGET MAN-POWER	MONEY	ACTION TO BE TAKEN: i.e.; Reduce Eliminate Keep

External resources necessary to perform activity:

Cause & Effect of a reduction of $_____ :

Cause & Effect of eliminating the activity:

Owens-Illinois, Inc. (Toledo, Ohio)

RANKING SUMMARY FORM

RANK	ACTIVITY PLAN	LEVEL OF EFFORT	PEOPLE		GROSS SPENDING		RECOMMENDATION
			Number	Cum No.	$	Cum.$	

Department Name

Manager

Date

Southern California Edison Company (Rosemead, Calif.)

DECISION PACKAGE FORM (Front)

Objective No. _____

Date _____

ACTIVITY (OR OBJECTIVE) NAME	DEPARTMENT	PREPARED	RANK

LEVEL NO. _____ OF _____

| | DIVISION | APPROVED | |

RESOURCES REQUIRED	CURRENT YEAR	BUDGET YEAR
Personnel		
Labor $		
Outside Services $		
Other $		
TOTAL $		

PURPOSE OF ACTIVITY

DESCRIPTION OF ACTIVITY

ALTERNATIVE WAYS OF PERFORMING WORK OR PROGRAM AND COSTS

ADVANTAGES OF RETAINING ACTIVITY

CONSEQUENCES IF ACTIVITY IS ELIMINATED

Southern California Edison Company (Rosemead, Calif.)

DECISION PACKAGE FORM (Back)

FUNCTION NO.	LABOR	OTHER	TOTAL
BUDGET YEAR EXPENDITURE DETAIL ($)			
Plant Work Orders			
Total			

BUDGET YEAR COST DISTRIBUTION ($)

FUNCTIONS	Operation and Maintenance—Including O/H	
	Research and Development—Expense	
	Other—Including O/H to Const. & Misc.	
	Total	
PLANT WORK ORDERS	Research and Development—Capitalized	
	Other	
	Total	
	Grand Total Expenditures	

Southern California Edison Company (Rosemead, Calif.)

SUMMARY FOR TOP MANAGEMENT PRESENTATION

This summary sheet is put together for the Management Committee's budget review. Each item is a decision unit in the classic sense, backed up by decision packages.

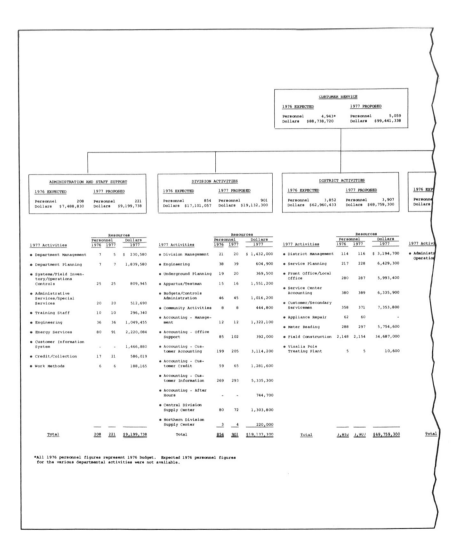

CUSTOMER SERVICE			
1976 EXPECTED		**1977 PROPOSED**	
Personnel	4,943*	Personnel	5,059
Dollars	$88,738,720	Dollars	$99,441,338

ADMINISTRATION AND STAFF SUPPORT			
1976 EXPECTED		**1977 PROPOSED**	
Personnel	208	Personnel	221
Dollars	$7,488,830	Dollars	$9,199,738

DIVISION ACTIVITIES			
1976 EXPECTED		**1977 PROPOSED**	
Personnel	854	Personnel	901
Dollars	$17,101,057	Dollars	$19,132,300

DISTRICT ACTIVITIES			
1976 EXPECTED		**1977 PROPOSED**	
Personnel	3,852	Personnel	3,907
Dollars	$62,960,433	Dollars	$69,759,300

	Resources		
	Personnel		Dollars
1977 Activities	1976	1977	1977
• Department Management	7	5	$ 230,580
• Department Planning	7	7	1,839,580
• Systems/Field Inventory/Operations Controls	25	25	809,945
• Administrative Services/Special Services	20	20	512,690
• Training Staff	10	10	296,340
• Engineering	36	36	1,049,455
• Energy Services	80	91	2,220,084
• Customer Information System	-	-	1,466,880
• Credit/Collection	17	21	586,019
• Work Methods	6	6	188,165
Total	208	221	$9,199,738

	Resources		
	Personnel		Dollars
1977 Activities	1976	1977	1977
• Division Management	21	20	$ 1,432,000
• Engineering	38	39	604,900
• Underground Planning	19	20	369,500
• Appartus/Testman	15	16	1,551,200
• Budgets/Controls Administration	46	45	1,016,200
• Community Activities	8	8	444,800
• Accounting - Management	12	12	1,322,100
• Accounting - Office Support	85	102	392,000
• Accounting - Customer Accounting	199	205	3,114,200
• Accounting - Customer Credit	59	65	1,281,600
• Accounting - Customer Information	269	293	5,335,300
• Accounting - After Hours	-	-	744,700
• Central Division Supply Center	80	72	1,303,800
• Northern Division Supply Center	3	4	220,000
Total	854	901	$19,132,300

	Resources		
	Personnel		Dollars
1977 Activities	1976	1977	1977
• District Management	114	116	$ 3,194,700
• Service Planning	217	228	6,429,300
• Front Office/Local Office	280	287	5,993,400
• Service Center Accounting	380	389	6,335,900
• Customer/Secondary Servicemen	358	371	7,353,800
• Appliance Repair	62	60	-
• Meter Reading	288	297	5,754,600
• Field Construction	2,148	2,154	34,687,000
• Visalia Pole Treating Plant	5	5	10,600
Total	3,852	3,907	$69,759,300

*All 1976 personnel figures represent 1976 budget. Expected 1976 personnel figures for the various departmental activities were not available.

Southern California Edison Company (Rosemead, Calif.)

RANKING SUMMARY FORM

State of Georgia

DECISION PACKAGE, MINIMUM LEVEL

With five years' experience under its belt, Georgia now requires four incremental levels for each activity. Decision packages on each level (minimum, base, workload, and new or improved) are depicted here.

OPB Budget 31
(Rev. 6-75)

F.Y. 1977

ZERO-BASE BUDGET REQUEST
DECISION PACKAGE – BASE LEVEL

Emergency Medical Health
Function

Human Resources — Department	Community Injury Control — Activity

Describe the Function in terms of its objective County and City Medical Centers are charged to meet emergency situations such as sudden illness, injury, natural or man-made disasters, and poison cases. The centers do not coordinate their efforts across county and city lines nor do they have exposure to the latest techniques and equipment in the emergency medical field. Some centers are highly successful due to a special innovation that other centers do not share.

Describe the Function in terms of service provided in F.Y. 1976 (Base Level) Utilize a central staff to conduct medical emergency courses around the State to monitor the operations of the Injury Control Program. The courses will provide instruction to the centers on the latest medical emergency techniques and methods. The Base Level provides service for the 100 most populated counties by conducting one medical emergency course at each.

Explain the Cost Increase or Decrease in the Base Level over F.Y. 1976
Personal Services – Within-grade increases and annualization of a part-year position
Regular Operating Expenses – Primarily due to rental contract increase for office space.
Travel – Increase in rate from 10 cents to 12 cents per mile.
M.V. Equipment Purchases – Replacement vehicle.
Equipment Purchases – 3 pocket calculators in addition to replacement of office equipment.

Positions This Package	Function F.Y. 76	This Pkg. F.Y. 77	Cum%
A. TOTAL PERSONAL SERVICES	25,624	9,276	105
1. Motor Vehicle Expenses and Repairs	900	326	
2. Supplies and Materials	1,900	700	
3. Repairs and Maintenance	500	200	
4. Communications	400	176	
5. Power, Water, Natural Gas	250	98	
6. Rents	273	77	
7. Insurance and Bonding			
8. Workmen's Comp. and Indemnities			
9. Direct Benefits			
10. Tuition and Scholarships			
11. Grants to Counties or Cities			
12. Assessments by Merit System	132	44	
13. Other Operating Expenses	450	244	
14. Extraordinary Expenses			
B. REG. OPERATING EXPENSES(Add 1-14)	4,805	1,865	104
C. TRAVEL	800	350	112
D. MOTOR VEHICLE EQUIP. PURCH.	4,680	5,112	109
E. PUBLICATIONS AND PRINTING	1,350	500	111
F. EQUIPMENT PURCHASES	750	1,550	206
G. PER DIEM AND FEES	2,000	750	112
H. COMPUTER CHARGES	2,900	900	100
I. OTHER CONTRACTUAL EXPENSE	1,600	1,050	100
J. AUTHORITY LEASE RENTALS			
K. GENERAL OBLIGATION BONDS			
L. CAPITAL OUTLAY			
M. LIST OTHER OBJECTS:			
TOTAL EXPENDITURES (Add A - M)	44,509	21,353	107
FEDERAL FUNDS	16,000	6,000	100
OTHER FUNDS	4,000		100
STATE GENERAL FUNDS	24,509	15,353	113

Quantitative Measures (Effectiveness, Workload, Efficiency)	F.Y. 1976 Function	F.Y. 1977 Base Level
Different Medical Centers Aided	100	100
Medical Emergency Courses conducted	100	100
Cost Per Course/Total funds	$445	$478
Cost Per Course/State funds	$245	$278

Package Name: Emergency Medical Health   Package 2 of 4

Prepared By: John Smith   Activity Rank 7

* Attach detailed schedule for F.Y. 1977 Base Level (Including Minimum Level) funds requested.
** Detailed schedule for the Base Level is to be developed at the Activity Level.

State of Georgia

DECISION PACKAGE, BASE LEVEL

F. Y. 1977

OPB Budget: 31
(Rev. 6-75)

ZERO-BASE BUDGET REQUEST
DECISION PACKAGE – BASE LEVEL

Human Resources	Community Injury Control	Emergency Medical Health
Department	Activity	Function

Positions This Package		Function F.Y. 76	This Pkg. F.Y. 77	Cum%
A. TOTAL PERSONAL SERVICES	**	25,624	9,276	105
1. Motor Vehicle Expenses and Repairs		900	326	104
2. Supplies and Materials		1,900	700	
3. Repairs and Maintenance		500	200	
4. Communications		400	176	
5. Power, Water, Natural Gas		250	98	
6. Rents	*	273	77	
7. Insurance and Bonding				
8. Workmen's Comp. and Indemnities				
9. Direct Benefits				
10. Tuition and Scholarships				
11. Grants to Counties or Cities				
12. Assessments by Merit System		132	44	
13. Other Operating Expenses		450	244	
14. Extraordinary Expenses				
B. REG. OPERATING EXPENSES(Add 1-14)	*	4,805	1,865	104
C. TRAVEL		800	350	112
D. MOTOR VEHICLE EQUIP. PURCH.	*	4,680	5,112	109
E. PUBLICATIONS AND PRINTING		1,350	500	111
F. EQUIPMENT PURCHASES	*	750	1,550	206
G. PER DIEM AND FEES	*	2,000	750	112
H. COMPUTER CHARGES		2,900	900	100
I. OTHER CONTRACTUAL EXPENSE	*	1,600	1,050	100
J. AUTHORITY LEASE RENTALS				
K. GENERAL OBLIGATION BONDS				
L. CAPITAL OUTLAY				
M. LIST OTHER OBJECTS				
TOTAL EXPENDITURES (Add A - M)		44,509	21,353	107
FEDERAL FUNDS	**	16,000	6,000	100
OTHER FUNDS	**	4,000		100
STATE GENERAL FUNDS		24,509	15,353	113

Describe the Function in terms of its objective   County and City Medical Centers are charged to meet emergency situations such as sudden illness, injury, natural or man-made disasters, and poison cases. The centers do not coordinate their efforts across county and city lines nor do they have exposure to the latest techniques and equipment in the emergency medical field. Some centers are highly successful due to a special innovation that other centers do not share.

Describe the Function in terms of service provided in F. Y. 1976 (Base Level)   Utilize a central staff to conduct medical emergency courses around the State to monitor the operations of the Injury Control Program. The courses will provide instruction to the centers on the latest medical emergency techniques and methods. The Base Level provides service for the 100 most populated counties by conducting one medical emergency course at each.

Explain the Cost Increase or Decrease in the Base Level over F. Y. 1976
Personal Services – Within-grade increases and annualization of a part-year position.
Regular Operating Expenses – Primarily due to rental contract increase for office space.
Travel – Increase in rate from 10 cents to 12 cents per mile.
M. V. Equipment Purchases – Replacement vehicle.
Equipment Purchases – 3 pocket calculators in addition to replacement of office equipment.

Quantitative Measures (Effectiveness, Workload, Efficiency)	F. Y. 1976 Function	F. Y. 1977 Base Level
Different Medical Centers Aided	100	100
Medical Emergency Courses conducted	100	100
Cost Per Course/Total funds	$445	$478
Cost Per Course/State funds	$245	$278

Package Name: Emergency Medical Health   Package 2 of 4

Prepared By: John Smith   Activity Rank 7

* Attach detailed schedule for F. Y. 1977 Base Level (Including Minimum Level) funds requested.
** Detailed schedule for the Base Level is to be developed at the Activity Level

State of Georgia

DECISION PACKAGE, WORKLOAD LEVEL

F.Y. 1977

OPB Budget: 32
(Rev. 6-75)

ZERO-BASE BUDGET REQUEST
DECISION PACKAGE – WORKLOAD

Human Resources	Community Injury Control	Emergency Medical Health
Department	Activity	Function

Describe the Function in terms of its objective County and City Medical

Centers are charged to meet emergency situations such as sudden illness, injury, natural or man-made disasters, and poison cases. The centers do not coordinate their efforts across county and city lines nor do they have exposure to the latest techniques and equipment in the emergency medical field. Some centers are highly successful due to a special innovation that other centers do not share.

Describe the Function in terms of service provided in F.Y. 1976 Utilize a central staff to conduct medical emergency courses around the State to monitor the operations of the Injury Control Program. The courses will provide instruction to the centers on the latest medical emergency techniques and methods. The Base-Level provides service for the 100 most populated counties by conducting one medical emergency course at each.

Explain the Workload increase in terms of service provided above the Base Level Conduct a medical emergency course in each of the 63 centers not covered in the State. Every center in the State would receive one course annually. This additional workload is demanded by the centers not now being served.

Explain the Workload Cost Over the Base Level
Personal Services – Two new positions, including fringes, less one month delayed hiring factor.
Related Expenses – To cover 63 additional centers, the new positions will need additional expenses and office space renovations.
Computer Charges – Expansion of the system to add 63 centers. Federal funds are available to help cover the additional centers.

	Function F.Y. 76	This Pkg. F.Y. 77	Cum%
Positions This Package 2			
A. TOTAL PERSONAL SERVICES	25,624	15,810	166
1. Motor Vehicle Expenses and Repairs	900	150	150
2. Supplies and Materials	1,900	600	
3. Repairs and Maintenance	500	100	
4. Communications	400	50	
5. Power, Water, Natural Gas	250		
6. Rents	273		
7. Insurance and Bonding			
8. Workmen's Comp. and Indemnities			
9. Direct Benefits			
10. Tuition and Scholarships			
11. Grants to Counties or Cities			
12. Assessments by Merit System	132	88	
13. Other Operating Expenses	450		
14. Extraordinary Expenses			
B. REG. OPERATING EXPENSES (Add 1-14)	4,805	988	124
C. TRAVEL	800	300	150
D. MOTOR VEHICLE EQUIP. PURCH.	4,680		109
E. PUBLICATIONS AND PRINTING	1,350	250	129
F. EQUIPMENT PURCHASES	750	100	220
G. PER DIEM AND FEES	2,000		112
H. COMPUTER CHARGES	2,900	300	110
I. OTHER CONTRACTUAL EXPENSES	1,600	200	112
J. AUTHORITY LEASE RENTALS			
K. GENERAL OBLIGATION BONDS			
L. CAPITAL OUTLAY			
M. LIST OTHER OBJECTS:			
TOTAL EXPENDITURES (Add A-M)	44,509	19,948	152
FEDERAL FUNDS	16,000	7,000	144
OTHER FUNDS			
STATE GENERAL FUNDS	24,509	12,948	166

* Attach detailed schedule for F.Y. 1977 Workload funds requested in this package.

Quantitative Measures (Effectiveness, Workload, Efficiency)	F.Y. 1976 Function	F.Y. 1977 Base-Level	F.Y. 1977 Cumulative
Different Medical Centers Aided	100	100	163
Medical Emergency Courses conduc.	100	100	163
Cost per Course/Total funds	$445	$478	$415
Cost per Course/State funds	$245	$278	$250

Package Name: Emergency Medical Health　Package 3 of 4

Prepared By: John Smith　Activity Rank 10

State of Georgia
DECISION PACKAGE, NEW OR IMPROVED LEVEL

Human Resources — Department
Community Injury Control — Activity
Emergency Medical Health — Function

Describe the Function in terms of its objective County and City Medical Centers are charged to meet emergency situations such as sudden illness, injury, natural or man-made disasters, and poison cases. The centers do not coordinate their efforts across county and city lines nor do they have exposure to the latest techniques and equipment in the emergency medical field. Some centers are highly successful due to a special innovation that other centers do not share.

Describe the Function in terms of service provided in F.Y. 1976 Utilize a central staff to conduct medical emergency courses around the State to monitor the operations of the Injury Control Program. The courses will provide instruction to the centers on the latest medical emergency techniques and methods. The Base Level provides services for the 100 most populated counties by conducting one medical emergency course at each.

Explain the New or Improved in terms of service Conduct an additional 37 medical emergency courses. This improvement will provide 37 centers with at least 2 courses. The centers serving the greatest population will receive more intensive instruction and more specialized courses. Improved coordination for local services will mean better emergency medical health statewide.

Explain the New or Improved in terms of Cost
Personal Services – Two new positions, including fringes, less one month delayed hiring factor.
Related Expenses – To conduct 37 additional courses, the new positions will need additional expenses and office space rental. No additional Federal funds are available for expansion.

Positions This Package 2	Function F.Y. 76	This Pkg. F.Y. 77	Cum%
A. TOTAL PERSONAL SERVICES *	25,624	15,810	229
1. Motor Vehicle Expenses and Repairs	900	500	
2. Supplies and Materials	1,900		
3. Repairs and Maintenance	500	50	
4. Communications	400		
5. Power, Water, Natural Gas	250		
6. Rents *	273	150	
7. Insurance and Bonding			
8. Workmen's Comp. and Indemnities			
9. Direct Benefits			
10. Tuition and Scholarships			
11. Grants to Counties or Cities			
12. Assessments by Merit System	132	88	
13. Other Operating Expenses	450		
14. Extraordinary Expenses			
B. REG. OPERATING EXPENSES (Add 1-14) *	4,805	788	141
C. TRAVEL	800	200	175
D. MOTOR VEHICLE EQUIP. PURCH. *	4,680		109
E. PUBLICATIONS AND PRINTING	1,350	100	137
F. EQUIPMENT PURCHASES *	750	100	233
G. PER DIEM AND FEES *	2,000		112
H. COMPUTER CHARGES	2,900		110
I. OTHER CONTRACTUAL EXPENSE *	1,600		112
J. AUTHORITY LEASE RENTALS			
K. GENERAL OBLIGATION BONDS			
L. CAPITAL OUTLAY *			
M. LIST OTHER OBJECTS:			
TOTAL EXPENDITURES (Add A-M) *	44,509	16,998	190
FEDERAL FUNDS	16,000		144
OTHER FUNDS	4,000		100
STATE GENERAL FUNDS *	24,509	16,998	236

* Attach detailed schedule for F. Y. 1977 New or Improved funds requested in this package.

Quantitative Measures (Effectiveness, Workload, Efficiency)	F.Y. 1976 Function	F.Y. 1977 Cumulative
Different Medical Centers Aided	100	163
Medical Emergency Courses Conducted	100	200
Cost Per Course/Total funds	$445	$423
Cost Per Course/State funds	$245	$289

Package Name: Emergency Medical Health   Package 4 of 4
Prepared By: John Smith   Activity Rank 14

State of Georgia
ACTIVITY RANKING

ZERO-BASE BUDGET REQUEST
DECISION PACKAGE RANKING

Human Resources Department

Community Injury Control Activity

RANK	PACKAGE NAME	F.Y. 1976 BUDGETED		F.Y. 1977 REQUESTED		CUMULATIVE LEVEL		
		State Funds	Positions	State Funds	Positions	State Funds	% 77/76	Positions
1	Executive Admn. (1 of 2)	32,420	2	24,200	1	24,200	14.9	1
2	Planning (1 of 1)	34,121	2	30,200	2	54,400	33.5	3
3	Patient Appraisals (1 of 2)	24,946	2	11,748	1	66,148	40.7	4
*4	Emergency Medical Health (1 of 4)	24,509	2	12,433	2	78,581	48.3	6
5	Food Service (1 of 2)	20,000	3	16,200	2	94,781	58.3	9
6	Housekeeping (1 of 3)	26,593	4	14,000	2	108,781	66.9	11
*7	Emergency Medical Health (2 of 4)			15,353	1	124,134	76.3	12
8	Executive Admn. (2 of 2)			15,200	1	139,334	85.7	13
9	Patient Appraisals (2 of 2)			17,000	1	156,334	96.2	14
*10	Emergency Medical Health (3 of 4)			12,948	2	169,282	104.1	16
11	Capital Outlay (1 of 1)			2,000		171,282	105.3	
12	Food Service (2 of 2)			19,000		190,282	117.0	
13	Housekeeping (2 of 3)			11,000	2	201,282	123.8	18
*14	Emergency Medical Health (4 of 4)			16,998	2	218,280	134.3	20
15	Housekeeping (3 of 3)			15,000		233,280	143.5	20
	Activity Totals	162,589	14	233,280	20			

$$\frac{233,280}{162,589} = 143.5\%$$

* Decision Packages in Sample

Frank Doe
Approved By

Activity Manager
Title

August 18, 1975
Date

Page 1 of 1

State of Georgia
DEPARTMENT RANKING

ZERO-BASE BUDGET REQUEST
DECISION PACKAGE RANKING

Human Resources — Department

Department Ranking — Activity

RANK	PACKAGE NAME	F.Y. 1976 BUDGETED		F.Y. 1977 REQUESTED		CUMULATIVE LEVEL		
		State Funds	Positions	State Funds	Positions	State Funds	% 77/76	Positions
1	Executive Adm. (1 of 2)	32,420	1	24,200	1	24,200	3.3	1
2	Administrative (1 of 2)	44,200	4	32,000	3	56,200	7.7	4
3	General Obligation Bond (1 of 1)	200,000		200,000		256,200	35.1	
4	Authority Lease Rentals (1 of 1)	100,000		100,000		356,200	48.8	6
5	Planning (1 of 1)	34,121	2	30,200	2	386,400	52.9	6
6	Emergency Facilities (1 of 3)	156,004	20	65,000	6	451,400	61.8	12
7	Housekeeping (1 of 3)	26,593	4	14,000	2	465,400	63.8	14
8	Administrative (2 of 2)			15,100	1	480,500	65.8	15
9	Patient Appraisals (1 of 2)	24,946	2	11,748	1	492,248	67.4	16
10	Emergency Facilities (2 of 3)			29,000	5	521,248	71.4	21
11	Food Services (1 of 2)	20,000	3	16,200	3	537,448	73.6	24
12	Staff Training (1 of 4)	62,200	6	7,000	1	544,448	74.6	25
13	Capital Outlay (1 of 1)	5,000		25,000		569,448	78.0	
*14	Emergency Medical Health (1 of 4)	24,509	2	12,433	2	581,881	79.7	27
15	Emergency Facilities (3 of 3)			110,721	9	692,602	94.9	36
16	Staff Training (2 of 4)			16,900	2	709,502	97.2	38
17	Housekeeping (2 of 3)			11,000	2	720,502	98.7	40
*18	Emergency Medical Health (2 of 4)			15,353	1	735,855	100.8	41
19	Executive Admin. (2 of 2)			15,200	1	751,055	102.9	42
20	Capital Outlay (1 of 1)			2,000		753,055	103.2	
*21	Emergency Medical Health (3 of 4)			12,948	2	766,003	104.9	44
22	Staff Training (3 of 4)			27,000	2	793,003	108.6	46
23	Housekeeping (3 of 3)			15,000		808,003	110.7	
*24	Emergency Medical Health (4 of 4)			16,998	1	825,001	113.0	47
25	Staff Training (4 of 4)			22,000	1	847,001	116.0	48
26	Food Services (2 of 2)			19,000		866,001	118.6	
27	Patient Appraisals (2 of 2)			17,000	1	883,001	121.0	49
	TOTALS	729,993	44	883,001	49			

Sam Doe
Approved By
* Decision Packages in Sample

Department Director
Title

August 26, 1975
Date

Page 1 of 1

Texas Instruments Incorporated (Dallas, Texas)

OPERATING DECISION PACKAGE

RANKING 10

PACKAGE NAME: Product X Planning (1 of 3)

PROGRAM AND GOALS:
Provide minimum level of planning effort for 5 million units of product X.
Maintain updated production and shipping schedules for two weeks in advance (currently maintaining schedules four weeks in advance).
Provide finished goods inventory level reports daily and in process inventory reports every other day (currently being done daily).
Maintain perpetual inventory system (computerized) on raw material to maintain a two weeks supply on hand and a two weeks supply on order.

IMPROVEMENTS: Reduce overtime and clerical effort due to perpetual inventory system. Replace professional with clerk.

TRENDS	1971	1972	1973
SM NSB/planner	1.2	1.3	1.6
Avg inv/M NSB	10%	12%	11%
Pkg cost/NSB	2.1%	2.0%	1.8%
Pkg cost/GPM	5.1%	8.0%	7.9%

BENEFITS: Activity required for minimum maintenance of planning function to deliver products on schedule.

CONSEQUENCES: Elimination of planners would force line foremen to do their own planning (zero incremental cost for foremen); but excessive inventories, inefficient production runs, and delayed shipments would result in excessive sales loss.

ALTERNATIVES:
- Combine production planning for departments X, Y, and Z.
- Package 2 of 3 ($15,000): add back long range planner.
- Package 3 of 3 ($15,000): add operations research analyst.

ASSUMPTIONS/MILESTONES:
1. Product X NUB at 5 million 10% below 1972 projected level.
2. X, Y and Z product mix will be essentially same as 1972.
3. New products (Q and R) not released to production until 4th Qtr. 1973 and then only in sample quantities.

RESOURCES	197 1 TOTAL	197 2 TOTAL	4 0 7 2 ANNUAL	TOTAL	1Q	2Q	3Q	4Q
						197 3		
GROSS	60	40	44	45				
NET ($000)	50	40	44	45	11	11	11	12
EXEMPT	4	2	2	2	2	2	2	2
NONEXEMPT	1	2	2	2	2	2	2	2

C C 287   ORGANIZATION DTL Planning   DIVISION Circuits   PREPARED BY   DATE/REV.

Texas Instruments Incorporated (Dallas, Texas)

LEVEL OF EFFORT ANALYSIS FOR DECISION PACKAGES

FUNCTION PCC ABC Production Planning		LEVELS				
ACTIVITY/TASK	1	2	3*	4	5
Compile Demand					
Customer Interface	F	D	C̲	C	B
International Inputs	C	B	B	B	A
Dallas Inputs	C	C	C	C	B
Derive Stocking Levels	D	D	D	C̲	B
Operating Planning					
Line Balancing	D	C	C	B̲	A
Demand Balancing	D	C	B̲	A	A
Work Scheduling	F	D	C̲	C	B
Photomask Operations	F	D	C	C̲	B
Forecasting					
Bar Billings	F	F	D	D	C
Mask Requirements	D	D	D	C	B
Materials	D	C	C	C	C
Excess Bar Inventory Control	F	C	B̲	A	A
Long Range Planning					
Capacity & Equipment Planning	F	D	D	C	C
Capital Investment Planning	F	F	F	D	C
Market Projections & Interpretations	F	F	D	D	C
Systems Development	D	D	D	C	C
			Current		
			Level		

QUALITY LEGEND		197 2	4Q 72		197 3			
A = EXCELLENT		TOTAL	ANNUAL					
B = GOOD								
C = SATISFACTORY	CUM. GR $K							
D = LESS THAN SATISFACTORY								
F = INSUFFICIENT	CUM. NET $K	74	76	25	53	78*	103	128
• (INDICATE CURRENT LEVEL	CUM. EX	3	3	1	2	3	4	5
USE ☐ TO INDICATE MOST IMPORTANT CHANGE IN LEVEL OF EFFORT.	CUM. NX	3	3	1	2	3	4	5

CC 300	ORGANIZATION ABC Production Planning	DIVISION Devices	PREPARED BY	DATE/REV.

Texas Instruments Incorporated (Dallas, Texas)

BACKUP SUMMARY FOR LEVEL OF EFFORT ANALYSIS

197 _3_	RESOURCES REQUIRED	LEVELS OF EFFORT				
		1	2	3	4	5
1Q	GROSS					
	NET	6	13	19	25	31
	EXEMPT	1	2	3	4	5
	NON-EXEMPT	1	2	3	4	5
2Q	GROSS					
	NET	6	13	19	25	31
	EXEMPT	1	2	3	4	5
	NON-EXEMPT	1	2	3	4	5
3Q	GROSS					
	NET	7	14	20	26	33
	EXEMPT	1	2	3	4	5
	NON-EXEMPT	1	2	3	4	5
4Q	GROSS					
	NET	6	13	20	27	33
	EXEMPT	1	2	3	4	5
	NON-EXEMPT	1	2	3	4	5
TOTAL	GROSS					
	NET	25	53	78	103	128
	EXEMPT	1	2	3	4	5
	NON-EXEMPT	1	2	3	4	5
CURRENT LEVEL — 4Q _72_ ANNUALIZED	GROSS					
	NET			76		
	EXEMPT			3		
	NON-EXEMPT			3		
197 _2_ ANNUALIZED	GROSS					
	NET			74		
	EXEMPT			3		
	NON-EXEMPT			3		
CC 300	ORGANIZATION ABC Production Planning	DIVISION Devices		PREPARED BY		DATE REV.

Texas Instruments Incorporated (Dallas, Texas)

RANKING SUMMARY FORM

R A N K	NAME OF OPERATING DECISION PACKAGE OR LEVEL OF EFFORT	4 Q ___ ANNUAL EXPENSE		197_ RESOURCES				197_ RESOURCES				CUM. RESOURCES			
				EXPENSE		PEOPLE		EXPENSE		PEOPLE		EXPENSE		PEOPLE	
		GR	NET	GR	NET	EX	NE	GR	NET	EX	NE	GR	NET	EX	NE
CC	ORGANIZATION	DIVISION				PREPARED BY				DATE/REV.					

Xerox Corporation (Rochester, N.Y.)

DECISION PACKAGE (page 1)

(1) Program Name:	(2) Department	(3) Budget Center	(4) Year	(5) Ranking
Data Capsule	ISG Region Operations Mgt.	S698	73/74	

(6) Statement of Purpose

Provide accurate run length Data Base of installed equipment

(7) Description of Actions (Operations)

Salesman completes label-installs Data Capsule
Mail in preaddressed envelope to Rochester
Rochester logs-enters header
Translator-Data Base
Report mailed back to salesman-data stored for reference

(8) Program Benefits

Customer Satisfaction
Sales Effectiveness
Professionalism-No guessing on the best Price Plan
Reduced Cancellations-Right copier for a given volume
Additional Business-Documentation for trade-up or accessory
Data Base for ISG (Pricing, etc.)

(9) Manpower Required

	TBA
3 Exempts	Mackenzie
2 Non-Exempts	Hagedorn
	Irving
	Kunes
	Fitzhugh

(10) Resource Summary ($ IN THOUSANDS)	1973	1974	1975
Total Expenses	$242	$194	
Manpower: Exempt	3	3	
Non-Exempt	2	2	

Xerox Corporation (Rochester, N.Y.)

DECISION PACKAGE (page 2)

(1). Program Name:	(2) Department:	(3) Budget Center	(4) Year	(5) Ranking
Data Capsule	ISG Region Operations Mgt.	S698	73/74	

11). Cost Assumption Worksheet of Non-Labor Costs:

General Travel
16 trips (8 trips MacKenzie, 8 trips Hagedorn)
@$250 per trip

XDX Equipment Maintenance
1973 Go Out-Transfer agreement
$1605 X 12 months = $19260

Dues and Subscriptions
1974-400 Data Capsule Units @$120 = $48,000
1973-800 Data Capsule Units @$120 = $96,000

(12) Other Unique Costs:

Depreciation
4 year straight line on Sigma 3 mainframe
$107,000/4 years=$26,750

(13) Detailed Costing ($ THOUSANDS)

#	Account	1973	1974
	Wages & Salaries	$95	$95
	Travel	4	4
	XDX Equip Maint	20	20
	Dues&Subs.	96	48
	XDX Depreciation	27	27
	Total	$242	$194

(14) 1974 Calendarization

Quarter	1	2	3	4
Expenses	$86	$36	$36	$36
Manpower: Exempt	3	3	3	3
Non-Exempt	2	2	2	2

Xerox Corporation (Rochester, N.Y.)

RANKING SUMMARY FORM

RANK	Package Name	1972 Resources			1973 Resources			1973 Resources Cumulative Total		
		Manpower (E/NE)	Spending ($000)	Capital ($'s)	Manpower (E/NE)	Spending ($000)	Capital ($'s)	Manpower (E/NE)	Spending ($000)	Capital ($'s)

Section Manager _____

Date _____

Page _____ of _____

Xerox Corporation (Rochester, N.Y.)

EDP ACCOUNT CALENDARIZATION

After a decision package has been approved, its account-level detail (page 2) is fed into a computer for consolidation and calendarization. This is the calendarized printout for the particular decision package shown. Other printouts are available for budget centers and departments to control against plan.

REGION OPERATIONS
BUDGET CENTER: S698

XEROX CORPORATION
INFORMATION SYSTEMS GROUP
EXPENSE PLAN
(AS OF MAY/21/73)

DATA CAPSULE

ACCOUNT / NAME	JAN	FEB	MAR	APR	MAY	JUNE	JULY	AUG	SEPT	OCT	NOV	DEC	YTD
6285 SUPR/EXEMPT-NO	4900	4900	4900	4900	4900	4900	4900	4900	4900	4900	4993	5000	58993
6295 CLERICAL-OTHER	2170	2170	2170	2170	2170	2170	2170	2170	2170	2170	2170	2170	26040
6405 BENEFITS COST-	800	800	800	800	800	800	800	800	800	800	800	810	9610
6411 PROFIT SHARING	954	954	954	954	954	954	954	954	954	954	967	968	11475
7801 GENERAL TRAVEL	325	325	325	325	325	325	325	325	350	350	350	350	4000
8039 XDS EQUIP. MAIN	3500	3500	3500	3500	3500	3500	3500	3500	3500	3500	3500	3500	42000
8604 DUES AND SUBSC	12000	12000	12000	12000	12000	12000	12000	12000					96000
TOTAL	24649	24649	24649	24649	24649	24649	24649	24649	12674	12674	12780	12798	248118

1975

ACCOUNTS	1st Quarter	2nd Quarter	3rd Quarter	4th Quarter	1975 TOTAL
SALARY AND WAGES	15	15	15	15	60
BENEFIT COSTS	3	3	3	3	12
GENERAL TRAVEL	1	1	1	1	4
XDX EQUIP MAIN	12	12	12	12	48
DUES AND SUBS	48	-	-	-	48
TOTAL	79	31	31	31	172

APPENDIX C

Zero-Base Budgeting
in the Federal Government

Since it scored several impressive successes in state and local government as well as in the private sector, interest in applying zero-base budgeting at the federal level has grown. Several reasons for this can be cited, including demands by the electorate to control government costs, regulation, and paperwork, and to make the bureaucracy more responsive to the needs of the American people. Other reasons are the growing assertiveness of Congress, which is reclaiming its constitutional mandate to control government spending, and the successful candidacy of President Jimmy Carter, one of zero-base budgeting's earliest and staunchest advocates. As a result, during 1976, both the Senate and the House of Representatives moved to legislate the use of the zero-base concept for federal policy planning and budgeting.

The hearings on the proposed legislation offer some practical insights; they illustrate not only how zero-base budgeting might be employed at the national level but also how common problems in applying it in industry and government have been handled.

At those hearings, many points of view were presented by dozens of expert witnesses. The testimonies of four witnesses are of particular interest, and edited transcripts of them are included in this appendix.

But interest in zero-base budgeting has not been limited to the legislative branch. At numerous times during the 1976 presidential campaign, Jimmy Carter promised to institute it in the executive branch as one of his first priorities. Accordingly, two of his key papers on the subject are included here. The first is a speech given at the end of his incumbency as Georgia's chief executive at the 1974 National Governors Conference. In essence, it reaffirms a recurring theme in the current professional literature on zero-base budgeting: The technique is invaluable if not indispensable, but be prepared to work hard and don't expect miracles. The second is a campaign paper written in mid-1976, parts of which appeared in the January 1977 issue of *Nation's Business.*

SENATE SUBCOMMITTEE ON INTERGOVERNMENTAL RELATIONS

March 17, 1976

TESTIMONY OF ARNOLD WEBER, DEAN, GRADUATE SCHOOL OF INDUSTRIAL ADMINISTRATION, CARNEGIE MELLON UNIVERSITY

Mr. WEBER. When I was at OMB, George Schultz always used to say the budget process was a fight of the parts against the whole, and the parts always won.

It seems to me that your earlier Budget Reform Act tried to establish the notion that the whole world have priority over the parts; S. 2925 [the sunset legislation] logically is an effort to make the parts consistent with the whole.

I endorse [its] principles. In an earlier incarnation, before I went to OMB, I was in the Department of Labor, where I served as assistant secretary for manpower and a program manager. So I suppose I have the perceptions of both the fox and the chicken.

It is correct and, it seems to me, almost inevitable that when a bureaucracy is left to its own resources, it will follow the path of incremental budget.

I was prepared to offer an immediate promotion to the first GS-8 that offered up his program for liquidation. When that does happen it is characterized as an act of whimsy rather than serious intent.

So, it seems to me that S. 2925 is a useful and meritorious bill which tells the Congress and the executive branch to do what we always hoped that they would have done.

Having said that, there are a few comments that I would like to make on the general thrust, if not the details, of the legislation.

First: It seems to me that the legislation should distinguish between programs to which the zero-base concept applies, and where it would be inappropriate.

If you did a zero-base study of the Justice Department and found out it was not very effective, it is inconceivable that you would abolish the department.

There are basic functions of government which should be recognized in the bill, such as the operation of foreign policy, the collection of taxes, and the administration of the criminal justice system.

It seems to me we can't treat them in the same way that we do a manpower training program for older workers or the Bureau of Apprenticeship training.

It would be inefficient and misguided to impose a law of the equality of millstones on every government program.

A second aspect of difference between programs is the expected period of maturity or performance.

For example, for some programs you can expect to have an outcome in a year. Other programs, such as the war on cancer or our efforts in the space area, may require a longer time horizon for performance.

Similarly, a program that has been in effect since 1906 is different from a program that was started last year.

To the extent that we are concerned with zero-base budgeting as an instrument to evaluate a particular program, it seems to me we should have some criteria which determine which programs should be higher on the roster for inquiry and examination.

Second, the workload inherent in the bill is just staggering, and it is really infeasible.

The last time I looked at the Catalog of Domestic Assistance programs, there were something like 1,200 programs. I don't know whether they have split by binary fission since then or whether some have withered away.

Almost each one of those programs constitutes a prospective dissertation for unborn Ph.D. candidates. One should not underestimate the work involved in evaluating even programs which appear to have a clear-cut objective—rural housing, sewage treatment in suburban areas, and what have you.

So it seems to me that in developing a system of zero-base budgeting, you have to trim your sails. The process of zero-base budgeting and evaluation should be subject to the same notions of cost-benefit analysis that you hope would apply to specific programs.

That indicates to me the development of some de minimis rule, such as limiting the process to a program involving a certain amount of money.

The third observation that I would make is that as I read the draft of S. 2925, it calls upon the president, presumably through OMB, to carry out the same exercise.

I think that would be terribly duplicative. It would probably put an excessive burden on OMB, and the evaluation process goes on in a continuous way in OMB, anyway. Not much appears on the surface, but that is what a budget examiner is supposed to do.

If in fact that standing committees do a zero-base evaluation, that probably would force OMB's hand, so to speak. The agency would have to deal with it, and in dealing with it they would replicate the important aspects of the evaluation.

Otherwise, a parallel track, it seems to me, would be highly cumbersome.

The fourth observation that I would make is that it should be understood that there is a very close relationship between zero-based budgeting, program evaluation, and government organization, but it is not confronted at all.

For example, particular agencies are single-program agencies and if, in fact, you determine that they are deficient, you still have the organizational substructure.

I remember one of the classic cases of this was a committee on safety in nonmetallic mines or something like that which did not have any program.

It was memorialized in the *Wall Street Journal* article in which the agency head reported that he played classical music because the Congress had done away with his program but not his organization.

The last point I would make is don't assume that zero-base budgeting is a form of magic. The development of overly precise objectives so you can hold an agency's feet to the fire is not always the best way to go.

The nature of government and particularly governmental programs is intrinsically ambiguous.

If you set very specific objectives, you deny the capacity of the administrators to modify and deal with new or different circumstances.

As you set objectives too specifically, bureaucrats will say to "game" them. I have learned if you work 1 hour a day trying to beat a fellow and he worked 10 trying to beat you, in most cases he will win.

One of the recommendations of the Ash council was to put the "M" in OMB, and I guess I was one of the first associate directors of management. We had tried to think of measures that we could use as a basis for subsequent evaluation.

I remember in analyzing one of the drug control programs we asked, "How efficient is Customs or the other agencies?" We looked for measures. We ended up with a spot price for cocaine in illegal markets in 20 cities.

We said that if the price went up, the enforcement program was succeeding because that indicated a curtailment of supplies.

Well, that was a very nice exercise, but in retrospect I am not sure it dealt effectively with the problem. So one of the difficulties we have in zero-base budgeting is a compulsion for particularity when it seems to me not all government programs lend themselves to this quality. Somehow we have to accommodate the unique aspects of government in the structure of our management and in the structure of our review.

With those suggestions, it seems to me a very constructive proposal; it is a natural companion to the budget reform legislation.

One additional matter.

I don't believe that pilot programs are necessary. We know enough about zero-based budgeting and evaluation, and if you have some sensible criteria for determining priorities, I don't see any useful purpose in setting up another pilot project. If you are going to do it, just go ahead and do it. [Emphasis added.]

Thank you very much.

HEARINGS BEFORE THE HOUSE TASK FORCE ON BUDGET PROCESS

Brock Adams, Chairman

July 27, 1976

The CHAIRMAN. The Budget Process Task Force will come to order. Our hearings this morning are on zero-base budgeting. We have a series of witnesses that we hope will bring to the committee both technical information and recommendations on this subject. Like many things, it is a subject which everybody seems to be for, but when you get to the particulars, it becomes very difficult.

I particularly want to welcome our witnesses for this morning's hearing. Testifying this morning are Allen Schick of the Congressional Research Service, Paul O'Neill, deputy director of OMB, and Peter Pyhrr, vice president of Alpha Wire Co., who implemented [zero-base budgeting at] Texas Instruments and, at Governor Carter's request, in the Georgia State government.

The goal of these hearings is to make recommendations to the full Budget Committee and Rules Committee regarding how we would implement a zero-base budgeting system.

I might say that personally I think that this is essential because we have faced a difficult problem this year. We cannot do anything substantial in terms of moving programs forward that are already in place. We have had a very difficult time with them, yet they continue.

I want to mention some specifics. How do you change the legislation on the 1-percent kicker, which has been voted by this committee and voted by the House? We have gotten it through two separate committees, but it is all contingent on a third committee. If that third committee does not act on it, then we cannot do anything about that program, even though its elimination has been a clearly expressed goal on the part of the House.

It is not the position of the Budget Committee or the chairman to pick on a particular group or particular program. I might note that we find this situation across the board.

Mr. Giaimo and I were just in the Democratic Caucus this morning where we are trying to do something about the mandatory programs in the GI bill extension and whether or not there will be an automatic extension of that bill. Once again, this bill goes to a committee that has very definite interests.

We are also struggling with the Highway Trust Fund, where the committee of jurisdiction does not wish to place a limitation on what will be spent in any one year. If it does not, then you create a budget resolution with little meaning. It is almost impossible to determine what will be spent each year.

The same has been true in areas of the defense budget. It has been true in areas in HEW. And our problem is how do you reach the ongoing programs which do not have a termination date and which have continued for many years. The Budget Committee must then either automatically take these programs into the budget—which tends to build in a very high fixed expense—or go in and struggle, trying to do what I call "pushing the string" to make a change.

We are very pleased this morning to have Mr. Schick, who is a recognized expert on budgeting.

As all of you familiar with zero-base budgeting know, it requires basically two things, a cycling process whereby you redo all the bills that are in place at some point, and second, that you look at the entire program from top to bottom, rather than just the proposed increment for a particular year.

We are hopeful that we can put one of these proposals into draft form so that as we are moving into the next budget cycle, we will be able to implement it and have this concept become part of the whole budgeting process of the Congress.

We think it can be done; we hope it can be done.

Mr. Schick, it is a pleasure to welcome you here this morning. We will be very pleased to hear your statement.

STATEMENT OF ALLEN SCHICK, CONGRESSIONAL RESEARCH SERVICE

Mr. SCHICK. Thank you very much, Mr. Chairman.

I have a prepared statement, but I think it would be more useful for the committee for me to place that statement in the record and instead concentrate on a few matters of concern with regard to the relationship between zero-base budgeting and the sunset legislation which is pending before the Congress, also with regard to various alternative approaches which may be considered by the Congress as it considers zero-base budgeting.

The CHAIRMAN. Without objection, the entire statement of Mr. Schick will be placed in the record.

Mr. SCHICK. Thank you.

I also would like to inject a note of realism into the debate on what zero-base budgeting and sunset might do if they were implemented.

We seem to have conflicting caricatures of both the existing process and of a zero-base budget process. We tend to underestimate what the current budget situation achieves for us, and perhaps we tend also to overestimate what might be accomplished under zero-base budgeting.

When we have inflated expectations about what zero-base budgeting might accomplish, it opens us to criticism and caricature, because of the likelihood that these expectations would not be realized.

On the one hand, many people insist that if something is placed in the budget, it never leaves the budget—despite the fact that there is considerable evidence that although federal expenditures have been trending substantially upward over the last decade, there has been a turnover in programs. Such change is not easy—it is not painless—but it is accomplished.

If one were to look at the budget of the United States of a decade ago and lay it side by side with the budget for fiscal 1977, we would find a considerable number of programs which now are funded at a lower level than they were a decade ago, or at a lower level in terms of constant dollars, and we would also find a number of programs which were in the budget 10 years ago and no longer are there.

We also will tend to find, if we were to place these programs under the microscope, so that we could look at them in more minute pieces, that even though the total program level does not appear to change, there are within federal agencies constant redirections of effort. It is, I believe, a simplification to insist that nothing gets removed from the base if it already is in the budget.

On the other hand, if we were to look at zero-base budgeting as a process which every year or two reexamines everything, without any selectivity, then we would expose ourselves to a different problem: It simply is not possible, within that time framework, to rediscover, reconsider, or reevaluate from the bottom up everything, every year or two.

Government continues, and its programs continue. Zero-base budgeting will not open us up to a government of sudden death, where according to an automatic budgetary or sunset process, we will phase the automatic termination of one-fifth, one-quarter, or one-half of all of government every year.

What is likely to be achieved under zero-base budgeting and sunset, however, is very important and very valuable. These processes may give the Congress and the executive branch a greater ability to reexamine the base, in terms of current priorities as well as in terms of the effectiveness and performance of programs established in previous years.

In this regard, zero-base budgeting and sunset should not be conceived as all or nothing propositions, but rather as enhancing and expanding the ability of the Congress to make program changes and redirections when it so desires.

This more modest viewpoint of zero-base budgeting and sunset certainly is within reach.

How do you implement it?

At the outset we ought to make a clear distinction between zero-base budget practices, particularly as they have developed in the States, and sunset as it is now being considered in legislation pending before the Congress.

These are two related processes trying to achieve the same result—that is, the reexamining of what the government has already committed itself to do. But they take rather different paths, and the differences are very important in terms of their relevance to Congress.

Zero-base budgeting tends to be an executive process, carried out by agencies in the course of budget preparation. In the dozen states, approximately, which have thus far implemented zero-base budgeting, the activity is almost exclusively an executive one because state practices tend to more liberally enable the state legislature to obtain executive budget data than is the case on the federal level; the state legislature often is able to get the zero-base data. But the review is done by the executive agency, not by the legislature.

Sunset, as it is conceived in pending legislation, however, is largely a legislative process. It is pegged to the termination of statutory authorization of programs. The reauthorization of programs, which requires new legislation, is a legislative as opposed to an executive process.

A second important difference between zero-base budgeting and sunset is that zero-base budgeting excels primarily as a management tool. Its utility increases as you go down the organizational ladder . . . zero-base budgeting can be an effective device for encouraging managers responsible for particular activities and programs to take a new look.

That requestioning can continue upward in the organization, but it is not likely to be done in the same manner at the very highest level.

A governor of a state cannot do the priority ranking, or other techniques of zero-base budgeting, which would be appropriate at the lowest level.

Sunset, however, is exactly the opposite. It concentrates on the highest level of program aggregation—that is, programs as they are authorized by Congress—a health program, a medicare program, a housing program, an educational program, on and on down the list. Although there are apt to be hundreds of these programs which might be subject to reauthorization under sunset, these compare to the many thousands of discrete activities which might be identified separately under zero-base budgeting.

The third and most relevant difference for this committee is that zero-base budgeting is a budget process and sunset is a process which works in relation to but relatively independent of the congressional budget process.

Let me explain. Zero-base budgeting takes advantage of the action-forcing qualities of a budget process—you have to budget every year, you have an ability, therefore, to force on the table certain matters for consideration which otherwise might be neglected. This is one of the reasons why throughout modern governments budgeting has come to command such an important and central position in the making of public policy.

However, budget processes are very limited. They tend to assume that laws already on the books requiring the expenditure of funds will continue on the books. If public officials work only through the budget process and try to make changes in those laws, they often run up against difficulties.

The chairman, in his opening statement, referred to the 1-percent kicker which is a good illustration of this phenomenon. If you look only at the budget you quickly discover that you have to go outside that process if you want to deliver on the changes which the budget calls for. The reason is that the budget process, all budget processes—whether it be a congressional process, an executive process, one in a state, or one in a city—excels as a procedure for continuing government in operation. A budget is perhaps the greatest triumph of routine known to modern government.

Sunset, however, has the limitation that it is not directly linked to the budget process; it concentrates instead on authorizations. But by being liberated in some measure from the budget process, it focuses on those things which have to be done in legislation to deliver the changes which the budget process calls for.

For example, if in its congressional budget resolutions Congress were to decide to shift priorities in a variety of programs already established under law, it would take some change in authorizations to implement those new priorities voiced by the budget process. Sunset focuses on the authorization process; it thereby is legislative in character and deals with top policy issues. By comparison, zero-base budgeting focuses on the budget process, is largely executive, and primarily managerial.

However, there is an advantage in relating zero-base budgeting and sunset.

From the perspective of zero-base budgeting, the advantage is that in order to carry out the dictates of the budget process, you have to reach to legislation, particularly when the legislation already is on the books and mandates an expenditure.

However, there also is something to be gained from linking sunset to zero-base budgeting, because if we authorize without being sensitive to budgetary realities, we might merely perpetuate the appropriation-authorization gap which has grown up over the last decade or so.

One illustration of this problem can be gleaned from the programs run by the Office of Education. In a recent year, the authorization level was approximately $10 billion, the appropriation level was about $4 billion, a gap of $6 billion. One of the reasons why this gap exists is that currently there is no reason to be realistic at the authorization stage when dollar amounts are being considered.

Perhaps one of the virtues of linking zero-base budgeting to sunset would be to inject a measure of realism about the dollar costs when authorizations are voted by Congress. It is a hope, but this is something which some people might think is apt to be difficult to achieve, even with sunset.

Now, in implementing zero-base budgeting and sunset, Congress is faced with a series of problems which are reflected in a number of the bills now pending.

If Congress gives the main responsibility to the executive branch, it might be departing from the trend of initiatives and taking the responsibilities reflected in the Congressional Budget Act of 1974.

On the other hand, if Congress, through sunset, says that "we are going to do the evaluation, we are going to undertake the zero-base review of programs," then Congress will simply be overloaded. No matter how much you augment the staffs of Congress, there will be no way for Congress to carry on its own backs, or the backs of its committees, the task of reviewing over a three-, four-, or even a five-year cycle the hundreds of programs which would terminate and come up for reorganization under a sunset procedure.

This problem has been wrestled with extensively in the Senate—in S. 2925, which has identical and companion bills in the House. It is for this reason that S. 2925 has now gone through, I believe, half a dozen committee prints—trying to find a balance between executive and legislative responsibilities, a balance between the other demands already placed on Congress and its authorizing committees, and the new demands which would be established via sunset.

And to go back to my starting statement . . . [about] . . . a concept of sunset which attempts to review everything, as if all problems were equal in urgency, as if they all were equal targets of opportunity for change: We must strike a balance between this comprehensive review and a more selective sensitive attention to those particular programs where there is indeed an opportunity. For example, again referring to the 1-percent kicker, the Budget Committee could have looked at a much larger range of programs this year, but it looked at 1, 2, 5, 10 major problem issues. Regardless of how comprehensively zero-base budgeting or sunset is applied, it is going to be selective. You cannot look at everything.

Without going into details on the current version which is being considered, an attempt is being made to achieve these balances between executive and legislative responsibilities, between the other legislative responsibilities of authorizing committees, and those reported under sunset, and between comprehensive and selected review.

Most of the sunset bills—there are about three dozen of them pending before Congress right now, including duplicates—focus exclusively on the authorization process. There are two additional candidates for sunset in various bills which might merit consideration. First, the regulatory activities of the federal government. Although regulatory agencies and their activities would be covered by a general sunset law, rules and regulations tend to require a different perspective and a different kind of evaluation than programs which are primarily expenditure ones.

So there are various bills and proposals to orient sunset specifically to regulatory activities.

The second candidate for extension is tax expenditures. The Congressional Budget Act of 1974 opened up a new concept for Congress in addressing the relationship between tax expenditures and direct expenditures. For various purposes, tax and direct expenditures are substitutes for one another. Governments can accomplish the same public policy on the spending side or on the tax side.

Without judging proposals to sunset tax expenditures, let me just point out that the state of art with regard to tax expenditures is much less developed than it is with regard to direct expenditures. This is a new concept, and the process of identifying, pricing out tax expenditures, and understanding how they operate, is not yet as advanced as it is for direct expenditures.

In conclusion, let me look at how sunset would function if it were implemented.

Let's assume you have a program—I will play it safe and not name the program—costing $100 million a year, in which the law already establishes various requirements and authority—"The Secretary shall" et cetera, et cetera. With sunset, all the basic statutory language would remain in effect. Sunset would not require the reenactment of the entire United States Code every 5 years. That would be a total impossibility. Sunset would simply reach the authorization provision, that little piece of the total statute which says that funds are authorized to be appropriated. Sunset would pull the plug on the money for the program without changing directly or automatically the basic language in law.

Once, however, sunset terminates the authorization, Congress would have a smorgasbord of options on how to proceed.

Congress might merely reconsider the authorization provision—how much money, how long, for what purposes—and reenact it. Or it might decide to terminate the whole program because it is not worth spending additional money. Or it might decide to use the sunset of the authorization provision as a means of reaching more extensively to the language already in law. For a particular program, Congress might inquire: Is this what we want the Secretary to do, is that the authority and the discretion we want him to have, is this the purpose and objective that we wish to cast for the program?

In sum, on the surface sunset seems to be a uniform process, in practice it will turn out to be something rather different for each of the programs subject to it. And the differences will be the ones determined by Congress.

Thank you.

[The prepared statement of Mr. Schick follows:]

PREPARED STATEMENT OF ALLEN SCHICK

Mr. Chairman, I appreciate this opportunity to discuss the purposes and proposed applications of zero-base budgeting (ZBB, in shorthand) and sunset legislation. Although they used different procedures, zero-base budgeting and sunset share a common objective: to compel the periodic review of every federal program in order to determine whether it should be continued. These are complementary—not competitive—approaches; they can coexist as a comprehensive set of procedures for legislative and executive review of government programs and expenditures. Features of ZBB and sunset are combined in a number of bills now pending before the Congress. . . .

COMPARISON OF ZBB AND SUNSET

Zero-base budgeting and sunset take different paths to the same objective. The differences are not merely matters of mechanics but go to the relationships between the legislative and executive branches as well as to the role of the budget process in the making of government policies.

As it has been applied in the states, *ZBB is primarily a managerial tool for program operators rather than a policy process for top-level decision makers.* Each manager responsible for a discrete activity develops his decision packages and ranks them in order of priority. This initial step in ZBB occurs at the lowest level of an organization capable of formulating a budget proposal. Even in a medium-size government, there are apt to be hundreds, if not thousands, of these separate decision units. The decision units are then consolidated into broader priority rankings at successively higher levels of the organization, in the same manner as agency budgets are conventionally prepared. This consolidation and ranking process can continue until it reaches the chief executive, but it is not feasible at this top level to comprehensively consider and rank all of the packages and alternatives. Budget review at this level is likely to concentrate on a comparatively small number of policy issues, and one cannot be certain that these issues will be considered much differently than if they were processed under more conventional budget procedures. [Emphasis added.]

Sunset is likely to operate at a high level of program aggregation, on issues of major concern to policy officials. The center of attention in sunset is on a terminating provision of law or a cluster of laws. The process is anticipated to work in a fashion almost the reverse of ZBB, beginning with highest-level issues and then being disaggregated to more particular matters. Sunset can penetrate to the details of program implemenation, but these can be considered in the context of the policy issues pending before the legislature.

A second distinction between the two processes is inherent in their modes of operation. ZBB is a budgetary activity, cycled to the one-year (or, in some states, two-year) timetable of the budget process, and it possesses the distinctive opportunities and limitations of budgeting. ZBB takes advantage of the action-forcing characteristic of budgeting, but it also can become just another set of budgetary routines, an additional chore that agencies have to go through in order to get their money. Because of its budget connection, ZBB is likely to be germane only for agencies and programs in which money is a main determinant of performance.

Sunset is linked to broader law-making functions, though it, too, can be oriented to the need of all programs and agencies for funds in order to continue in operation. Most federal versions of sunset are tied to the authorization process in Congress, to the particular provisions of law which authorize Congress to appropriate funds for programs and agencies.

The most important difference between zero-base budgeting and sunset is that the former is primarily an instrument of executive budgeting while the latter necessarily is a legislative device. ZBB activity occurs during the preparation of the budget by government departments and agencies. The appropriations process need not be directly affected by the ZBB activities of the executive branch. By itself, ZBB would not necessarily enrich or alter the form or quality of data available to Congress. In a number of ZBB states, the legislature has been involved in the new process primarily because it already has a formal role in executive budget preparation. But in other states where executive budgeting is practiced, neither the content of the budget nor the form of appropriations has been affected by ZBB.

This issue is potentially more serious for Congress than it is for most state legislatures. In over half of the states, copies of agency budget requests are made available to the legislature, either when the request is submitted to the governor or at a later date. Most state legislatures, therefore, have access to the ZBB alternatives considered by the executive branch as well as to the priority rankings and at least some of the performance and analytic data marshaled by the agencies in support of their budget requests. Congress, however, generally obtains only the budget recommendations submitted by the president, though for an increasing number of programs and agencies it is managing to get agency estimates as well. If ZBB were introduced under this arrangement, Congress might be cordoned off from the consideration of alternatives and priorities by the executive branch.

The sunset process, by contrast, could be legislatively controlled, with congressional committees determining the kinds of reviews that should be conducted of expiring programs. The authorization process offers a broader scope for congressional participation and direction than does a ZBB process operated in the bowels of executive agencies.

RELATIONSHIP OF ZBB AND SUNSET

I have already noted that although the two approaches differ, they also have the potential to complement one another. Sunset can compensate for some of the limitations of ZBB and vice versa. The main limitation of ZBB is that of the budget process itself. No matter how thorough and objective an evaluation is made of a program, it simply might not be possible to shift funds from one use to another. In all governments, the budget process excels as a means of assuring continuity and stability in government; it works to smooth out the zigs and zags which might arise from political changes and other circumstances. One of the laudable aims of ZBB is to countervail against this static feature of budgeting, to encourage more change rather than inexorable continuation and growth of base programs. But it is not surprising that the few studies of ZBB in operation have suggested that it does not significantly affect the efficient allocation of a government's financial resources, that the content of the budget is not necessarily different after ZBB than before.

The federal budget offers a compelling explanation of why ZBB often fails to affect the allocation of resources. Almost $200 billion in new budget authority for fiscal 1977 is in the form of permanent appropriations which become available without any current action by Congress. Since Congress doesn't have to do anything in order for these permanent appropriations to be available for obligation, it is quite possible that their budget status will not be altered by ZBB. Much the same applies to the almost three-quarters of the budget which is officially classified by the Office of Management and Budget as "relatively uncontrollable under existing law." Without changes in basic legislation, these outlays will have to be made during fiscal 1977, even if a ZBB evaluation were to challenge their effectiveness. As a matter of fact, much of the remaining 25 percent of the budget also is not likely to be substantially impacted by ZBB because these funds go largely for salaries and other costs of operating the programs of the federal government. Perhaps the only segment of the budget where ZBB alone might make an immediate and substantial difference is in federal grants to state and local governments, and one must question whether the budget process should be biased in favor of only this type of change.

The budget process has two characteristics which impair its ability to convert ZBB reviews into budgetary outcomes. One of these is the fact that basic legislation often has to be modified in order to implement the ZBB findings; the other is that the budget process tends to fix its attention on the forthcoming fiscal year rather than on a larger-term view of things. Both of these problems can be ameliorated if ZBB is applied in tandem with sunset. Sunset goes to the basic legislation so that it can deliver the changes prompted by the zero-base budget. Moreover, most sunset schemes envision a multiyear authorization cycle, thereby liberating ZBB from the limitations of a one-year-at-a-time budget process.

But sunset has some problems of its own for which ZBB can bring relief. A significant number of the federal programs which now have multiyear authorizations experience what has come to be known as an authorizations-appropriations gap. Program authorizations for each year of the cycle are pegged at one level while appropriations often are made at a much lower level. This gap can make it difficult to establish realistic objectives for programs or to evaluate their results. If ZBB were coupled to sunset, it might encourage the authorization of programs at a level consistent with budgetary expectations. . . .

The CHAIRMAN. Thank you, Mr. Schick, for an excellent presentation.

I am personally very grateful to you for laying these points out for us. I have only one question. . . . I am concerned about your comment on the enormous amount of paperwork. We cannot review all these programs. We are overburdened now just doing the regular annual appropriations. . . . What do we do?

Mr. SCHICK. There are a variety of alternatives which have been considered. One is pilot testing. My own view is that where pilot testing has been tried, it has not worked, because agencies get the message that it really doesn't count. You are not in business when you pilot test.

A second option is to spread the sunset or the zero-base procedure over a number of years—2, 5, 7 years—as many as is deemed appropriate.

A third possibility is . . . as follows:

First, the sunset procedure applies to all programs of the federal government with certain exceptions like social security, retirement, and interests on the public debt.

Second, sunset is scheduled over a five-year period, so that, as the chairman just suggested, four functions might be up for review one year, two another year, two or four a third year, et cetera.

Third, the authorizing committees at the start of the sunset process would determine which programs up for termination in the next cycle would be given priority in their review.

In other words, they would file a formal report which would acknowledge: "We know everything has to be reauthorized, but we cannot look at everything, that is sheer impossibility. Therefore, for the next year, as we reevaluate the programs which are scheduled for termination, we will give priority to the following programs." As part of this setting of priorities of the agenda by the authorizing committees, they also would issue instructions to the executive branch agencies and to congressional support agencies, such as the GAO, the Congressional Research Service, and the others, as to the assistance and data which should be provided in the course of the next year, to enable Congress to do its job selectively.

Selectivity I believe offers the best hope of coping with what would otherwise be an impossible workload.

The CHAIRMAN. Thank you, Mr. Schick. . . .

Mr. LATTA. You mentioned in your statement that New Mexico had tried zero-base but had abandoned it. Can you give the reasons for this?

Mr. SCHICK. Yes. There were actually at least two reasons in New Mexico.

One was that about the second or third year that New Mexico was in zero-base budgeting, they had a huge budget surplus.

Mr. LATTA. That is good, isn't it?

Mr. SCHICK. Yes, but it is very hard to maintain the . . . budgetary discipline in this circumstance. Let me explain.

The instructions in New Mexico required state agencies to separately justify their programs as if they only would receive, I think, 75 percent of last year's level of expenditure. The state treasury had enough to fund them at perhaps 130 percent. Every one knew the 75-percent exercise was unrealistic. . . . That was one reason. A second reason is much more pervasive. Zero-base budgeting in some states has created an enormous amount of paperwork, perhaps because it has not been tried selectively enough, perhaps because of the techniques used in some of the states. The combination of surplus funds and concern about the extra paperwork led New Mexico to abandon it.

Mr. LATTA. You mean all the surplus they had the first year was eaten up in paperwork the second year?

Mr. SCHICK. Not quite in paperwork—in budget requests.

Mr. LATTA. I think that would be interesting to the taxpayers, not only in New Mexico, but in Ohio and other states as well, that if they would turn to that system, they would come up with a 25-percent surplus in 1 year. I think it is something that has to be tried. And I think it has to be tried by this Congress. You indicated that zero-base budgeting is something more for the executive branch rather than the legislative, whereas the sunset process is for the legislative branch.

I don't see it that way. I think we have a job to do on zero-base budgeting. I know the members of the Appropriations Committee could take on a certain responsibility. I think that a lot of these programs have to be looked into. As you indicated, they go on on the books, and they are never looked at again—only on the increase side; they want more money. And I think it is time that we do something about this, if we are ever going to get a handle on this budget. Everybody in Congress is hearing from back home. People believe the budget is out of hand. We have to cut it back. There is no doubt in my mind that we do have some programs that should be terminated. Let's take a look at them. If they cannot justify their existence, do away with them. . . .

Mr. GIAIMO. Mr. Schick, isn't the problem one of time? In effect, when you speak of zero-base budgeting, and when you speak of sunset, you are suggesting remedies to do something that we really should already be doing and that we obviously are not doing; isn't that correct? I mean when we go to evaluate the budget and enact appropriations, we should be looking at the total budget. And you are saying we do not. Under zero-base budgeting we would do this. Do you think the reason we do not is that we have overloaded the decision-making process and we cannot do it on a yearly cycle?

Are circumstances going to be any different under zero-base budgeting, or sunset? Aren't we going to have to have a great deal of additional staffing? And isn't that going to further complicate our problem?

What I am really asking you is, "What is going to make it work?" It sounds great. And we are all becoming enchanted by it, because we recognize the present unhappy situation that literally we are losing control over budgets because of their magnitude. But what is going to make it work? How is it really going to be different?

Mr. SCHICK. There is only one thing that can make it work, and that is the Congress of the United States. It is perfectly possible to have a zero-base budget system or sunset in operation, with the results the same as before. . . . But you are right that there is no automatic benefit to be delivered by these new techniques.

Mr. GIAIMO. What is the magic ingredient that is going to make us so much better under ZBB?

Mr. SCHICK. I think the best response is to say that Congress will still be selective, and it will sharpen the ability of Congress to make program changes when it wants to.

I want to avoid the overexpectation that Congress will look at everything every year, or every 5 years. Even if Congress had the time, it would not have the disposition to reopen every question, or every program issue.

All zero-base budgeting and sunset will do is to give Congress, for those programs where it wants to, a better opportunity to take a different tack and to change the course of the program.

Mr. GIAIMO. They really have that power now, don't they?

Mr. SCHICK. Not always.

Mr. GIAIMO. They certainly have the power right now to look at the total budget of any given agency.

Mr. Schick. Yes; but—

Mr. Giaimo. Isn't it a problem of time, that you have only enough time in the yearly budget cycle to examine the increases and add-ons, much less the basic programs?

Mr. Schick. That may be part of it. But I am optimistic.

Mr. Giaimo. And doesn't the same apply to the executive branch, when they are putting their budget together?

Mr. Schick. Well, no one asks about how the millions of hours of work are invested in the executive branch in preparing the current budget. My own view is that it is possible to combine zero-base budgeting with current executive practices in a way which does not overburden the Congress.

Mr. Giaimo. What evidence of success can you present to us?

Mr. Schick. I do not know. The only thing I can offer you is from a very recent survey of the states; there are approximately 11 states which already have experienced zero-base budgeting, and they are happy with it. I do not know whether they are happy because they are getting better results, or because they are marching under the banner. . . .

Mr. Giaimo. Is there any available evidence?

Mr. Schick. Yes; and the evidence is not favorable. The evidence suggests that if you merely do zero-base budgeting, attached to the budget process itself, the likelihood is that it may turn out with roughly the same results, the same amount proposed program by program that you would have in the absence of zero-base budgeting. And the reason why that occurs relates to what I said before about the difference between zero-base budgeting and sunset.

In the context of a budget process itself, it is very hard to make changes. Most changes which have to be made require changes in legislation. No matter what you put in the budget, unless you follow through with legislative changes, the spending will continue on the same course. This is one of the reasons why I think that sunset combined with zero-base budgeting might be a more appropriate approach than zero-base budgeting alone. . . .

Mr. Smith. You said that only Congress could make this work, and I agree with that.

But a study has shown that the average Member of Congress now works 59 hours a week, which means some of them must be working 70. And so Congress is only going to be able to do things like this and improve if it can operate more effectively and efficiently. And I submit that there is a culprit here that you did not mention, that goes in the opposite direction, really, and that is that we have too many annual authorizations. These authorizing committees in the last 10 or 12 years have gone to annual authorizations, and they are so busy passing an annual authorization that is already 6 months late, and they have to put in all kinds of hold harmless clauses, and they are so limited with what they can do with the program anyway, that they just barely keep their heads above the water. And it is not enough to talk about sunset, and having a maximum number of years, but in addition to that we are talking about a minimum number of years on these authorizations, perhaps 3 or something like that, so they can make some meaningful changes, and not be so hemmed in with "hold harmless" clauses and worrying about what is going to happen to some school district that has already made plans for next fall, and you are affecting them. We have to do something about minimum authorizations as well as maximum.

Mr. SCHICK. You are putting your finger, sir, on one of the most difficult and touchy problems here. On the one hand many committees complain of workload. On the other hand, they move toward annual authorizations which augment their workload. The attractiveness of annual authorizations—this has been the trend, as you pointed out—is that it enables Congress to pinpoint immediate and close control over executive agencies and actions. Congress can write into the annual authorization bill, if it wished, a variety of limitations on what an executive agency can do in the year ahead.

Now, I am a little skeptical as to whether the committees which have discovered the advantages to themselves of annual authorizations will readily surrender it in favor of a long-term sunset provision. Consequently, although you may be right that the most advantageous use of congressional time would be to create a floor and a maximum on authorization periods, it might not be possible to do. . . .

Mr. SMITH. Well, just to put it a different way, a little more succinctly perhaps, if Congress is to have the time to study the program that is going to be terminated unless it is extended, they are going to have to find the time somewhere, and to find the time they are going to have a minimum number of years on authorization, otherwise they will be buried in annual authorizations.

Mr. SCHICK. That is a very logical statement, yes, sir.

The CHAIRMAN. Thank you very much, Mr. Schick, for an excellent presentation. . . . Our next witness is Paul O'Neill, deputy director of OMB. Mr. O'Neill is here to present the administration's view on zero-base budgeting and sunset legislation. . . .

Again, the committee is pleased to have another recognized expert in budgeting procedures.

STATEMENT OF PAUL H. O'NEILL, DEPUTY DIRECTOR, OFFICE OF MANAGEMENT AND BUDGET

Mr. O'NEILL. Thank you, Mr. Chairman. . . . I appreciate the opportunity to testify before this task force.

We in the administration, following the president's strong leadership, are firmly committed to the stated purposes of these bills [H.R. 11734 and S. 2925]:

> To eliminate inactive, unnecessary, duplicative, or outmoded programs, and to see to it that every dollar of the taxpayer's money is spent as efficiently as possible to produce the best possible product.

The president's commitment to these purposes is fully demonstrated in his legislative and budget program. . . .

In turning more specifically to H.R. 11734 and S. 2925, I would first like to raise a caution. Perhaps growing out of too many years of experience, I am frequently reminded of one of H. L. Mencken's pithy observations. He said: "For every human problem there is a solution: neat, simple . . . and wrong."

That is not to suggest that you put aside the legislation you are considering. But it is intended to urge caution.

I believe a good case can be made for legislative action by observing the progress that has been made under the Congressional Budget Act. But at the same time our experience with the planning-programming-budgeting (PPB) systems of the 1960s suggests we proceed with great care. In my judgment, our experience with PPB demonstrates the problems that can be created with a rigidly specified system. Those of you who were close to it will recall, as I do, the mountains of paperwork it produced. One saving grace was the fact that it was a creature of the executive branch which we were able to redirect without legislative action, preserving its fundamental ideas while doing away with its process burden. And so, I think it is extremely important, as this legislation is considered, that we try very hard to say precisely what it is we think will be accomplished by its enactment and what its cost will be. In other words, we should apply the ideas of sunset and zero-base review in considering this legislation.

Last spring, in testimony before the Senate Government Operations Committee, we offered an analysis of S. 2925 in its original form, which at that time was identical to H.R. 11734. Those comments are, I believe, still valid and I have therefore attached them to my prepared statement.

There is one concern not covered by the attachment that I want to mention. It has become apparent that the program identification required to be made by the GAO under the existing bills may lead to a paperwork process that is mind-boggling—even by Washington standards. We have indications that the GAO approach may result in the identification of 20,000 or more programs. These programs would then become the basis for determining the number of reviews to be made and of objectives to be covered in the budget.

[The attachment referred to follows:]

EFFECT OF PROVISIONS OF S. 2925 [SUNSET LEGISLATION]

Some of the specific provisions of S. 2925 could work at cross-purposes with the basic intent of the bill. A discussion of some of these problems follows.

LIMITING AUTHORIZING LEGISLATION TO FOUR YEARS

Title I imposes a 4-year limit on authorizing legislation for most federal programs and activities. This means that these programs must be reauthorized every four years or be terminated. . . .

The provision ignores some realities. The functions of some agencies (as opposed to the efficiency with which these functions are carried out) are not subject to dispute. For example, there seems to be no disagreement that Justice must enforce federal laws, Defense must maintain the national security, and the Bureau of Census must count the population.

Tying the mandatory reauthorizations to the functional classification will insure that the programs in each category will be reviewed simultaneously. However, this does not provide for focusing review and reauthorization on government-wide issues that may cut across functions or subfunctions. In addition, it is unlikely that any fixed classification could provide for such focus. Use of the functional classification would also make restructuring of that classification more difficult to accomplish.

The processing and paperwork that would be required each year for those federal programs being reauthorized would be mountainous. The end result of this provision would be to divert time from focusing on those programs or activities for which changes should be made. The necessity to prepare detailed justifications and evaluations for all reauthorizations would impose an unnecessary workload and paperwork burden on those agencies whose functions are not subject to dispute and those agencies whose efficiency is not questioned.

The means already exist for concentrating our evaluation efforts on those areas for which they are most needed. The legislative committees of the Congress clearly have it within their power to specify that evaluation studies will be made in conjunction with new authorizing legislation or amendments and extensions of existing law. Moreover, the Government Operations Committees and Budget Committees would appear to have both the authority and the interest to suggest areas of study. Of course, the appropriations committees have a strong interest in program evaluation, too, but the horizon of the appropriations process is generally too short to encompass a complete evaluation cycle. This is not to say that progress reports to appropriations committees are not appropriate. Finally, the executive branch, particularly OMB, has ideas on where program evaluation is most needed and would welcome working with the Congress to develop program evaluation plans.

ZERO-BASE REVIEW AND EVALUATION BY THE EXECUTIVE BRANCH

Section 321 of the bill requires the executive branch to conduct zero-base review and evaluation every year for about a fourth of the federal programs. A very complex and technical evaluation would have to be conducted to assess the level of program quality and quantity that could be purchased at various expenditure levels. The results of the reviews conducted by the executive branch would be required to be transmitted to the Congress at the same time as the president's annual budget. To accomplish this each year in connection with the annual budget would either very seriously degrade the quality of the regular budget review of the programs not subject to zero-base evaluation, or it would require significantly greater resources and more time than [are] now available for the budget review process.

If the type of zero-base review and evaluation defined in . . . the bill is to be made, program impact levels must be measured accurately—in terms of service output—and related to resource inputs in terms of incremental amounts of budget authority. The initial program analysis and evaluation of this bill coupled with the reauthorization process will suffer the same data and paperwork problems experienced for the Planning-Programing-Budgeting system in the late 1960s. It proved impossible to use effectively the considerable amount of information provided by that system.

The magnitude of this task for most, if not all, programs can be illustrated by the following example of a two-step process.

Step 1: Measurement of Effort. Determination of the program impact of a specific level of budget authority is frequently so difficult that it is virtually impossible to anticipate how much time it will take to have useful results.

An excellent, though not extraordinary, example of these problems is provided by an elaborate evaluation of Title I of the Elementary and Secondary Education Act (ESEA). The measurement instruments for this evaluation are now undergoing tests. Title I of the ESEA is aimed at meeting the special needs of educationally disadvantaged children. The evaluation study is expected to take 7 years—at a cost of approximately $7 million for the first 2 years. Design and measurement techniques in such an evaluation present a formidable task due to the diversity of projects that have been undertaken under Title I. State and local educational jurisdictions have taken highly varied and individualized approaches in designing corrective programs for the educationally disadvantaged. Moreover, the measurement of educational attainment is clouded by the absence of standard tests for which there is agreement among educators as to their validity, and by the unavailability of adequate comparison groups. All of these uncertainties about the success of this long-term expensive evaluation project are set against a background of previous efforts, which frequently have been unable to demonstrate conclusive evidence concerning the effect of such special educational programs. The difficulty and expense of measuring program effects is not to be taken lightly.

Step 2: Production Functions. Even if these vexing measurement problems can be solved—and we are constantly seeking solutions—true zero-base review and evaluation as outlined in the bill require a good deal more. [They require] relating such efforts to varying dollar and employment levels.

Even with more program impact data than it is reasonable to expect, the development of such production functions would be a challenging analytical task in itself. It is likely that sophisticated mathematical models will be required. We are not aware that such techniques have been successfully developed for any significant social programs, not because of a lack of will on the part of those who have attempted to develop them but because of the great methodological difficulties inherent in them and excessive costs alluded to previously.

At this point, it is not more evaluations but better evaluations that are needed.

There are also reservations to the indiscriminate use of the zero-base technique. This technique may be inappropriate to many federal programs, and in such cases less complex, less detailed techniques may better serve the purpose while at the same time requiring fewer resources. A study was made of the indiscriminate use of zero-base budgeting for a whole agency, the Department of Agriculture, some years ago. In the view of one writer a major conclusion of this study was that:

> . . . The main result was a mountain of paperwork. The experiment failed both because no one could figure out how to make the comparisons and because no one was willing and able to make the drastic reallocations that would have been required.

It is doubtful that the basic purpose of this bill is best served by requiring in law that across-the-board zero-base evaluations be performed every four years. The resultant lack of flexibility may not be worth the added emphasis that a statute would provide. It may be that despite its noble intent, enactment of the bill as presently written would cause more harm than good. It would so systematize a very complex and sensitive process and so diffuse our current efforts to encourage quality evaluations that it might cause a net loss of usable data to evaluate and manage federal programs.

Nothing now prevents either the executive branch or the appropriate legislative committees from conducting zero-base reviews and evaluations of the basic purposes and functions of agency programs.

The Congress should allow the heads of agencies to work with the authorizing committees to determine where evaluations are needed as well as their frequency. It should be possible to impose a discipline without the rigidities and inefficiencies involved in taking the across-the-board statutory requirement approach.

ANNUAL OBJECTIVES INCLUDED IN THE PRESIDENT'S BUDGET

[The bill] . . . requires that the President's budget include specific annual objectives for each federal program or activity and an analysis of how the objectives set forth in previous budgets were met. In addition, [it requires] that the President and the Congress specify—in quantitative terms—the objectives of the programs and activities as part of the four-year reauthorization process.

Considerable care must be taken in the proper development of performance measures. Otherwise, these measures often show how busy people are rather than the cost benefit of their activity. The development of a meaningful performance measurement requires significant managerial effort and reorientation. In addition, the maintenance of the process requires that Congressional and executive decisions be based on these analyses or the process will be discredited.

This effort would be staggering. There are more than 1,000 federal domestic assistance programs alone. The amount of information to be included in the President's budget would be so great that detailed analysis by the OMB and agency staff would necessarily give way to "pro forma" examination. OMB policy officials could not possibly do an adequate job of reviewing such a large mass of material and devote the time and effort required during the already overloaded budget review process. Agency accounting systems, many of which are computer-based, would have to be redesigned and reprogrammed. These crushing data requirements would be superimposed on those added by the Congressional Budget and Impoundment Control Act, which have stretched the abilities of OMB considerably. The requirements of [the bill] are more—much more—than the system should be expected to meet.

OVERLAPPING WORK BY THE LEGISLATIVE AND THE EXECUTIVE BRANCHES

The bill requires evaluations to be conducted by Congressional committees, the GAO, the CBO, and the executive branch. . . . A great deal of overlap would be inevitable. An alternative is to reach an understanding on the design of the evaluation—which should be fully coordinated at the start—then have either the executive or the legislative branch conduct the evaluation and avoid duplication of effort.

SUMMARY

The development of an effective process that provides a systematic mechanism for periodic full-scale review and evaluation of federal programs is complex and difficult.

Legislation that provides the flexibility that is needed to make the process work could well be too broad to be meaningful. On the other hand, specificity in the legislation could result in an unduly restrictive and inflexible approach. Rather, it would appear that legislation is not necessary to accomplish needed evaluations.

A more fruitful approach would be to reach agreement with the appropriate legislative committees on a limited number of major program areas that should be evaluated, develop cooperatively a study design for evaluating the programs included in those areas, and then work closely together to make certain that the studies are completed on schedule. OMB could suggest program areas for these committees to consider. It would also make a great deal of sense if the legislative committees were to impose evaluation requirements whenever new programs are instituted or the authorizations for old ones are extended.

This approach differs considerably from the plan outlined in the bill. But it should be possible to find a more appropriate way to accomplish the objectives of this bill without a legislated mechanical and inflexible approach.

The CHAIRMAN. Thank you very much Mr. O'Neill. I have only one question, . . . the same one that I directed to Mr. Schick. My experience in working with the budget process this year, last year, and the year before leads me to a certain amount of caution such as you mention. I don't want to see a big mountain of paper come up here and when we are finished have the same result we get now. I need to know your suggestions for alternative ways to trigger or select under this process. . . .

Now if we enshrine this into a statute of selective process what are your suggestions as to what is possible? I don't want to overpromise and underproduce in this area.

Mr. O'NEILL. . . . I certainly agree with your concerns, and perhaps it would be helpful to start back up the logic stream someplace and talk about what it is this bill seeks to do that is different from what we are now doing.

I think frankly many of those who have talked with such fervor about sunset and zero-base review haven't any idea what the executive budget process is all about. . . .

In the years I have been in the executive branch I cannot recall one when the sum of spending suggested to the President when he was beginning to formulate his budget was not more than $20 billion or $30 billion more than prudent people would reasonably believe should be spent by the executive branch. Given that circumstance, which I frankly do not see changing very dramatically over the next 10 or 15 years, *I think the executive branch is always going to be in a position where it must in effect do zero-based budgeting.* [Emphasis added.]

We do not have a choice because spending demands on the President overwhelm the amount which fiscal policy indicates can reasonably be spent. I think you see the proof of that in the short list of examples in my prepared statement.

Many of the reform, restructuring, and elimination proposals that have been made by the President were not easy proposals to make. It would have been much easier to take the easy road and say, "Let's fund all of these things and not offend any interest groups or any committees or any of the other interested parties that have some attachment to these things."

But I think without regard to partisan politics, Presidents have had to, and will have to in the future, practice zero-based budgeting.

If you agree with me in that assessment then it seems to me the correct question is: What is it we are trying to accomplish with this legislation? . . .

Let me give you an example where the Congress has not been very interested in asking questions that need to be asked. It is one I know you have some experience with. That is, the Public Health Service hospital program, a program created in 1789 when admittedly we had a limited number of hospitals available in the country and we had a problem with our merchant marine bringing infectious diseases back into the country. We had a relatively low-paid merchant marine. So we thought we ought to have a special hospital care system to take care of those people and those problems. In spite of the fact we have a merchant marine that is rather handsomely paid by comparison with most other people in the economy and the fact that we have thousands of general hospitals which can take care of people and we know how to deal with infectious diseases, we still have eight Public Health Service hospitals run by the government for a purpose that escapes me. And yet, in spite of efforts beginning in 1965 with Lyndon Johnson, we have not been able to stop doing that job.

As I say, I think if this bill were successful in doing what it proposes to do, we would stop doing that, but only if this legislation were truly to cause the Congress to ask the question, "Why are we doing this at all?"

It frankly is not clear to me with all the ins and outs of the data requirements and the procedural requirements for canceling programs that that essential purpose will be accomplished by this legislation. That is to say, that the right questions will be asked which will lead to the elimination of outmoded, duplicative, or unnecessary programs.

The CHAIRMAN. Thank you very much. I am concerned about it because of what I see occurring in the budget process this year. In a democracy you must learn from the way a process proceeds, not from some theory of what you thought or hoped it was going to do or anything else. What I see occurring is this. There are many programs already in place through either permanent legislation or because they are in areas where they have enormous political clout—and I use that again in a nonpartisan sense. When you place a ceiling on some programs as we do in the budget process, these other long-lived programs survive at the expense of the programs that are required to be appropriated each year. . . .

I am trying to determine a way to make it fair for all programs that are faced with the ceiling. I would appreciate your answer.

Mr. O'NEILL. Mr. Chairman, I have thought about it quite a bit. We have been in discussions with the Senate Government Operations Committee that has been looking at this legislation since they began last February, and frankly I have come to the conclusion there is no mechanical way we can force people to ask the right questions.

To take your example, GI bill benefits for postwar volunteer armed services people: It is not clear to me that the fact of the sun setting on the GI bill program would lead to a different result than the one you suggest we may be faced with this year. That is to say, there is nothing in the notion of sunset that will cause the members of the committee to ask why are we doing this, and there is nothing in the sunset idea to force them to ask public witnesses to come forward to say that this is a rotten idea.

It really does seem to me that trying to solve what I agree is a very fundamental public problem right now doesn't seem to be subject to the kind of mechanical process that is suggested by these bills. . . . I don't think there is anything built into this legislation the way it has been drafted, nor has anyone identified a way to insure that members ask witnesses who come before them, "Why are we giving you any money at all?" When the witness says, to take a narrow example, "Because we have an infant mortality problem in the country," to press beyond that and say, "All right, I agree with you, infant mortality is too high, we are 13th in the world in our rates. You tell me how the dollars you are proposing to be spent in this program are going to have a direct and decided effect on the problem of infant mortality. Then tell me, Mr. Witness, how it is that we prevent the dollars the Congress appropriates for this infant mortality program from simply replacing dollars that are being spent by state or local governments or by the private sector so that we can see what is going on in the national sense."

One of the difficulties we have had for many years in the way we approach budgeting in this country from a federal level is an egocentric view that says if we appropriate $200 million for some purpose, that adds $200 million to the margin as to what the country is spending in totality. I think you can look at program after program and be hard put to draw the conclusion that dollars appropriated from the federal till actually end up being 100-cent dollars by the time they were spent through our society. We have been kidding ourselves.

Looking at the witnesses' testimony before committee after committee, I find very, very infrequently any indications where the witnesses are put on the spot beyond the kind of superficial first question I suggested.

The CHAIRMAN. Thank you very much. . . . The committee will now hear from Peter Pyhrr who implemented the Georgia State government budgeting process. We are most interested since this is a case where zero-based budgeting has worked. . . .

STATEMENT OF PETER PYHRR, VICE PRESIDENT, ALPHA WIRE CO.

Mr. PYHRR. Thank you very much. . . . What I would like to do is relate to you some of my experiences with zero base and use that as a framework to addressing two main problems which I think all of you have addressed here today. . . .

Let me drop back to draw perspective to give you a feeling of how zero-base budgeting works, how it was designed, where it has succeeded in most areas, why it has failed in others. At the end of my text I will go back to New Mexico, with which I am well familiar.

Zero-base budgeting, the way the process is now known, is really sort of a new animal originating at Texas Instruments in 1968. Texas Instruments is a large electronics manufacturer. Over a long number of years they have been known as being a textbook case for business schools around the country because of their well-advanced management systems, which were predicated on the high-technology type of the industry.

So Texas Instruments started out before my relationship with them, and before the development of zero-base budgeting, as a company that was already noted for its excellent planning and budgeting systems. But I think what tends to happen in those high-technology companies is they develop even better systems to do a job. Prior to the development of zero-base budgeting we followed the incremental budgeting approach. In some years we looked at decreases from the prior budget, in other years increase. Obviously, during all these times of either increase or decrease on a selective basis because of management understanding and feel of the organization, we would selectively go in and basically do a thorough review of selected program areas.

So when people as knowledgeable as Paul O'Neill, and many other people I have talked to since we started zero base, point to examples of areas they have gone in and done a review, I will certainly agree that in selective areas a thorough review has been done. But in my experience, I categorically disagree that the majority of programs, the majority of questions, have been raised.

This has been true from when I started at T.I., when everybody said, "Why do this zero-base budget?"

The answer is we have only done a zero-base review in very selected areas. What the zero-base approach tends to do in a systematic manner is review all operations, review the expenditures, of which the majority . . . are in the so-called base of ongoing operations. What we are trying to do is develop a process which basically said two things: No. 1, the budgeting process has to be the focal point of most management analysis and decision making because this process determines how the resources get allocated. Any pragmatic manager knows he should spend his time and effort in something that will produce results, and the budgeting process results in getting money. . . .

Zero base tries to identify the whole iceberg rather than just the tip. In listening to Paul O'Neill, I disagree on some points in the criticism that Congress does not ask the right questions. I would say I agree Congress does not ask all the right questions, as well as OMB. I would also say in agencies all the right questions are not asked because people do not have the information with which to ask questions on all programs.

Also with a feel the Congress may have or the President may have or agency directors may have, they have predetermined problem areas . . . they may wish to select. Part of this may be on specific problems that arise. . . . But my contention is that there are a great deal of problems which never surface, and the purpose of zero-base budget is to try to surface these questions for review at all levels, of which the first level has to be within the agency.

Problems may also be raised at the Presidential level or OMB or in the Congress, but I think the majority of these questions have to surface out of the agencies in some way so that existing staffs at all levels of government can handle the analysis and paperwork.

I will get into the question of selectivity and paperwork in a minute, but I would like to drop back and talk a little more about the practical implementation of zero-base budgeting. . . .

There are two basic users of zero-base budgeting. The first user that I will mention is to me the key user and probably has the longest-term and most beneficial impact in either government or industry. That is the man responsible for operating the program or activity. . . . This is why this budgeting was developed at Texas Instruments, not the president or board of directors level. Zero base was developed in two operating divisions because we had problems that we could not address through the typical management or budgeting techniques. [Emphasis added.]

I think what we found in the state of Georgia, selective agencies in the state of Illinois, most other states which are now starting to use the process, and in most industries, [is that] *zero base is primarily an operating tool of your line managers.* [Emphasis added.]

I think part of this gets into the question of workload. The question that has been raised continuously is, how can the existing staffs in the Congress—and I will expand that to include the executive, OMB, and all the large agencies—handle the clerical tasks of trying to identify what is happening, what the alternatives are, how efficient and how effective the programs are. The answer is, no staff at any level can answer all these questions. What we have found is the man who is most knowledgeable, and actually can provide many innovative suggestions if he is given the opportunity and the challenge of doing so, is the man who knows the problem and who has operational responsibility for the program. To me, it should be his basic function, if not the most important one, to effectively plan and evaluate his program.

So one of the questions is the workload question. What we are trying to do is take that workload of 90 percent to identify what is happening and put that workload on the program manager where it belongs. We can then free the existing staffs to spend the majority of their time on analysis.

For example, when we were working in the state of Georgia, I happened to spend a lot of time [on] mental health institutions and prisons because these were the toughest areas to get at and the toughest to evaluate. We found that we had many problems within the institutions that typically never surfaced. What happened is that over a period of years there was an inflationary increase to some of the institutions. One of the favorite strategies in any state or in federal government tends to be to run the press through the institution prior to appropriations or authorization hearings. Part of what we found in Georgia and Illinois, throughout institutions in all levels of government, city and state, is that in many cases the cries of inadequate rehabilitation services [were] absolutely true. But part of the redirection that has happened in zero-base budgeting, which doesn't always appear at the surface and is not always at a conscious level of top-level executives and legislative bodies, is that *there can be massive redistributions within institutions, pulling unnecessary maintenance costs out and redirecting these same moneys into more effective and additional services.* [Emphasis added.]

For example, in the *Milledgeville* case they got the traditional inflationary increase. However, rehabilitation increased by four times throughout the institution. We found this happening throughout the states, whether they were mental health or prison institutions. So part of the benefits that occur from zero base are really subsurface [and] may not approach the congressional level of decision that has to be made.

What zero base will certainly do in the long term, it will tend to reduce the inflationary nature of spending in those areas.

Now, the second use of zero-base budgeting is certainly at the top-level management of whatever organization you are talking about. In industry, it is at the division level, the presidential level, the board of directors. Certainly in government I will put into that category of top management, if you will forgive me, both executive and legislative bodies because both really have the same problem. Both have certainly different viewpoints but have limited resources by which to get down and discover what is happening with the agencies and evaluate the effectiveness of the programs and efficiency of the expenditures.

We are taking a look at another set of users. In my mind, the zero-base budgeting is an internal agency mechanism which basically identifies program efficiency and effectiveness, takes a look at different ways to deliver similar services. This internal agency analysis leads to a macroeconomic summary for the top-level executive analysis. This macroeconomic summary basically focuses at direction of resources and a macroeconomic program evaluation. So I see this process as a feeding mechanism, the basis of the data coming from the agencies, being summarized at agency levels and presented to the executive and legislative committees.

However, there is total independence of OMB, the President, the Congress, to disagree with policies, to disagree with some of the analysis presented. But I think the Congress and OMB will find [that] with this information provided to them, they can much more effectively select those issues which they wish to focus their time on.

In the workload question I should also add that in my experience, in any industry or any state government that has implemented zero-base budgeting, there has been no additional increase in staff. The only qualification is in Georgia: In each case I was added for a period of about 9 months. We decided at that stage to implement the process throughout the whole state the first year.

So I think that what we have found at all staff levels is that the budget staffs have determined that zero-base budget is one of the most powerful tools they could ever be given, primarily because it surfaced so many questions and so many problems within the agencies that they could now focus their attention on the problem areas rather than being inundated with reams of numbers which they did not know how to evaluate.

The disappointing thing about some of those reams of numbers that tend to boggle the mind of anyone at this level of government—certainly in the Congress or OMB, and . . . in the big agencies—is that the reams of numbers do not focus on the key policy issues or program delivery issues. So the agencies have a problem, the problem is compounded at higher levels, at OMB and Congress, so what we are trying to do is develop a system which will not add significantly to any staffs but will provide a system which is an ongoing management process developed primarily in the agencies with the overview at both OMB and congressional levels.

What we are trying to do with zero base is develop an analysis, and if you can take a look at the components of the analysis which are identified in the Senate bill, it is basically a macroeconomic view of what would happen at lower organization levels within the agencies. The two critical elements of zero-base budgeting [are] an analysis that we call a decision package, and the . . . setting of priorities. Those priorities which have initially been set at the agency levels can obviously be modified at either OMB or congressional levels. The key is the analysis in what we call the decision package, which does a variety of things, none of which are new. The main difference is that the analysis has been wrapped together in a process which is a little bit broader than the traditional budget process, which tends to be a numbers-oriented clerical task, a process which brings in several components, such as identification and establishment of objectives (which should identify duplicate programs which may tend to serve the same constituencies); description of the proposed programs; quantitative workload performance measures (what kind of population has a given program been serving, how effective has it been in program delivery?).

There are two key items in the decision package analysis. One is an identification of alternatives of different ways of program delivery—taking a look at the best way of delivering services. In this process what we have done is given the incentive to program managers to identify the best way to deliver the program, whether this be the method that has been going on for the last 50 or 100 years or a new method.

What we found in this analysis—and what I think [is] a major advantage, as viewed from program managers who may have had the tendency of telling the administration for years and years "We are not getting the money's worth and we ought to redirect the program" and therefore become quite often disillusioned—[is] that they now have a golden opportunity to identify and commit to improving a program, changing method of delivery, improving perhaps cost-effectiveness as well as delivery. They are going to stand behind those recommendations, and they have a ready opportunity to make those recommendations and changes.

The other thing that we are going to look at is different levels of funding, of which one level is obviously zero. What happens if we eliminate the program? However, being pragmatic people, we know we will find a few of those, but certainly we are not going to eliminate the majority of government programs. What we may want to do is reduce the program level, either because the workload has decreased or because we have started to solve problems. What tends to happen is that you keep the same staff that existed at the peak of the problem. . . .

So we want to take a look at a level of funding less than current. In doing this, in taking a look at different cost levels and different benefits we receive from those cost levels, we now have a large variety of alternatives in which the agencies can recommend their priorities—priorities can be reviewed or modified by both OMB and the Congress.

Once we have an analysis of each program and activity, we come to a ranking process by which we want to find out where different levels of organizations wish to spend their funds. Since we have a limited amount of funds, *we have often found that agencies have come up with rather major shifts in where they want to spend their money.* They might want to take funds out of an area where the problem has been reduced, or because of changes in policies or priorities they wish to reduce funding in order to fund today's current problem. [Emphasis added.]

Agencies can fund today's current problem and address it partially or even wholly by reducing or eliminating those programs which are now no longer justified in the set of priorities.

How do we review all this? How do we take some decision packages which identify a very sophisticated . . . analysis, how do we then review these and the priorities set by the agencies?

I said in the beginning I don't think any of us are smart enough to know before we take a look at an area all the questions to ask. I don't think anybody is that smart in the Congress, or in the OMB, or in the agencies.

I think what we have found is as these decision packages and priorities have surfaced, many, many questions have popped to the surface that no one anticipated. For example, in Jimmy Carter's first review, which is our first experience with such a massive volume, we found the budget staff at the state was very capable in its preliminary working analysis with the agencies to identify the key policy issues and questions which should have been raised. I think all major organizations work this way in some degree because you cannot at this level look at everything in a major organization. So what you are basically doing is giving the staffs a tremendous base of information which they can spend 90 percent of their time analyzing, rather than only 10 percent analyzing and 90 percent fact finding, to identify not only the issues they have been directed to investigate, but other issues which will work their way out of the woodwork as problem areas.

Many of these problems will be identified and highlighted by the agencies. . . .

In going back to Allen Schick's comments on what expectations we should have, should such a process as presently envisioned come into being, I think what we have found is *the zero-base review or budgeting process is an evolutionary process.* We are not adequately knowledgeable of all programs to begin with, and we will raise many, many questions which we will not be able to immediately resolve. [Emphasis added.]

What we have done is focus on those questions and tried to come up with a solution which may be accomplished during the immediate year before the budgets are finalized, or more frequently over a period of years.

I think a very interesting example, and satisfying example to me, relates to something I heard in Illinois 3 years after my Georgia experience. When we were first in Georgia, the first year of Jimmy Carter's administration, we did exactly what I said, raised a lot more questions than answers. One of the questions we raised was in the welfare area in the social-services programs, where we had no data or mechanism to evaluate workload and performance of social-services programs throughout the state. We had had the problem, didn't have any answers, which put us in sort of a tough position to make budgetary decisions. We set aside some money to try to develop a social-service recording system to identify where these millions of dollars were spent, and how effectively. I happened to be doing work about three years later in the state of Illinois, where they have installed zero-base budgeting throughout their correctional system and were testing it in their welfare department. I ran into a major project effort which was funded by HEW that was installing a social-service reporting system around a variety of states throughout the United States. The model they were using for this was Georgia. So what we did in Georgia was identify the problem. We didn't have a solution, but knew it was worthwhile to get the answers, so we set aside appropriate moneys. In the long-term attempt it was a very excellent investment and was used as a model throughout many states.

The other thing that I would like to discuss, which was raised during Allen Schick's testimony, is what happened in New Mexico. It failed there. I think . . . we need to take a look at the weak points as well as the strengths of a system and learn from others' mistakes to make sure we don't repeat them.

What happened in New Mexico is a classic example of what can happen when the executive agencies are pulling in one direction and the legislative in another. I will come back and emphasize this point in my summary.

In New Mexico you had a strong legislative budget staff who wanted to implement zero-base budget, and an executive staff that did not want to. Therefore the agencies were given two completely different sets of budget instructions, and they had to prepare two budgets. I pity the agency managers who had to do that.

One of the reasons of it failing was that the main proponent in the legislature retired in about the second year of implementation. So some of the basic incentives on the legislative side were reduced, and all of the problems therefore overwhelmed the process.

The other part of the problem was maybe a technical one, but a significant one nonetheless, and that is the way the process was physically administered . . . the design of the forms and budget manuals was extremely poor. Although it is perhaps not the appropriate question to address at this level, I think as in any system, effective design of a system—if it is a good system—will help it succeed. The ineffective design of a good system will almost surely result in failure. As we take a look at the implementation [of] both the sunset law and the zero-base review in the federal government, I think we need to keep these points very much in mind.

What I am encouraged to see so far is that there appears to be strong support, bipartisan support, in the legislature for this type of program. I think this type of program needs bipartisan support. It should not be a Democratic system versus a Republican system. I think also as we get into this, if it is to work, it must be embraced both by the legislature and the executive so that we have one system in the United States that everyone will learn to use, rather than a multitude of systems of which some people use one system, some use another.

What happens in the agencies is that different systems absolutely kill them. It gets them involved in a paperwork machine that will doom the best of processes to failure.

Also, in designing the paperwork system I have a great sensitivity, because I have been at the other end of the stick on the workload end, to insure that the amount of paperwork is reduced. I think that everybody has mentioned this problem, and it is a very valid concern. *However, when we take a look at whether zero-base budgets produced more paperwork, we have to compare it with the paperwork which already exists,* and my experience is that it has not produced more paperwork. In some cases it has saved a great deal of paperwork, but this saving was predicated on revising some other systems which were duplicative or which were not justified after zero base has been introduced. So there has been a very conscious effort in all my experiences to reduce other paperwork considered nonproductive. So in total we have reduced the amount of paperwork. [Emphasis added.]

Also within the agencies, once you talk to some of the people at the program levels and below, what we find out in the budgeting systems is that there are a variety of systems within agencies that are different among agencies. If you talk to some of the program people they may have two systems they budget: One they use internally, and one they pass to the top of the agency.

There are a variety of systems. To successfully implement zero base you must eliminate those duplicative systems, and in some cases conflicting systems, with a comprehensive zero-base system which can be designed to meet the needs of each agency. There is nothing that says one set of forms or instructions needs to be used in each agency because we have found in states around the country, or among different agencies, there are slightly different needs which we allowed each agency to incorporate to meet their internal needs as well as the needs of the executive or legislative branches.

That takes care, I believe, of paperwork. Let me go to the workload of the staff question. I will repeat a comment that I made previously, that to my knowledge *none of the states or none of the industrial organizations that have implemented zero-base budgeting have added significantly to their staffs*. With the amount of information developed by the agencies the staffs can then use this information and cover a much wider ground in the same period of time, selectively identifying those areas which they wish to focus on. [Emphasis added.]

I think the selectivity question is a natural evolutionary process and I have found that staffs have felt much more comfortable with zero base because they can spend the majority of their time picking out policy issues they wish to focus on rather than mere fact finding, which is the bulk of [what] most staffs usually spend their time on in the traditional budgeting process.

I think that zero-base budgeting has a variety of incentives, and to implement such a system in such a massive bureaucratic organization as the federal government, we need a variety of incentives, some of which are carrot and some of which are stick.

I believe that the proposed legislation has some of both. I believe that zero base offers a major incentive to management within the agencies. Rather than looking at zero base as a negative or a threat—which happens in some areas and maybe is the initial reaction to a process such as zero base, which challenges what has gone on in the past and does not automatically assume everything in the past is well and good—there are many managers throughout government who want to do an effective job. They have good ideas. What zero base does is provide an incentive for them and an opportunity to evaluate their programs in a positive sense, to make changes, to increase their program effectiveness, and to have a say in what they do, how they do it, and what their priorities should be.

I think one of the biggest frustrations of any manager trying to do his best job is that he cannot impact the system. He gets locked into a system that over a period of time, if he cannot change, does one of two things: He leaves or he gets indifferent to the system itself and to the job he is trying to do.

I think a zero-base system can be an incentive. We are not looking in government to using a system to eliminate or fire government employees, although it may be used that way in some businesses. Both in industry and government the predominant feeling is to take areas where programs have been reduced and take those funds and people and transfer them into other programs which are increasing in scope, or to replace turnover.

In Georgia, Governor Carter made a decision he would not fire government employees. The majority of some major organizational changes and some major redirections of programs and funds from one program into another were accomplished through a variety of methods. The major method was transferring people from one program area into another where there were comparable skills; No. 2, retaining where possible. No. 3, turnover took its fair toll. No. 4, after all those alternatives, what we did was redline positions, saying on an ongoing basis, once this position turns over, it will not be refilled.

So hopefully these types of implementation procedures will eliminate the threat of job loss of an employee who is doing his best to perform, and will show him only the side which says here is a mechanism to give you a better tool to do a better job and to have a major say in how a program should be implemented.

On the stick side of it, which we also need a bit of to counteract those forces which do not like to see changes, I think we have a stick in the sunset provision. The stick is one on both the executive and the legislative bodies that says that over a certain period of time we are going to force ourselves to zero an authorization and reconsider. I think that this is a tremendous incentive to make all of us review programs on a systematic basis. It is a tremendous incentive and reinforcement for zero base because agencies will know they have to present a well thought-out case to have their authorization approved or to generate the authorization from zero. This is a tremendous incentive for any manager, for any individual, to do a good job to present his case.

Obviously even with this we are still not taking away the independence. Although we may have one zero-base budgeting system used in the executive and agency levels, this does not take away any independence of the groups because although we are providing an analysis which in some cases may be biased by the agencies, we have the energies to go back and challenge those biases.

We have the information to pick out key policy issues which are stated and recommended that individuals may disagree with, so that there is no mechanism built into this system which says we cannot go back to the agencies or we do not have the information to overturn policy recommendations coming out of the agencies or coming out of OMB. So I think the legislature does not lose anything in working with the executive for one uniform process for the federal government, but I think the process of zero-base review is sort of a macroeconomic program review for the OMB and legislative level.

The zero-base budget, which is more of a micro review, and the zero-base review are all self-supporting systems. Each system, in and of itself, lends to the success of the other systems. So I think that what Congress is presented with is a workable package, which can succeed with some intelligent and well thought-out management of the process, which is needed for any system to succeed. I think the basics are there, and from my employment as a professional manager and as an individual who has had an opportunity to be deeply involved in this, and also as a taxpayer, I think that the package that is being proposed is a very workable one. With the good efforts of people throughout the federal government, the Congress and executive branch, the agencies which will bear the brunt of the analysis responsibilities, it will be a very workable system.

The CHAIRMAN. Thank you very much, Mr. Phyrr, for an excellent presentation.

Mrs. HOLT. I think you have spelled out your views very well.

One thing I would like you to repeat for me very briefly was your example of the *Milledgeville* case.

Mr. PYHRR. Milledgeville was the biggest mental health institution in Georgia. When I was there, I believe, it had 7,000 patients. It was, from a political standpoint, what I might term a hot potato. It was a very sensitive subject. With limited resources throughout the whole mental health program throughout the state, there is really a question of No. 1, how much are we going to spend and No. 2, where are you going to spend it. The way the final result came out in Milledgeville, the first year I was there, they got approximately the same amount of money they had traditionally: a 6- or 7-percent increase. What we did is we increased by a magnitude of 4 times the amount of rehabilitative services that institution provided per patient by reorienting some moneys from other operations into rehabilitation. I give you an example in the area of pathology. Doctors are very sensitive when you get into medical areas. When we got there they had three pathologists.

I know absolutely nothing about pathology, but in comparing Milledgeville to other institutions and doing a little bit of outside discussion with other pathologists, we found there were major differences in workload among hospitals. We found we could only justify the need for one pathologist where we had three. In a couple of other hospitals they were woefully understaffed and normally would have hired pathologists. What we did was transfer the pathologists out of Milledgeville to other hospitals who would have hired them anyway.

We did the same thing in other services. In the little town right next door they had a fire department and one on the premises. The typical argument presented to the legislature is the horror of what would happen if they had a fire at the hospital. Everybody conjured up visions of patients jumping out windows. This was the traditional method by which they justified their existence. What we ended up doing was make negotiations with the local town who could provide adequate equipment which reduced another piece of funding which then went into rehabilitation.

It is not any one specific thing which saved millions and millions of dollars in this example, but it came from [different] departments and operations in the hospital and was reoriented.

The thing that was encouraging about it was a lot of this was done by the hospitals themselves. They had never had any system which brought these things to the surface. You have other examples where they do save millions of dollars in one shot. At that time another example in the health area is the question of community mental health centers versus institutions.

At that stage, in 1970–71, community mental health was not the program that it is today. People did not rush into a community mental health program. But it didn't take us long, looking at the cost per patient in the institution (for which they just finished six regional hospitals) versus a very embryonic community mental health program just getting started, which had nobody backing it or pushing it. We saw this from a state level, looking over the whole program, and totally shifted the direction of the state from institutions to community. Other states also have seen this. But zero base brought it to our attention in Georgia. And there are all types of examples . . . where nobody knew the problems and the system brought problems to the surface.

The CHAIRMAN. I have just one question concerning the mechanics of this process. I directed this same question to the prior two witnesses. You have given me a different insight on how you would set up your sunset provisions.

Suppose we gave the executive branch the opportunity to come up with a list of proposed changes. The Congress would then have a period of time to reject them. By proposed changes I mean a proposed series of areas to be triggered for sunset-style termination. The alternative, of course, is for Congress to create its own list.

Would this be a way of determining the sunset rotation, because what you seem to be saying is that the way that the system works for the executive side is to have the areas of necessary examination filter up from the program managers. Is that what you are saying?

Mr. PYHRR. Let's take it in each of the steps. Let's start at the agency who initiates the bulk of the data. They would put forth an analysis based on a zero-base budget, which would be a program review or summary called the zero-base review, as per the existing legislation, which is to the program level. In this review they would identify major changes in policies, changes in objectives, overlapping objectives among programs, identify major shifts in policy or operations, or shifts in funding, in those programs that they are proposing. So you would have focused in a very concise way for the executive branch, or for the legislative branch, what their recommendations and changes were.

The executive branch, after they received the agency analysis, can either accept or reject, or modify, the agency recommendations. They would then submit a modified zero-base review to the legislature, identifying the major changes from the existing programs so that the legislature would be given in summary an identification of major changes in policy operations, funding levels, which they could review and accept or reject. They would also have the base data to back in and raise their own questions. So the answer is, yes.

The CHAIRMAN. How do you physically transfer the information from the operating level to the higher levels in an organization as big as the federal government?

Mr. PYHRR. The basic timing procedure follows the existing budget procedures within the agencies. The agencies develop their internal budgets prior to focusing on an agency-level submission to OMB. So most of the big agencies start internally at a lower level first and naturally build up prior to submission to OMB.

The CHAIRMAN. Now, how would you change what they do now to implement what you propose at that level?

Mr. PYHRR. I would not change the timing at all.

The CHAIRMAN. How would you change the submission form?

Mr. PYHRR. The submission form would be zero base rather than the traditional incremental budget. So I am saying I would keep the same time sequence that exists. I would change the content of the budget submissions to zero base.

The CHAIRMAN. All right.

Now, shifting from the mechanics at this level to the substance at that level, how do you produce a change in the budget process so that the program manager or the person operating at that level is not made so vulnerable to the clientele that the program manager is dealing with? Will his decisions be affected by fear of losing a job or having more difficulty with the clientele they are involved with? . . . How do you know whether you are getting good information from the lower level? Do you try it for a while and see what happens?

Mr. PYHRR. I guess there are two ways to answer that. Right now, the same thing, the same prejudice, whether you think prejudice is good or bad, takes place within the agencies, although you do not see it.

You see reams of numbers coming up. You have no idea what decisions have or have not been made.

The CHAIRMAN. Agreed. . . .

Mr. PYHRR. You do not know what the position that has been agreed upon is in most cases.

The CHAIRMAN. And we have never been supplied with that information by any executive. What happens, then, is that you do get a coherent presentation of budget issues. This is not surprising considering the number of agencies there are in the federal government and the numbers that are involved.

Mr. PYHRR. Absolutely.

The CHAIRMAN. Do you do it anonymously at the program levels, or do you expose everybody to their people above and people below?

Mr. PYHRR. Basically you expose the people for whatever their prejudices are. During the traditional budgeting processes, you do not have an identification of the decisions that are made and built into the budget. But I would also say that problem, although perhaps less severe, exists at OMB, and exists within the agencies. In all the organizations that I have dealt with, the amount of [information] that managers, who may have been in departments for their whole career, . . . found out during the first zero-base budgeting process, most of them have said, is more than they have learned in their experience in the agency, because . . . as long as you get the identification of what is going on at a reasonably low level, so that it is not hidden, then you are a step ahead.

Then the question is, how good is the analysis, or what is the bias of the individuals?

The CHAIRMAN. Before you turn to that, how good is the underlying information?

Mr. PYHRR. We have found in the past that because of the way it has been formated, and knowing that there is a threat of people checking on the information since it is explicitly stated, . . . *most managers won't go along with known falsehoods, either because they are good managers or because they are afraid of being caught.* If it is on a piece of paper, that means you, or I, or any individual could go pick it up and challenge the information. As long as it is explicitly stated, it is very difficult to falsify, or certainly much more difficult to falsify, because it is easy enough to check. [Emphasis added.]

So we have found that although, when I entered Georgia, for example, I was deathly afraid of that same problem, [it] did not materialize—that the agencies pretty well policed themselves, and the information was straightforward enough that it did not take a lot of analysis to say something doesn't look right. So we did not have that problem.

The CHAIRMAN. The reason that I asked about the quality of the underlying information is that I served in the executive branch, in the Department of Justice, and I guess I would qualify as what you would call a program manager. I was a U.S. attorney running a particular office—so many assistant attorneys, so many secretaries, so many clerical people, with a budget to be presented. I know this repeats itself over a myriad of areas. I use this as an example only because it's an area I am familiar with.

You would then be relying upon me as a U.S. attorney to say, which happened to be the case, we are going to condemn the highway, so we need a landman. But we should not be handling all these cases below $500, because you are never going to catch the people anyway, so we ought to settle all those cases for whatever money you can get and clean our docket. And that would be submitted as part of the budget presentation of how many lawyers, how many secretaries, and how many clerks. Is that what you are talking about? . . . I am just trying to look at the mechanics of what physically occurs out there.

Mr. PYHRR. The answer is yes. But let me take you, if I can, a step further and raise the questions that would be raised to you. So let me just reverse roles here a second, if we might.

And looking at you, as a program manager, I would probably ask you the following questions on this program.

What alternatives do you have to deliver it?

Should this be implemented from a federal standpoint or local?

The CHAIRMAN. Is this in your form?

Mr. PYHRR. Yes, built into the form.

The CHAIRMAN. And how low a level does that go to? . . . I'm up here in an apparatus which just staggers my imagination. There is an incredible number of people in the federal government doing all kinds of things, some good, some bad, and some in between. That is why we are concerned about the paperwork problem.

Mr. PYHRR. We would probably start out, and we have in the states, going down within the agencies to whatever the agency defines as a budget unit . . . which probably is below the activity of your program level, the way the legislation is written. This information would be analyzed by the budget unit manager, submitted to the program manager, who would then provide the overview analysis on the entire program or activity. That is the document which would then pass up into OMB or the legislature.

However, all those internal agency analyses, which are the basis of the analysis, would be available to anyone who wanted to go back and take a look at them. Or they could be submitted as a part of the total submission if desirable.

The CHAIRMAN. Suppose you conflict? Let's say in the defense area, for example, which I mention because you have three obvious areas that always fight—Air Force, Army, and Navy. They fight in the sense that they each want their share of the total budget. The budget program manager for tactical aircraft is likely to say, "We need them to do this, and they will cost that amount," and then the program manager for the unit next to it says, "We need this many aircraft and they ought to do that." And the two come up. Those produce some classic fights up here on Capitol Hill—where everybody lines up behind their own. That is what I mean by "conflict." There will be so much money available, and both want it. . . . Now, where do you reconcile if you have all that material?

Mrs. HOLT. Mr. Chairman—would you let me add one thing at this point, because I think this is what we were talking about earlier.

Where do you provide the incentive? Because that is the key to the thing. There has to be some incentive to accomplish what we are trying to accomplish. Otherwise you are going to have this conflict right down the line. We see it over and over in the federal government. We build the outreach programs into everything we legislate here, and so therefore there is an incentive to increase, to continue, to grow bigger.

So I am not sure I understand where your carrot and stick fit in this process that we are talking about right now.

Mr. PYHRR. Let me see if I can continue the hypothesis and try to envision with you how this might work.

Let's assume that each of the program managers that we talked about, the three, who are then going to come to a conflict at some stage, have an incentive and believe in their programs, and have an incentive to evaluate it, recommend it, and would obviously like additional funds. Now the analysis that you [get] out of zero-base budgeting would take a look within each of the three areas—let's keep the three separate now—identify what happened if you eliminated it, what would happen at a lower level of funding than current, current level of funding, or some increased levels of funding. So now this program manager is identifying his alternatives, or identifying what the consequences are, and benefits are, of different levels of funding.

The CHAIRMAN. He must answer all four.

Mr. PYHRR. He must answer all. He must also identify what other alternatives are available.

The Navy has a similar program. . . . In your case, in the judicial part . . . maybe the states should be doing it rather than the federal government. What is the objective of the program in the first place? Maybe the objective is not valid. Maybe you should not cut off at $500. Maybe what you should say is, at a minimum level I will cut off at $500,000, and I only have to have so many lawyers for that. Then the question at a higher level of lawyers, higher level of spending is, I am going to cut off at a lower level and take cases at $100,000 and above. This is what we start to see coming out of the analysis.

Somewhere in that organization in the Department of Defense, you have some individual or group responsible for all three programs. And we put the burden of proof on them to rank in priority order the programs of these three organizations. They do not end up saying group 1 is first priority, group 2 is second, and group 3 is last priority. What they basically have to do is take the increments in the package, and say, "At a reduced level of spending for this one area, that is my top priority." So what they have to do is successively rank in order of decreasing importance what they consider to be the most important programs in increments of expenditure, and increments of benefit.

Now, obviously, if they present 20 decision packages, of which you have these three air arms, or whatever, broken up into pieces, they would probably like all 20. The question is: What you forced on them was to say which was most important. So even though you did not give them all 20, assuming you bought their argument on priorities, which you don't have to do, you eliminate the biggest problem, their biggest complaint. They will always complain they didn't get enough money. But an even more severe point to me is, "You gave it to me in the wrong places. You didn't give me enough money, plus you gave it to me in the wrong places." So you are putting the burden on them to say, "Here are our priorities."

In Georgia, for example, the amount of increases requested were 50 percent less than the prior year. And the governor did not give them anywhere near that. But I am saying the amounts of increase that the agencies came forth with were 50 percent less.

Paul O'Neill talks about the federal government at the OMB level [getting requests for] 20-, 30-, 40-percent increases, which the president automatically cuts. But the name of the game in incremental budgeting [is], the more you ask for, the more you are going to get, because you wear them down. And there is not a state budget agency, a federal budget agency, or city or industrial budget agency that does not take requests and pare them down. *In incremental budgeting the name of the game is you request more, you get more* [emphasis added].

In zero base, you find out, with the analysis we are asking for, that some of those increases look stupid. And what managers quickly learn is if they look stupid in one area, because they request ridiculous increases which they cannot justify on a programmatic and evaluation basis, everybody else will think all their other programs are the same way. So what they do is police themselves, because they do not like to look stupid. None of us likes to appear ridiculous. If you are submitting numbers, it is easy to crank in all kinds of people increases, cost increases, because you are not forced to really evaluate and justify [them].

So zero base does an awful lot of its own policing. And we are putting the burden back on the agencies to say, "You recommend the priorities, you show us the analysis, and we can then determine the level of funding."

The CHAIRMAN. Mr. Pyhrr, I want to thank you. You have made an excellent presentation. I'm particularly pleased that you have gone into the details of some of the very practical ways in which it has worked and explained where it has worked and where it has not, because that is one of the things that concerns me. I have learned that if the process is flawed, no amount of good wishes or good intentions will make it succeed. And I appreciate what you have said to us this morning. I think it was excellent.

PLANNING A BUDGET FROM ZERO

A *Speech Delivered by*
JIMMY CARTER
at the National Governors Conference

JUNE 1974

On the campaign trail, a lot of promises are made by candidates for public office to improve economy and efficiency in government if they are elected. This pledge has a natural appeal to the financially overburdened taxpayer. But when the winning candidates take office, they too often find that it's easier to talk about economy and efficiency in government than to accomplish it. Entrenched bureaucracy is hard to move from its existing patterns.

Taxpayers, on the other hand, hear the promises but see few results. It seems to them that for every new program in government there must be a tax increase. Each government—whether federal, state, or local—seems to have an insatiable financial need. No matter how much money is collected, it never seems to be enough.

When I campaigned for governor, I promised that if elected there would be no general statewide tax increase during my four-year term in office. At the same time, I outlined a platform of eight general goals and 97 specific objectives that I wanted to accomplish. The twin promises, in my estimation, were not incompatible. I felt that this administration could reverse the past pattern of ignoring campaign promises.

Immediately upon election, I began planning a program to keep my commitments. I knew that simple appeals for greater productivity in government were not the answer. Economy and efficiency must come from basic, subtle changes that slice across the complete spectrum of a government's activity. The two areas that seemed to offer greatest possibilities of success were budgeting and planning. Through tight budgeting, more services can be squeezed out of every tax dollar spent. Through planning, the groundwork can be laid for implementing new programs and expanding existing ones in ways that will avoid possible pitfalls and launch the programs directly towards their goal from the beginning.

As a citizen interested in government and as a former legislator, I had long believed that too many governmental programs are botched because they are started in haste without adequate planning or establishment of goals. Too often they never really attack the targeted problems.

The services provided by Georgia's state government are now greatly improved, and every tax dollar is being stretched further than ever before. There has not been a general statewide tax increase during my term. In fact, there has been a substantial reduction in ad valorem tax. Neither will a tax increase be necessary when my successor takes office next year.

REORGANIZATION MERGES PLANNING AND BUDGETING

In budgeting, we initiated a new concept called zero-base budgeting to help us monitor state problems better and attain increased efficiency. In the area of planning, we merged the roles of planning and budgeting—which had previously operated completely independent of each other—so that they could work together in promoting more economy in government. At the same time, we clearly defined the various roles of planning and assigned the proper roles to the appropriate organizational unit.

The functions of planning and budgeting were merged in a broad reorganization program that completely streamlined the executive branch of Georgia's state government. Much of our success during the past three years in improving state programs is a direct result of reorganization.

We reduced the number of state agencies from about 300 to 22 major operating agencies and combined functions to eliminate duplication and overlapping of services. For instance, 33 agencies were combined to form the Department of Natural Resources. Reorganization is a separate story of government in action. My interest now is to stress how we changed our budgeting and planning procedures to help accomplish the previously stated goals.

Georgia was the first government to implement a program of zero-base budgeting. Under this novel concept, every dollar requested for expenditure during the next budget period must be justified, including current expenditures that are to continue. It also provides for examining the effectiveness of each activity at various funding levels. This is a dramatically different concept from that followed by most governments, which concentrate almost totally on proposed new expenditures when considering a new budget. Except for non-recurring programs or expenditures, the continuing expenditures in a current budget get little attention.

Take as an example a government with a budget of $1 billion. Projections are that the new budget will grow by $50 million during the next budget cycle because of growth in the economy, a tax increase, or other factors. Department heads submit their budget requests with proposed increases to get a slice of the $50 million in new funds, either to expand existing programs, launch new programs, or to cover increases in costs through inflation. The governing officials rarely look at the existing expenditures to judge whether they are meeting their objective. The officials are concerned only with carving up the $50 million in new funds. If graded, a new program actually might become a greater priority than an existing program, but it doesn't get funded unless it can get a slice of the $50 million in new money.

Zero-base budgeting changed this practice in Georgia. Every program, existing and proposed, must now vie for funding in the new budget on an equal level. Every single dollar spent by a department in the current year must be justified if it is to be recommended by the governor for funding in the following year's budget.

Until the concept was implemented in Georgia, only one Texas corporation had ever used zero-base budgeting. The new technique was developed by that corporation as a means of reducing the costs of its overall operation. This was done by ranking every single function within the company's operations and abolishing the lowest-priority functions. Thus, the company was able to reduce expenses as required in a manner that retained the most-needed functions.

DECISION PACKAGES ESTABLISH PRIORITIES

On a larger scale, zero-base budgeting in Georgia has peeled the veil of secrecy from around bureaucracy by opening up for inspection and scrutiny the activities of every single state employee. For the first time, a governor, legislator, department head, or anyone else can study in detail what is being accomplished at the lowest level of state activity.

The heart of zero-base budgeting is decision packages, which are prepared by managers at each level of government, from the top to the bottom. These packages—10,000 in Georgia—cover every existing or proposed function or activity of each agency. The packages include analysis of the cost, purpose, alternative courses of action, measures of performance, consequences of not performing the activity, and benefits.

Merely compiling these packages would not accomplish any purpose other than to provide information. Therefore, they are ranked in order of importance against other current and new activities. This ranking forms the basis of determining what functions are recommended for funding in the new budget, depending, of course, upon the amount of money available. If less funds are appropriated than requested, the lowest-ranking functions and activities are cut out.

PLANNING REQUIREMENTS

Besides placing priority on spending programs and revealing more information about actual governmental operations, zero-base budgeting achieves one more important action: it forces planning into levels of government where planning may never have existed. It forces all levels of government to find better ways of accomplishing their missions. It also gives a voice in governmental direction to the rank-and-file state employee who is responsible for delivering services. Besides making him a more integral part of the planning process, it elevates his own sense of importance of his position and prompts him to work harder and deliver more efficient services.

There are three ingredients necessary for successful implementation of zero-base budgeting: (1) unqualified support from top executives, (2) effective design of the system, and (3) effective management of the system.

Zero-base budgeting has been well received in Georgia. It has become an important planning tool to insure that we are placing our priorities on the proper programs and are constantly seeking the maximum services for every state dollar.

I don't want to mislead you and leave the impression that implementation of zero-based budgeting has created miracles in Georgia's state government. Obviously it has not. But it has been subtly at work for three years making basic changes in the operations of our government and will continue to pioneer further improvements in the years ahead.

The merging of budgeting and planning services into one cohesive organization has worked so well that one wonders why they were ever located in separate, non-cooperating agencies.

State planning was a function of the Bureau of State Planning and Community Affairs when I took office, while the Budget Bureau handled all budget matters. Although both agencies were under control of the governor since he appointed both agency heads, they operated separately with no cooperation between them—a fact that minimized the probability of the planning output being implemented.

One of the most critical problems was that the Bureau of State Planning and Community Affairs, which had been created in 1967, had never really established its mission in Georgia's state government after four years of operation. Legislators didn't understand its functions and were skeptical of its entire operation. They felt that the planning bureau and the individual state departments were overlapping in their responsibilities. In some instances this was true. More importantly, the planning bureau was doing most of the program planning in state government without adequately synchronizing its efforts with the state agencies. When it came time to implement the planning efforts, department heads were skeptical and too often were reluctant to push for implementation of the proposed improvements. This created an impasse that made the work of state planners generally ineffective.

As soon as reorganization brought the budgeting and planning functions together into the same agency, the Office of Planning and Budget, changes began to occur. For the first time, planners and budget analysts worked side by side and began to coordinate their efforts.

Over a period of another year, further changes took place that changed completely the role of state planning. Through reorganization, most state agencies began to do their own functional program planning. This was made possible by creation of planning divisions within these departments for the first time, and also by the fact that the reduction in number of departments made them large enough to justify their own program planning divisions.

A New Role for the Planning Division

Concurrently, planners in the Planning Division of the Office of Planning and Budget assumed a new role of policy planning rather than program planning. By restricting program planning to the agency level, there is now a greater chance that it will be implemented.

Georgia state law charges the OPB Planning Division with the responsibility for assessing accurately Georgia's physical, social, and economic needs. On a periodic and timely basis throughout the year, these needs are identified, documented, and analyzed.

One method that I have used to secure citizen participation in the state planning process was the Goals for Georgia program. This was a year-long program in 1971 in which Georgia citizens were given a chance to outline the types of programs they wanted their state government to emphasize in the years ahead. Since that time, state planning has been updating the results of this program continuously in the formulation of the state's goals and policies.

The role of OPB planners in preparation of the 1975 budget tells the story of how state planning is now done in Georgia.

Long before the state's budget analysts got deeply involved in preparation of the proposed fiscal year 1975 budget that would be submitted to the General Assembly, OPB planners started meeting with department heads to determine their program priorities for the following year. Detailed analyses were prepared and submitted to me for review. At the same time, I was meeting with the planners to outline my priorities. Later, I met with the planners and each department head to discuss both of our priorities. We reached a mutual agreement on many programs to be pursued and disagreed on others. Even though we didn't reach unanimity, we established a common ground of understanding about our conflicting goals. Later, when the budget analysts started putting together the actual budget proposals in dollars and cents, the spadework done by the planners proved to be an immense help.

OPB's Planning Division didn't stop at this point. Its staff continued to attend every budget meeting and provide assistance in ironing out details of the actual budget proposal to be made. Although planners had been involved in preparation of the proposed fiscal year 1974 budget, this was the first time they had actually been involved with a clear-cut role established for them. I can only say that I wish we had had this type of budgeting-planning relationship available when I became governor. I am more than pleased with the working rapport that has been established. The relationship between me and all department heads concerning budgeting preparation has been improved considerably.

The work of the planners is reflected in our printed budget documents as well. One of the three budget documents we prepare in Georgia is an outline of proposed spendings on a program basis with a four-year projection of future needs for each program. This document is keyed by page number to the main financial display document for easy cross-reference.

One role of planners has been retained—program evaluation. This involves determining whether each program has attained its objective and making a thorough analysis of the strengths and weaknesses of each program.

OPB planners were left with this function because an objective, outside-the-agency evaluation is needed, and because many programs cross agency lines. It would not be fair for one line agency to evaluate the effectiveness of a related program in another line agency.

Along with the new objectives of OPB's Planning Division, one major change has taken place in our recruiting efforts. Instead of recruiting trained planners, we hire experts in the various areas of governmental activity such as education, law enforcement, mental health, etc. We provide them the in-house training necessary to work within the framework of our planning organization. This policy has been successful. By virtue of being experts in their activity of assignment, OPB planners can discuss programs on a level with department heads. They have an expertise that is creating more trust in state planning and is helping to establish better rapport between the governor's office and the various state departments.

Georgia's state government still has a long way to go to achieve the quality of service that I would like to see. But we've come a long way since I took office in 1971.

The innovations involving zero-base budgeting and merging of the budgeting and planning staffs will be felt in Georgia for a long time. We are leaving a legacy to our next governor that will allow him the flexibility and mechanism to move quickly into the decision-making process of a new administration that hasn't been available to Georgia's past governors.

ZERO-BASE BUDGETING

by Jimmy Carter

Since first presented in the *Harvard Business Review* six years ago,* zero-base budgeting has enjoyed a widespread and growing acceptance.

♦ The concept has been successfully implemented in over 200 organizations of all types and sizes. In business, these range from such giants as Texas Instruments and Southern California Edison to several smaller functions within Xerox and Tektronix. In the public sector, its value has been acknowledged in organizations ranging from the state of Georgia to the city of Garland, Texas, and the Greece, New York, school district.

♦ A zero-base budgeting seminar offered by the American Management Associations is the most successful of all new courses launched in the last two years, with attendance running three to four times expectations. And the fact that many participants are attending as part of company teams suggests more than just a casual interest on their part.

♦ The concept is the subject of a growing body of professional literature, with one book—as well as numerous articles—already published and two in preparation. Hardly a day goes by without some mention of it in our national media.

♦ Finally, zero-base budgeting, or variations of it (such as "sunset budgeting"), are being actively discussed at the federal government level in the Congressional Budget Office, the Office of Management and Budget, and the United States Congress. And zero-base budgeting has been advanced in the political plank of a prominent Georgian.

While the great majority of organizations attempting zero-base budgeting characterize their experience in warm, positive, even glowing terms, others have found their fond expectations of it still a distant, unrealized hope and internal conflict alleged to it an oppressive reality. Now that zero-base budgeting has emerged from its infancy, it's appropriate to find out—

* Peter A. Pyhrr, "Zero-Base Budgeting," *Harvard Business Review*, November–December 1970.

based on my experiences as one of its many godfathers—why the baby is up and running in some organizations while still kicking and crawling in others.

WHAT ZERO-BASE BUDGETING IS

On a *procedural* level, zero-base budgeting represents a dramatic departure from traditional approaches. Here is what could be called the "traditional budgeting syndrome" that many organizations experience. Does it apply to yours?

- ◆ During the initial phases of the budget cycle, staff managers take the current year's spending level, increment it for inflation, and fold in a myriad of new programs.
- ◆ The results are submitted to the budgeting staff (normally well past the eleventh hour) for consolidation and presentation to the chief executive.
- ◆ Their analysis and presentation to him clearly show that the initial effort is totally unrealistic and usually unaffordable if not irresponsible.
- ◆ But because they're lacking a thorough understanding of which efforts are really critical, a rather distressing scenario now unfolds. Arbitrary across-the-board cuts are made, and considerable muscle and bones are sacrificed with the fat. Last-ditch Byzantine lobbying occurs between the CEO and his key subordinates. The controller runs out of time and patience, not to mention scarce political capital.
- ◆ Yet somehow (usually several weeks after the deadline) some sort of budget is finalized and blessed. All parties congratulate one another, and the exhausted ones slip away for a quick vacation, quietly suppressing nervous feelings of doubt. But all share a determined commitment that next year will be different—if nothing else, they will start earlier or increase the planning and budgeting staff!

Under the traditional approach, once a staff or agency has been established, it is almost immune from later scrutiny. If approved, programs either grow like cancers or retreat into self-perpetuating obscurity. Zero-base budgeting starts from a very different premise. Rather than incrementing the new on the old, the system demands a total rejustification of everything from scratch—from zero! It means chopping up the organization into individual functions and analyzing each annually, regardless of whether it is fifty years old or a brand-new proposal for a future program.

The budget is broken into units called "decision packages," which are prepared by managers at each level, from top to bottom. These packages cover every existing or proposed activity of each department. The packages include an analysis of purpose, cost, measures of performance and benefits, alternative courses of action, and consequences of not performing the activity. But merely compiling these packages would not accomplish any purpose other than to provide information. Therefore, all packages are ranked in order of priority. After several discussions between department heads and the chief executive, the rankings are finalized, and packages up to the level of affordability are approved and funded.

Zero-base budgeting has had a rather long gestation period and a brief infancy. Some have traced its origins to the Program, Planning, and Budgeting (PPB) system originated in the Department of Defense Office of Systems Analysis in the early 1960s and refined in our nation's space program. In the mid-1960s, similar approaches were being adapted and employed in various functions at such companies as Texaco, Ashland Oil, INA, and Xerox. The concept was fine-tuned at Texas Instruments in the late 1960s.

When I became governor of Georgia in 1970, one of my first jobs was to prepare the budget for the coming year. Piled on a table were departmental funding requests that amounted to more than half again as much money as would be available. No one had made any attempt to assess their worth or arrange them in any sort of priority. I quickly saw the need for zero-base budgeting and moved to implement it by executive order.

As the professional literature on the subject grew, and prompted by the recession of 1973, dozens of public and private organizations began to climb on the bandwagon. And the roster of its disciples has continued to grow. They shared a need for more rational planning and allocation of resources in that fuzzy and challenging area called "staff"; for zero-base budgeting is not intended for line operations, where accounting standards can be meshed with projected volumes to quickly put together a budget. Rather, zero-base budgeting is intended for staff functions ranging from manufacturing quality control to personnel administration and from the tax department to public agencies.

SOME KEY SUCCESS FACTORS

One of the first steps an organization takes to implement zero-base budgeting is to contact another with some experience in it. Indeed, the staffs of most organizations pioneering in this concept—including my own—have been inundated with such requests in recent months. Usually, the basic procedures and forms are requested. Somehow, I suspect that those making the requests hope someone else's approach will be the magic touchstone that can be readily modified and implemented in turnkey fashion in their own.

Such requests represent a good first step but fall wide of the mark, for they overlook three other critical ingredients. And these represent, to me, the substance of a successful zero-base budgeting effort. In order of importance, they are:

Top management's personal involvement and commitment. Zero-base budgeting procedures are among the best tools for ensuring constant reassessment of staff programs, new as well as old. But no system will work unless the chief executive officer understands the workings of a large bureaucracy, is willing to work long hours to find out what is really going on, and has the political courage to make tough decisions. To be sure, the budgeting staff will play a key role in orchestrating the effort. But delegating the responsibility for final decisions to them clearly dilutes commitment by everyone while diffusing accountability for results. In short, it is an invitation to disaster. I personally know of no organizations that have successfully pulled off zero-base budgeting without meeting this need.

Imagination. Zero-base budgeting demands the best creative energies of the managers involved in it. Nothing is sacred: New and innovative techniques must be conceived, evaluated, and compared to business-as-usual approaches. At the outset, those undertaking zero-base budgeting should carefully assess their managements' capabilities in this area. Those enjoying the luxury of a strong, incisive, broad-gauged management cadre recruited and nurtured over many years are safe in broadly involving all in the process. Texas Instruments and Georgia are key examples of this approach. Others have found a select task force of their best talent better suited to the effort. Many municipalities and smaller companies have followed this approach. Still others have used both techniques to check and balance each other where appropriate.

Persuasiveness. Finally, where new approaches (including zero-base budgeting) represent clear improvements over the old ways, all managers involved must employ their best persuasive and human-relations skills to gain approval and manage change. A business friend of mine responsible for implementing zero-base budgeting in his own organization in fact required all his key budget managers and analysts to attend the company's basic sales course. His logic was interesting: While most staffs are excellent wellheads of ideas and innovation, few have ever had to really convince others to implement them or, more important, live with the results. Therefore, the basic persuasion skills of probing, listening, talking benefits rather than features, and, most important, *getting commitment* are mandatory for any sound zero-base budgeting effort.

Successful zero-base budgeting, then, requires more than just a set of procedures and forms: It in fact demands a wholly new mental attitude and management style throughout the organization. And only with that mentality and style can its promise be fully realized.

Some Common Concerns—and How to Overcome Them

Many seasoned executives, however, have raised specific and sometimes well-intentioned concerns about zero-base budgeting. In virtually all cases, the broad principles outlined earlier can be applied. But here is a summary of some of the most frequent objections and how I and others have handled them:

Zero-base budgeting is threatening. Staff managers will be less than candid in their budget submissions. This challenge is not unique to zero-base budgeting. Even among those employing traditional techniques, I know of few that enjoy completely open and frank discussions during the budget cycle. And your own experience in handling this problem in the past is a worthwhile starting point. All key men involved in the process must dust off their basic skills in human relations, discussion, and persuasion. Reluctant participants should be approached using a healthy dialogue that focuses on what the process can do *for* them rather than *to* them. For unlike traditional approaches (which, incidentally, do focus on the *to* rather than the *for*), zero-base budgeting in fact offers them a genuine opportunity to *increase* their resources where they can clearly demonstrate greater cost-effectiveness or improved delivery of their services. In fact, another of my business friends in the automobile industry who tried zero-base budgeting found himself inundated with resource requests for new and better ways to run the operation.

Administration and communications become more complicated as more people become involved. In zero-base budgeting's formative years, this concern was probably valid. But it is less so now because procedures and forms have been refined and tested and a substantial cadre of planning executives experienced in the technique have won their spurs. But in a more fundamental sense, I find the best ideas for improvement often come from the rank-and-file managers, who know their operations intimately and are seriously committed to improving them. Besides making them a more integral part of the planning process, the zero-base budgeting process elevates their sense of importance and prompts them to work harder to deliver more efficient services. Zero-base budgeting can provide these people a channel of communications for their day in court. Notwithstanding administrative difficulties, the tradeoff is clearly worthwhile.

Zero-base budgeting requires more time than traditional approaches. This unfortunate perception does not fit the experience of most successful organizations. That more time is required may be true during the learning process. But in comparison to the old ways, my own experience suggests that the time required is substantially lessened, often by as much as a third. The reason is quite simple: By lumping everything together, traditional techniques do not lay out in understandable pieces what's being done and at what cost. Thus, the key decision maker wastes much time flailing in darkness and confusion to arrive at the final budget. The zero-base approach in large part eliminates this by documenting everything in advance for quick decision—and in so doing obviates many of the headaches and heartaches associated with traditional methods.

Zero-base budgeting requires work measurement and evaluation data to assess cost-effectiveness. Often they are simply not available. Yet a good amount of data on the economics of improved operations is indeed available to those willing to dig it out. Supplier salesmen, for example, are always eager to discuss the advantages of their products, and usually in hard terms. And one company has worked out a firm procedure for such traditionally soft areas as job enrichment and training. Lacking firm data, resource requests must be justified by the results achieved for similar efforts in other companies or by a broad review of the available professional literature. Lacking either of these, pilot tests are usually approved for those efforts of most significant promise. All approved programs, though, are rigorously scrutinized at a follow-up checkpoint review or performance audit.

Zero-base budgeting forces decision making. Forcing decision making is one of zero-base budgeting's greatest strengths, and an obviously healthy one for the organization. But it is often a bitter pill for those of long incumbency, ossified in staffs or under leaders not demanding the best. A carefully devised implementation plan, worked out well in advance and rigorously adhered to, that identifies such areas and how they will be handled can minimize this risk. In Georgia, we amended the Constitution to permit the payment of incentive rewards amounting to up to ten percent of first-year savings. Again, tactful attention to human relations, to the issue of what zero-base budgeting can do *for* you rather than *to* you—and not the "whose ox can I gore" attitude—can go a long way toward ensuring success.

Large volumes of decision packages place an unmanageable burden on the budget staff. Again, this was probably a valid concern in zero-base budgeting's early years. In Georgia, we overcame this problem with a computer routine. Each decision package was assigned a code number to describe the kind of service being delivered. Then, we could detect duplication automatically when these package numbers were printed out sequentially. To offer a couple of examples, we identified *seven* agencies responsible for the eduction of deaf children and *twenty-two* responsible for the utilization of water resources. Even if we could claim no benefits from zero-base budgeting in the first year (which we certainly could) the technique provided us with a massive data base that was a critical information source for a major reorganization. And for smaller operations like my campaign staff, we've devised a small 5×8 card that captures a decision package with up to four alternatives. Using it, we could quickly reallocate resources by flipping, reordering, or dropping cards.

Evaluating and ranking dissimilar functions is not feasible. In its early stages, zero-base budgeting required the consolidation and ranking of packages from different departments; all had their requests meshed and ranked together. This has caused obvious problems to some, for who can objectively say that a developmental training program is more important than a new computer system? Many organizations have skirted this issue by simply not doing such a global ranking. Where they're not faced with a fiscal crisis, their experience indicates that it's simply not necessary. Most chief executives know intuitively how much they want to spend on each function. To mesh the rankings of the various staff efforts is wasteful of time if not counterproductive. It invites a fratricidal warfare among the departments or agencies, with each fighting for the other's resources. But in a crisis situation, it will still be necessary.

Indeed, this need dictated moving to zero-base budgeting at Texas Instruments. In Georgia, there was intense opposition from the bureaucrats who thrived on confusion, from special interest groups that preferred to work in the dark, and from a few legislative leaders who did not want to see their fiefdoms endangered. But with forceful leadership and persuasiveness by our key people, almost all accepted the new approach with gratitude that the state's resources were being allocated openly, decently, and free of political intrigue.

Evaluating the priority or legal status of decision packages represents a political nightmare for the budgeting staff. Among organizations in the private sector, packages to fund efforts required by law (such as payroll operations, SEC reporting, or affirmative-action programs) obviously go to the top of any ranking scheme. And many have in fact already modified their evaluation and ranking techniques to meet this need. Of greater challenge is how the budget staff should handle the chief executive's sacred cows: The corporate retreat and aviation program come to mind. Their dilemma is not unlike that of the mice in the nursery story: All agree that the cat should wear a bell, but none can agree on who should hang it on him. Here, the staff must maintain intellectual honesty with a full and open analysis; the final decision and responsibility must of course rest with the CEO. I find that when all packages are laid out with costs and benefits for each and are ranked, most executives will have serious misgivings about approving patently self-serving personal amenities in lieu of demonstrably beneficial efforts. In this regard, recent developments in director liability are intriguing: The boards of two large companies have begun to demand full justification of all spending for clearly discretionary programs.

In the final analysis, though, each of these concerns has been raised with traditional approaches. And, effective management of them hinges on employing the traditional tools: disciplined procedures, top management involvement and commitment, persuasion skills, and imagination.

SOME BENEFITS

From my own experience as well as that of a number of other companies, several clear-cut benefits can be gained from an effective zero-base budgeting effort.

1. It focuses the management process on analysis and decision making rather than inordinate "numbers crunching"—in other words, the "what, why, and how" questions as well as the "how much."
2. It combines planning, budgeting, and operational decision making into one process.
3. It forces managers to constantly evaluate in detail their operations, efficiency, and cost-effectiveness. This includes discretionary spending and start-up costs, as well as those for specific programs—both new and old—all of which are clearly identified rather than functionally buried.
4. It provides a system to trade off between long-term and short-term needs during the budget, as well as a follow-up tool on cost and performance during the year.
5. It allows for quick budget adjustments during the year if revenue falls short. In so doing, it offers the capability to modify goals and expectations quickly and rationally to correspond to a realistic and affordable plan of operation.
6. It identifies similar functions in different departments for comparison and evaluation.
7. And most important to me, it can broadly expand management participation and training in the planning, budgeting, and decision making process.

In Georgia, the tangible results for the taxpayers truly demonstrated zero-base budgeting's bottom line benefits. Here are some of them:

◇ Before installment of the system, every major department had its own computer system. Through zero-base budgeting, we identified this as a problem and created just one central system.
◇ Each large or small agency had its own print shop. We merged forty-three into one.
◇ In many cities around the state there were three, four, or five radio repair shops for different state departments, each one overstaffed and underworked, sometimes in adjacent buildings.
◇ At enormous expense, Georgia patrolmen were trained, uniformed, and provided an automobile. Yet often they were assigned to admin-

istrative chores or radio dispatching. We moved almost 100 of these troopers out to patrol the highways and replaced them with handicapped Georgians trained in vocational rehabilitation programs. The many benefits are obvious.

In total, these and other achievements resulted in a 50-percent reduction in administrative costs. And zero-base budgeting was our secret weapon to identify the opportunities and make them happen.

A FINAL WORD

Zero-base budgeting has proved its value for those organizations endowed with a will to manage, to engage in a productive dialogue founded on mutual trust during tough planning and budgeting decisions, and to find new and better ways to serve their constituents or customers. But like most new management tools, success requires balancing the approach with classic, common sense human-relations and creative problem-solving techniques.

Where that balance is achieved, however, the hard efforts required have indeed generated more light than heat, with greater efficiency and resource allocation to boot. In the public sector, there is no inherent conflict between careful planning, tight budgeting, and constant management reassessment on the one hand and compassionate concern for the deprived and afflicted on the other. Waste and inefficiency never fed a hungry child, provided a job for a willing worker, or educated a deserving student. Similarly, in the private sector, misdirected or redundant staff efforts never paid a dividend, provided a meaningful, rewarding job for a competent employee, launched a successful product on time to specification, or satisfied a demanding customer.

Selected Readings

Anderson, Donald N. "Zero-Base Budgets Offer Data, Spending Control." *Industry Week,* January 12, 1976, p. 48.

Anderson, Donald N. "Zero-Base Budgeting: How to Get Rid of Corporate Crabgrass." *Management Review,* October 1976.

Anthony, Robert N. "Zero Base Budgeting is a Fraud." *The Wall Street Journal,* April 27, 1977. See also replies by Paul Stonich and Robert J. Lipstein of May 16, 1977, and by Peter A. Pyhrr and George Minmier of May 23, 1977.

Austin, L. Allan. "Zero-Base Budgeting: An Integrating Concept." *Management Counselor,* January 1977.

Bensahel, Jane G. "Zero-Base Management." *International Management,* January 1977, pp. 36–37.

Bonsack, Robert A. "Zero-Based Budgeting: A Blueprint for Better Operations?" *Chicago Tribune,* December 22, 1976.

Brueningsen, Arthur A. "SCAT—A Process of Alternatives." *Management Accounting,* November 1976.

Brueningsen, Arthur A., David Robinson, and John Yagielski. "Using Zero-Base Budgeting in Effecting Cost Reductions." *Educational Economics,* Vol. 1, No. 4, September 1976.

Business Week. "What It Means to Build a Budget from Zero." April 18, 1977.

Carter, Jimmy. "Start from Zero." In *Why Not the Best.* Nashville, Tenn.: Broadman Press, 1975.

Carter, Jimmy. "Jimmy Carter Tells Why He Will Use Zero-Base Budgeting." *Nation's Business,* January 1977, pp. 24–26.

Cheek, Logan M. "Cost Effectiveness Comes to the Personnel Function." *Harvard Business Review,* May–June 1973, pp. 96–105.

Cheek, Logan M. "Zero-Base Budgeting: Priorities Tool for Planners." *Newspaper Controller,* January 1977, pp. 4–5.

Congressional Quarterly. "Zero-Base Budgeting Undergoes Limited Test." March 12, 1977, pp. 441–443.

Davis, K. Roscoe. "Budgeting by Level of Activity." *Managerial Planning,* May–June 1975, pp. 10–14.

Davis, Otto A., M.A.H. Dempster, and Aaron Wildavsky. "A Theory of the Budgeting Process." *American Political Science Review,* September 1966, pp. 529–547.

Farnsworth, Clyde H. "Next Time, Zero-Base Budgeting." *The New York Times,* February 27, 1977.

Granof, Michael H., and Dale A. Kinzel. "Zero-Base Budgeting: Modest Proposal and Reform." *Federal Accountant,* December 1974, pp. 50–56.

Gross, Bertram M. "The New Systems Budgeting." *Public Administration Review,* March–April 1969, pp. 113–137.

Hayward, John T. "Buzz Words Galore!" *Government Executive,* September 1976, pp. 19–21.

Large, Ailen J. "Applying Zero-Base Budgeting." *The Wall Street Journal,* May 24, 1977.

Leone, C. "How to Ride Herd on the Budget." *Nation,* May 22, 1976, pp. 625–627.

Leininger, David L., and Ronald C. Wong. "Zero-Base Budgeting in Garland, Texas." *Management Information Service,* April 1976, pp. 1–6.

Levin, Merwin. "Zero-Based Budgeting." *Boardroom Reports,* December 30, 1976, p. 14.

MacFarlane, John A. "Zero-Base Budgeting in Action." *Chartered Accountants,* December 1976, pp. 28–32.

MBA Magazine. "Zero-Base Budgeting: Peter Pyhrr Defends His Brainchild." April 1977, pp. 25–31.

McGinnis, James F. "Pluses and Minuses of Zero-Base Budgeting." *Administrative Management,* September 1976.

Minmier, George S. *An Evaluation of Zero-Base Budgeting as a Tool for Planning and Control of Discretionary Costs in Government Institutions.* University of Arkansas, 1974.

Minmier, George S. *An Evaluation of the Zero-Base Budgeting System in Governmental Institutions.* Research Monograph No. 68. Georgia State University, 1975.

Minmier, George S., and Roger Hermanson. "A Look at Zero Budgeting: The Georgia Experience." *Atlanta Economic Review,* July–August 1976, pp. 5–12.

Murray, Thomas II. "The Tough Job of Zero Budgeting." *Dun's Review,* October 1974.

Neuman, John L. "Time for Lasting Cuts in Overhead." *McKinsey Quarterly,* Summer 1975.

Novick, David. "Long-Range Planning Through Program Budgeting." RAND Corporation, 1968.

Peterson, Walter E. "Zero-Base Management System." *Military Engineer,* September–October 1975, pp. 371–373.

Pyhrr, Peter A. "Zero-Base Budgeting." *Harvard Business Review,* November–December 1970.

Pyhrr, Peter A. *Zero-Base Budgeting.* New York: John Wiley, 1973.

Pyhrr, Peter A. "Zero-Base Budgeting: A Management Tool to Evaluate and Control Expense." In *Budgeting for Profit,* Chandra Gyan and Swrenda Sing Hvi, eds. Planning Executive Institute, Oxford, Ohio, 1975.

Pyhrr, Peter A. "The Zero-Base Budgeting Process." In *How to Improve Profit Ability through More Effective Planning.* Thomas S. Dudick, ed. New York: John Wiley, 1975.

Pyhrr, Peter A. "Zero-Base Budgeting: Where to Use It and How to Begin." *SAM Advanced Management Journal,* Summer 1976.

Pyhrr, Peter A. "The Zero-Base Approach to Government Budgeting." *Public Administration Review,* January–February, 1977, pp. 1–8.

Salpukas, Agis. "Pitfalls of Zero-Base Budgeting." *The New York Times,* May 31, 1977, pp. 39–40.

Singleton, David W., Bruch A. Smith, and James R. Cleaveland. "Zero-Based Budgeting in Wilmington, Delaware." *Governmental Finance,* August 1976, pp. 20–29.

Stein, Herbert. "How About Zero-Based Revenue?" *The Wall Street Journal,* January 3, 1977.

Stonich, Paul J. "Zero-Base Planning—A Management Tool." *Managerial Planning,* July–August 1976.

Stonich, Paul J., and William H. Steeves. "Zero-Base Planning and Budgeting for Utilities." *Public Utilities Fortnightly,* September 9, 1976, pp. 24–29.

Tufty Communications. *Zero-Base Planning and Budgeting Digest.* Washington, D.C.

U.S. House of Representatives, Committee on the Budget. *Zero-Base Budget Legislation.* Washington, D.C.: Government Printing Office, 1976.

U.S. News and World Report. "Zero-Base Budgeting—A Way to Cut Spending, or a Gimmick?" September 20, 1976.

U.S. Senate, Committee on Government Operations. *Government Economy and Spending Reform Act of 1976.* Washington, DC.: Government Printing Office, 1976.

Utah Foundation—Research Brief. "Zero-Base Budgeting and Sunset Laws." November 8, 1976.

Vancil, R. F. "Texas Instruments Incorporated." *Harvard Business School Case,* 9-172-054, September 1975.

The Wall Street Journal. "Zero-Base Budgeting." November 20, 1975, p. 1.

The Wall Street Journal. "The 'New Generation.'" May 17, 1976.

The Wall Street Journal. "Governor Carter's Experiment." October 12, 1976, p. 5.

The Wall Street Journal. "Zero-Base Budgeting." March 14, 1977, p. 1.

Wentling, Tim L., and Tom E. Lawson. *Evaluating Occupational Education and Training Programs.* Boston: Allyn and Bacon, 1975.

Wildavsky, Aaron, and Arthur Hammond. "Comprehensive versus Incremental Budgeting in the Department of Agriculture." *Administrative Science Quarterly,* December 1965, pp. 321–346.

Index